# MIND YOUR OWN BUSINESS

## The Best Businesses You Can Start Today for Under $500

# MIND YOUR OWN BUSINESS

## The Best Businesses You Can Start Today for Under $500

### By Stephen Wagner & the Editors of INCOME OPPORTUNITIES Magazine

**BOB ADAMS, INC.** PUBLISHERS
Holbrook, Massachusetts

Published by Bob Adams, Inc.
260 Center Street, Holbrook, MA 02343

ISBN: 1-55850-153-3

Printed in the United States of America

J  I  H  G  F  E  D  C  B  A

This publication is designed to provide accurate and authoritative information with regard to the subject matter covered. It is sold with the understanding that the publisher is not engaged in rendering legal, accounting, or other professional advice. If legal advice or other expert assistance is required, the services of a qualified professional person should be sought.

> — From a *Declaration of Principles* jointly adopted by a
> Committee of the American Bar Association and a
> Committee of Publishers and Associations.

The editors of *Income Opportunities*® magazine wish to express their appreciation to the many contributors whose articles were used in this book. Credit for their contributions is acknowledged at the end of each article.

# CONTENTS

Introduction ............................................... 7
PART ONE: Starting On a Shoestring Budget .................. 11
PART TWO: Keeping Costs Low ............................. 17
PART THREE: Low- and No-cost Advertising and
        Promotion ........................................ 25
PART FOUR: 100 Businesses to Start for $500 or Less........... 35

1. Adult Education.......................................... 35
2. Aerobics Classes ......................................... 37
3. Airport Express Service................................... 39
4. Alterations Business ...................................... 41
5. Apartment Cleaning....................................... 44
6. Apartment Preparation.................................... 46
7. Appliance Repair......................................... 47
8. Aquarium Maintenance ................................... 49
9. Auto Glass Repair ........................................ 51
10. Auto Striping............................................ 53
11. Balloon Decorating Service............................... 56
12. Bike Repair ............................................. 58
13. Cake Decorating ......................................... 61
14. Calligraphy Service....................................... 62
15. Candle Making .......................................... 65
16. Car Opening Service ...................................... 66
17. Community Maps ........................................ 68
18. Consulting............................................... 70
19. Cookbook Publishing ..................................... 73
20. Crafts: Local Shows ...................................... 75
21. Crafts: Home Parties...................................... 78
22. Crafts: Party Plan Classes ................................ 81
23. Credit Repair............................................. 83
24. Crossword Puzzles ....................................... 85
25. Dating Service, Specialized................................ 90

26. Day Care ............................................... 92
27-30. 4 Delivery Services ................................. 95
31. Defensive Driving Instructor ........................... 98
32. Drop Shipping ......................................... 100
33. Electronics Consultant ................................ 103
34. Estate Sales .......................................... 106
35. Farm-Sitting .......................................... 109
36. Firewood: Apartment Delivery .......................... 111
37. Flea Market: Consignment .............................. 114
38. Flea Market Stand ..................................... 116
39. Flyer Delivery Service ................................ 119
40. Garage Cleaning Service ............................... 121
41. Garden Consulting ..................................... 122
42. Genealogical Service .................................. 125
43. Gift Baskets .......................................... 127
44. Gift-Buying Service ................................... 131
45. Greeting Cards, Creating .............................. 132
46. Greeting Card Verse ................................... 136
47. Hair Care, Mobile ..................................... 138
48. Handwriting Analysis .................................. 142
49. Herb Farming .......................................... 145
50. Home Party Sales ...................................... 148
51. House-Sitting Business ................................ 153
52. Junk Business: Turn Trash into Cash ................... 158
53. Lawnmower Reconditioning .............................. 160
54. Literary Agent: Income from Authors ................... 162
55. Longaberger Baskets ................................... 164
56. Lot Clean-Up .......................................... 167
57. Mail Receiving/Forwarding ............................. 168
58. Meeting Planner ....................................... 171
59. Mushroom Magic ........................................ 173
60. Music ................................................. 176
61. Odd Jobs .............................................. 179
62 Outdoor Collectibles ................................... 182
63. Outdoor Guide ......................................... 188
64. Paper Recycling ....................................... 191
65. Pet Care ............................................. 193
66. Photo Buttons ......................................... 195
67. Photo Postcards ....................................... 197
68. Potpourri ............................................. 200
69. Recycled Glass Art .................................... 203
70. Researching Birth Dates .............................. 206

71. Résumé Service........................................ 209
72. Self-Published Booklets ................................ 211
73. Sharpening Saws and Tools............................. 214
74. Silk Plants............................................ 216
75-80. Six Ways to Pickup Truck Profits ...................... 218
81. Snail Ranching ....................................... 220
82. Swimming Lessons.................................... 224
83. Tag Sales............................................ 228
84. Talent Agency for Tradespeople ......................... 231
85-94. Ten Ways to Earn Vacation Money ..................... 233
95. Travel Writing ........................................ 239
96. Tutoring............................................. 244
97. Typing Profits ........................................ 247
98. Video Services........................................ 250
99. Worm Farming........................................ 253
100. Writing/Editing Service............................... 257

# INTRODUCTION

When you first read the title of this book, a doubtful smirk might have broken upon your face. After all, perhaps you thought, what kind of business can you really start with only $500? Well, we've uncovered no fewer than 100 of them.

When most of us hear phrases like "start a new business" or "start-up costs," our minds immediately conjure figures with lots of zeros in them. While it is true that most businesses do require several thousand dollars to start up, there are certainly many that don't. They really do exist; it's just a matter of focusing in on them.

The impetus behind this book was realizing what the current financial situation is for many people like you. You're struggling. Every paycheck has to be stretched just to make ends meet—even though your spouse may be working, too. You need extra money, especially if you have a family and a mortgage to pay.

Sadly, that's how things are for a growing number of Americans. The United States is no longer a nation with a "comfortable" middle class. And with the lengthening recession we've been hit with in the last few years, our finances are tighter than ever. Many wonder if their jobs are secure, and saving money for the future, once a cherished tradition, has receded to futile wishing.

We won't discuss here what the causes of this dismal economic climate are. There are many, and you'll be hard-pressed to find two financial experts who will agree on them. Suffice it to say that this is the current reality.

Things being what they are, you have probably considered starting your own business, even as a sideline, to supplement your income. Perhaps you never acted on that consideration because you lacked what you thought would be adequate start-up funds. While it's true that the more start-up funds you have available, the better your chances are for early success, you *can* start a satisfying, profitable business with no more than $500.

## How is it possible?

One of the reasons that all 100 businesses suggested in this book require such a low investment in that all can be operated out of your home. There's no need to rent office space, so your initial overhead is minimal. Later, when your business begins earning decent profits, you might want to consider renting office space, but at first, it's not necessary.

These businesses also have in common that whatever tools and materials needed to start can be purchased for less than $500—sometimes for much less. There are businesses listed here that require an initial investment of as little as $5!

It's true that some businesses assume you already own some important piece of equipment. For instance, to operate a light hauling business, you would need a pick-up truck; to start a computer consulting business, we assume you would already have a computer. Chances are, if you didn't already have this equipment, you wouldn't be interested in these businesses anyway.

It's also true that these businesses probably won't make you rich overnight, and we certainly wouldn't promise any such thing. We do, however, propose that each one has the potential for substantial earnings. What the earnings will actually be will depend on a number of factors, not the least of which is the effort you put into the business. No business, large investment or small, makes money by itself. It will require time, patience, enthusiasm, and determination on your part to achieve the level of profitability you desire.

It's probably best to start on a part-time basis. You'll get to learn the ins and outs of the business, you'll find out whether you really like running the business, and, of course, you'll keep your costs as low as possible. Once you've gotten your feet wet, determined that there's a good market for your product or service, and increased your profits to the point where you can adequately support yourself and your family—then you might want to make the switch to full-time.

The biggest cost for most businesses just starting out is advertising. This is where the ideas listed here have a big advantage. Virtually every one of them can get off the ground with a simple, inexpensive classified ad in your local shopper paper. Naturally, if you have more money to invest, you'll want to put it into advertising. No business is going to go anywhere unless potential customers know about it. However, there are lots of low-cost ways to get exposure, and these are described in Part 3 of this book.

Want more proof that you can start a business for $500 or less? The best proof is in the ideas themselves. In most cases they are based on actual case histories—people just like you who, without a lot of money to invest, decided to "take the plunge." To protect their privacy we have changed the people's names and the location of their businesses, but we guarantee that the stories in this book are true.

## The key to low-investment success

We recommend, once you get the business going, that you re-invest the profits in the business. That may be hard for you to do, since one of the reasons you started the business was that you needed the extra money. Try to think of the long term, however. Those initial profits can buy better or more equipment, improve your ad campaign, and spruce up your image. Only in that way will your business grow and yield even more profits.

## Which business to start?

When deciding which business to start, choose one you will enjoy and with which you have some familiarity, if possible. Many people turn hobbies into money-making ventures, for example, while others create off-shoots from their regular jobs.

Some people operate small manufacturing businesses out of their garage or basement; others set up service-oriented businesses in their kitchen or from their van; some have discovered the lucrative field of importing goods, and others have tucked mail-order companies into spare rooms, since you don't need a store front for this kind of business but only a mail box and space for inventory.

As you think about what kind of business to operate, consider where you live, what your job skills and hobbies are, what equipment you own, what the needs of your community are, and certainly, what work you enjoy doing.

# PART ONE:

# STARTING ON A SHOESTRING BUDGET

The best low-cost opportunities are the ones you make for yourself, right in your own home. Starting a business on a very small budget is not only possible, it is being done every day. Everyone has heard that undercapitalization is the reason most small businesses fail. Wrong. Most small businesses fail because their owners lack experience and business knowledge, not money. If you have a marketable product or service, a basic understanding of small business principles, and a lot of common sense, you can begin to work right now. Once you do, you will realize that money is only one of the tools you need to start a business at home.

Possibilities can make us all rich. Starting a business at home lets us explore these possibilities without spending a great deal of money. Of course, it is always easier to have working capital, but lack of it does not mean that you must give up your dreams. A low-budget business means that you begin gradually and that all income goes back into the business. It also means that you must use creativity and initiative instead of cash to help your business grow.

Believe it or not, having little working capital can actually be a benefit for the new business owner. When your investment is small, you gain the time and flexibility to learn as you go. Large investments require fast growth and an owner who knows exactly what he or she is doing.

Keeping a low overhead will increase your chances of success and allow your venture to yield profits faster. There are many ways you can cut costs in your day-to-day operations. Keep in mind, however, that it's not *always* wise to scrimp; spending a little more initially to get better quality will save you money in the long run.

The following tips will help you to maximize the money you can spend and compensate for the money you don't have to invest.

## Knowledge is power

One of the most basic ingredients for success in business—knowledge—doesn't cost any money at all. Your opportunities for acquiring business expertise are virtually unlimited. Everything you need to know is in your library and bookstore. Spend your time, not your money, learning how to plan your business, then learn how to market your product or service inexpensively. Read every relevant book and publication you can get your hands on and then speak with anyone and everyone who is willing to answer your questions. Analyze successful small businesses and determine why they have thrived where others have failed. The knowledge you gain will provide power that money could never buy.

## Start two businesses

Some business ideas have long-range potential but will not provide immediate income. If you need quick cash, a temporary pursuit can help you finance your dream venture. Do home typing or become a sales representative for an established company. It doesn't matter what you do, as long as it leaves enough time and some extra money for working at your real goal.

## Use money wisely

Don't spend the money you have on a fancy desk or expensive equipment that your target audience will never see. Instead, buy the best business cards and stationery and invest in a separate telephone line and good answering machine. If you must buy a desk and a filing cabinet, however, get the best quality you can for the money, furniture that's not going to fall apart after three months of use. Don't buy more equipment than you really need.

Projecting a professional image to the public is essential to the growth of your business, so use your money to enhance that image. Don't spend for a photocopy machine or a fax machine if you'll hardly ever use them. The faxes you need to send or copies you need to make can be handled elsewhere. It may be inconvenient to be working at the kitchen table, but a fancy home office is a luxury you can't afford yet. When funds are limited, spend money to develop your product or service and reinforce the public's positive perception of your company.

Computer systems and necessary software can be expensive (although the price continually decreases), but they can serve a multitude of functions: typing, filing, invoicing, accounting, record keeping, and more. Computers can save time, which often translates into saving money for your business. (More on this in Part 2.)

Get the most out of the equipment you do buy. Keep a file of warranties and guarantees and a strict record of repairs. Get estimates on any repair jobs and decide whether it's wiser to repair or replace the item. You should also schedule periods of regular preventive maintenance.

## Office supplies

To save on supply costs, keep your purchases at a minimum, but with enough volume-per-order to be eligible for discount prices. Also, try to anticipate your supply needs, then double up on orders to minimize the time and money spent on writing individual orders.

## Correspondence

It costs 29 cents to mail a business letter, right? Actually, it's much more when you consider the paper, envelopes, time and filing involved. To cut costs:

- Use window envelopes. This eliminates having to re-type the address on the envelope.
- If you have a computer, keep names you write to frequently in a database. You can run off multiple labels in this way and use a program's mail merge function to print out form letters with each customer's name automatically embedded.
- For reply letters, use a ruled-off reply box at the bottom of the letter instead of enclosing a separate sheet. This will speed up the reply and save paper.
- Use pre-printed form letters.

## Mailing costs

There are several ways to reduce your overall mailing costs, especially if your business requires a lot of correspondence. For mail-order businesses, these are a must:

- Control stamp use by metering mail whenever possible.
- Don't use expensive air mail unless you must.
- Consider faxing a letter instead of sending it overnight mail.
- Use certified mail rather than registered mail; it's cheaper and serves the same general purpose.
- If you make massive mailings, consider investing in a machine that folds the letters and inserts them in envelopes. Cheaper still, get your kids to help with this chore.
- For mass mailings, consult your postmaster about bulk rate. You'll have to sort the mail by zip code, but a computer system can do this easily before it prints out labels.

## Don't advertise—publicize

The public needs to know about your business, but new business owners with little money to invest cannot afford to advertise. Spending all of your money on one expensive ad in the hope that a larger response will launch your business is a foolish move. Advertising can only be effective when it is placed in exactly the right publications and consistently repeated. When you are just starting out, spending needed cash on advertising is as risky as gambling the rent away.

Instead of advertising, find ways to let the maximum number of people know about your business without spending a lot of money. Distribute appealing flyers, or develop a telemarketing or direct-mail marketing plan that will help you reach the people who are most interested in your business. Most new business owners don't even think of the least expensive method of promotion, which also happens to be the most effective: publicity. Newspapers and magazines as well as television and radio stations need to fill up space and time with interesting items. Your business can be featured if you can give expert advice, offer a benefit to the public, or develop a newsworthy angle to your product or service.

A press release is usually the first step to becoming a guest on a talk show or the subject of a feature article. Create news by sponsoring a contest or donating your time or products to a local charity. Offer a free fact sheet about your specialty to anyone who sends a self-addressed, stamped envelope; the responding names will be the beginning of your own mailing list. Be creative, learn all you can about publicity procedures, and remain persistent in your attempts to attract the media's attention. You'll find lots of low-cost promotion and advertising ideas in Part 3.

### Barter

Doctors do it. Plumbers do it. Anyone who can offer a desirable product or service can do it too. When you exchange goods or services without exchanging money, you are bartering. This is an excellent way to obtain what you need and save cash. A typist could barter with a printer and exchange typing for the cost of business cards. Small publishers can exchange advertising space in each other's publications. Remember, though, even though no money changes hands, the IRS wants to know about bartering arrangements. Before you make any kind of exchange, it might be wise to check with your tax adviser.

### Networking

Networking has been defined as "getting together to get ahead." Joining local and national organizations will put you in touch with others who either share your goals or would be interested in buying your product or service. Contacts with people who have businesses similar to yours will give you the opportunity to ask questions and learn techniques that have been successful for them. You will find many opportunities to offer and receive assistance. But remember, networking is a two-way street. Be prepared to give assistance to others as often as you receive it.

Investing thousands of dollars in a business is no guarantee that it will be successful. Nor is a small investment of cash reason enough to prevent a good business idea from taking hold. You may have to save up to have business stationery printed and cash in your loose change in order to pay for your listing in the Yellow Pages, but you will be laying a strong foundation for the future.

## Other tips:

- During busy times of the year, hire a temporary worker instead of taking on a full-time employee.
- Don't keep or file things that are unnecessary. Try to keep your operation as efficient and streamlined as possible.
- Consider leasing some equipment rather than buying it outright.
- Avoid debt. Pay your bills on time and avoid penalty and interest charges.
- If you need advice, first try obtaining it free from books or from government agencies before you turn to high-fee lawyers and consultants.

**PART TWO:**

# KEEPING COSTS LOW

### Put your new business on a budget

When starting a small business, a budget is essential. It will help you determine what your profit goal should be and whether it is within your reach. Budgeting also helps you plan to earn more than you thought you could before you took the time and trouble to put these figures on paper.

For now you can look at this paper and know—even if your new business is nothing more than a dream—approximately what your net profit may realistically be. You will also be able to see ways to increase it.

Another name for this kind of budget is a projected profit-and-loss statement. Here's how to set up:

1. Start by listing the annual income you expect to receive. This is called your gross profit.
2. List and total all anticipated expenses, including salaries, supplies, rent, equipment, utilities, interest on borrowed money, and other costs.
3. Subtract the expense total from the estimated gross income to determine your probable net. Net is your actual profit.

SAMPLE BUDGET
(PROJECTED PROFIT-AND-LOSS STATEMENT)
Year commencing January 2, 1993 and ending December 31, 1993.

TOTAL REVENUE                                    $ _____
        (income from sale of merchandise or services)

FIXED EXPENSES:

| | |
|---|---|
| Owner salary | $ _____ |
| Employee(s) salary (-ies) | $ _____ |
| Rent | $ _____ |
| Utilities | $ _____ |
| Advertising | $ _____ |

| | |
|---|---|
| Interest on borrowed funds | $ _____ |
| TOTAL FIXED EXPENSES | $ _____ |
| VARIABLE EXPENSES: | |
| Office supplies | $ _____ |
| Manufacturing supplies | $ _____ |
| Equipment purchases, rental, repair | $ _____ |
| TOTAL VARIABLE EXPENSES | $ _____ |
| TOTAL FIXED AND VARIABLE EXPENSES | $ _____ |
| NET INCOME: | $ _____ |

(revenue less total fixed and variable expenses)

*Use this as a worksheet. Add or delete items as necessary.*

The form above can be used as a model. Figures are omitted so that you can fill in your own. Add and delete any expenses and revenues as they apply to your particular situation. Such a budget can also help you increase your anticipated earnings: study it carefully and make changes after considering ways in which you might gain profits and cut costs. Find answers to the following questions:

## To increase revenues . . .

■ Can you charge more for merchandise or services than originally planned? Can you check your competition's prices first, so you don't go too far?

■ Can you cut prices below those of nearby competitors with the same merchandise or service in order to make more sales?

■ Can you do this without starting a price war with your competition?

■ Can you offer more varied goods or services to tempt customers away from the competition or to increase their purchases? If you plan to sell women's watches and bracelets, can you also offer other jewelry items?

■ Can you offer such services as free gift wrapping, deliveries within a certain area, or free parking to encourage customers to trade with you?

## To decrease costs . . .

There are many ways to decrease costs, and some accountants suggest these be divided into two areas: "fixed" and "variable." Fixed costs are those that stay the same regardless of the business income, such as rent, salaries, interest, and advertising. Variable expenses include buying or repairing equipment. The important thing is to list them all so that you can decrease costs.

## Cutting fixed costs

If business rents are excessive, you might cut this cost by locating in a less desirable area than you originally planned, unless you think this will jeopardize potential profits. You might consider using a room in your home or a garage as an office until your enterprise takes hold and you can afford to rent expensive commercial space. If you'll require considerable selling or warehouse space, you might save renting costs by carefully planning space-saving layouts.

If interest on borrowed money is high, can you borrow from a relative at no interest or lower interest, rather than a bank? Can you use your own savings comfortably—if you have enough? You might cut the fixed expense of salaries by doing more work yourself. If you're planning to hire two employees for your new enterprise, can you handle the tasks of one and cut this expense in half? If your projected business requires the help of a specialist, can you save by learning to do this work yourself? Can you work without a salary by starting your new business in your free time while you hold down an outside job?

To cut down on your utility costs, can you start your day an hour earlier and stop when darkness falls to save electricity? Can you replace incandescent lighting with less expensive and brighter fluorescents?

You can advertise with a smaller budget by placing ads in smaller local papers and by posting handbills or distributing flyers yourself.

## Cutting variable expenses

There are ways to cut variable expenses as well. Can you use cheaper but acceptable grades of office supplies and stationery instead of costlier items? Can you purchase in quantity? Would it be better to lease certain equipment rather than purchasing it? If your need for a particular piece of equipment is uncertain, you can rent it for a time to see if you really need it or not. Another benefit to renting equipment is learning what features you may or may not need—on a fax machine, for example. You should also consider purchasing used equipment and furnishings for your office.

A way to cut costs in both areas is by improving your management of the business. Consider speeding up production time with more efficient machinery, if you are manufacturing a product.

You might also cut costs by taking in goods on consignment or dealing with suppliers who are willing to carry you until a specified date when you expect the goods will be sold. Money is tight when you are starting out, and the costs for merchandise can be overwhelming.

In order to decide on the best alternatives, you will have to answer a number of questions concerning each, and may have to work up several tentative and revised budgets before coming to a final plan.

## Increase profits by preparing a projected budget

1. Don't forget taxes. Take your finished budget to a tax counselor to learn which expenses are deductible or can be revised to be made deductible.
2. Use your imagination. If you can't locate in the best part of town, can you advertise there by billboard or distribute material directing customers to your location?
3. Take advantage of any help others may offer. For example, there are manufacturers and suppliers who offer free advertising and display materials to retailers.
4. Be exact. Don't try to "guesstimate" your costs. If you plan to hire a bookkeeper, find out what the average salary for a book-keeper is beforehand. When dealing with rental costs, don't forget accessory expenses such as deposits, commissions, and decorating and maintenance charges, if any.
5. Remember, no budget is etched in stone. Even if you've drawn up many budgets, the final version should still be open to revision. Your main goal is profit, and you'll gain the most by keeping expenses low.

## Invest in a computer—eventually

Certainly, the business that is starting on a shoestring budget will not be able to purchase a computer right off the bat. There goes your $500 investment—and then some. However, once you've gotten your business off the ground, purchasing a personal computer should be a serious consideration. In the long run it can save you time and money. Not all businesses can benefit from a computer in the home office, but many can. In fact, your small business can be more profitable if you use a computer to help you in the following ways.

### Bookkeeping

If you currently do business bookkeeping with a ledger book and calculator, or if you pay an accountant or someone else to do your books, consider replacing them with a personal computer. New software packages provide all accounting functions in one computerized package. You can computerize your general ledger, accounts receivable and payable, inventory, invoicing, job costing, and payroll. As you gain experience, these functions will become automatic and accurate, saving you time and money.

### Customer files

If you keep information about your customers in an address book or on pieces of paper crammed in a file drawer, you could be using a computerized database instead. In fact, a database on computer is very much like your address book or file of papers. However, computers do a much better job of organizing information and getting it back when you need it.

With a database management program you can set up your own specific filing systems. You can create mailing lists, inventory lists, lists of customers, and lists of suppliers. This system also makes it easier for you to sell your customer mailing list to other businesses.

### Word processing

You can use a personal computer to create and print letters, lists, forms, and advertising flyers. With the right kind of printer attached to your personal computer, you can print items sharp enough to be copied by a photocopier or your local print shop. This can save on printing costs as well as valuable time.

Accounting, database management, and word processing are perhaps the three most important operations that a personal computer can do. With a personal computer, you can do these operations yourself and do them more efficiently. That means your small business will be more profitable.

### Hardware

IBM makes the most common kind of personal computer. Copies of IBM's computers, known as "clones" or "IBM-compatibles," are made by many other manufacturers, such as Radio Shack, Hewlett-Packard, AST, and a host of foreign manufacturers like Hyundai, Toshiba, and NEC. Such computers are also known by the kind of operating software they use. All IBM and IBM-compatible computers use MS-DOS software. Another name for these computers is "MS-DOS-compatible."

A personal computer stores information on removeable disks or on a storage system built into the computer. Removable disks are called "floppy disks," while a built-in unit is called a "hard disk" or "hard drive." Storage space on a floppy disk and hard drive is measured in kilobytes (1,000 bits of information) and megabytes (1,000,000 bits of information), respectively. A typical hard disk contains from 20 to 80 megabytes of storage space, enough for hundreds of pages of text, customer information, spreadsheets, or inventory information. A floppy disk can hold 360, 720,

1,200, or 1,440 kilobytes of data.

To best serve your business, a personal computer system should include a hard drive and at least one floppy drive. The software you will run on your personal computer will come on one or more floppy disks. Usually the programs are copied from the floppies onto your hard drive. Then your computer will operate at its maximum speed, using the programs on the hard drive and storing data there.

"Memory" refers to your personal computer's capacity to run programs. Memory is also measured in kilobytes. Today, most computers have 640K of memory. Memory is also referred to as "RAM" which means Random Access Memory; 640K is required to run many of today's more sophisticated business programs.

Computer prices range from a low of about $500 up to $3,000 or more. At prices below $1,000, a personal computer should offer a minimum of 640K of memory and two floppy disk drives. Adding a hard disk drive pushes the price to at least $1,500. More expensive computers offer more memory, more storage on a larger hard drive, and better monitors to display your work.

For a full range of business applications, you should buy a computer with a hard disk drive and color monitor. Plan to spend from $1,500 to $2,000 for the computer, monitor, and keyboard.

### Printers

There are three kinds of computer printers: laser, daisy-wheel, and dot-matrix. Each has advantages and disadvantages but can be judged according to two overall characteristics: print quality and printing speed.

Print quality can be measured in "dpi" or dots (of ink) per square inch, or it can be stated as "draft-quality, near-letter quality, or letter quality." As the quality of the output increases, so does the price of the printer.

Dot-matrix printers are usually the least expensive; they are fast and have a range of modes, from draft quality to near-letter-quality. Daisy-wheel printers, which are slower, work like standard typewriters, producing letter-quality pages. At the high end of the price scale, laser printers range in price from $1,000 to $7,000 and can produce high-quality pages with graphics. Laser printers are quiet, fast, and produce pages that will add a professional image to your business. If your business depends on the high-quality appearance of sales letter, forms, flyers, and brochures, a laser printer is a must.

### Software

Your computer can't do anything without software. Specific software programs for your business fall into three broad price ranges.

$125—These programs usually are for one job and offer only a few functions.

$125 to $399—Most programs for your small business are in this price range.

$400 and up—There are many programs with a variety of features in this price range. As your business continues to grow and profit, you will want to get more powerful programs for important functions like accounting and payroll.

*Learn all you can*

Before investing your hard-earned money in a personal computer, consider taking an introductory class in computer use at your local community college, public library, adult education center, or retail computer store. With the investment of a few hours of your time, you can explore some of the basic functions of a personal computer. You can also learn about the performance of various models.

During an introductory class, get to know the instructor and explain your business. Ask the instructor to recommend a particular computer and software to help you. By learning about computers in an adult education class, you can gain valuable knowledge at a very low cost.

After carefully studying hardware and software, you will be ready to make a wise purchase. Many personal computers are purchased through mail order. Again, a computer magazine will have many ads for computers that can be purchased by mail. On the other hand, buying a computer from a local computer store should give you access to training and service after the sale. A third option is to buy a used computer through classified ads in your local newspaper or *Computer Shopper* magazine. A local computer club may also have a "computer swap meet" where used equipment is available to the public. Check it out.

Although a personal computer sounds expensive when you figure all costs, it will soon start paying for itself by helping you get more sales, keep in touch with current customers, and turn out more accurate billing.

## PART THREE:

# LOW- AND NO-COST ADVERTISING AND PROMOTION

No matter what kind of business you choose to start, advertising is essential for getting new customers and selling more to the customers you already have. The entrepreneur who is operating on a shoestring budget must spend every advertising and promotion penny wisely. There are, in fact, many ways of promoting your new business without spending a lot of money, but each requires effective planning.

The first step in planning an effective program is to decide who your potential customers are. Do your prospects read magazines or newspapers? Will flyers or word-of-mouth draw potential customers? Are you selling in a specialized field, so that some particular trade journal will reach the majority of your buyers?

In addition to considering your regular customers, determine who your potential buyers might be and how you can expand your prospect list through advertising. Study various magazines and local newspapers to see what kind of advertising is being done by competitors or producers of related products.

After you have isolated your customers, you must then decide what you want them to think about you, your product, or service. This will enable you to target your advertising where it will do the most good.

The next step is to consider what kind of advertising will be most effective for you. Study the different advertising media available, tabulating data on comparable costs and results. Your study should cover signs, notices and bulletins, business cards, and display or classified advertising in newspapers and magazines.

How often you should advertise depends on your service, product, or business. Seasonal advertising is sufficient for some operations, but generally it is a good idea to keep your name or logo before the public at all times. The most cost-efficient way to do this may be to run continuous classified ads.

When you plan your advertising program, be sure it will completely cover your territory. It is better to cover too large an area than too small.

The basic purpose in advertising, of course, is to sell your product or service. This is accomplished by attracting your prospects' attention and holding it long enough for them to get your message.

Following are several ways to advertise and promote your business on a shoestring budget.

## Word-of-mouth

Word of mouth simply means satisfied customers spreading the word about your product or service. This is the oldest and perhaps best form of advertising. It is also, of course, the cheapest, since it's free. Don't think it will come automatically, however. You have to initiate it. Try to develop warm, friendly relationships with the customers you already have, and remind them to tell their friends about you. Be honest. Tell them you are trying to build up your business and you'd appreciate their help. People really do like to lend a hand when given the opportunity. If your profit margin is high enough, you can also offer "freebies" or commissions as incentives for referrals.

## Press releases

This is another form of "free" advertising. Sent to the various media—newspapers, magazines, radio, and television—the press releases you write will describe your service, product, or some special promotion. There is no guarantee that the media will use your press release for publication or broadcast, so it is important to make the contents of the release as "newsworthy" as possible. It should create interest, be unusual, or make an extraordinary offer.

## Signs

Simplicity and visibility are the keys to business signs. They don't have to be boring, just legible and to the point. You can afford to be a bit more decorative if you have a sidewalk store, but for roadside businesses, "less is more." Use bright, bold lettering with only a few main words, and perhaps an arrow directing customers to your place of business. Commercial signs can be quite expensive, so consider making them yourself. Check with local authorities about sign ordinances in your area. After legal permission, do a little research. Drive down the road to determine where your sign should be in order to give motorists enough time to see it, read it, and stop safely.

## Business cards

These are a must for most businesses. They don't cost much and will make your business look much more professional.

Don't wait for people to ask for a business card; give them to everybody! Even those who don't seem to be very interested just might have a friend who needs your service. Tack your cards on bulletin boards, stack them on counters, include them with everything you mail—even when you're paying your personal bills. The person opening your envelope may be able to use your service or product.

When you're having cards made, remember that offset printing costs less than engraving. It's helpful to make your cards a little bit unusual. Try a different size, a color other than white, or printing all to one side or all around the edges. Anything to make them stand out.

## Bulletin boards

Tack up notices of your service or product on bulletin boards in apartment complexes, condominiums, recreation halls, club meeting rooms, office buildings, laundromats, shopping centers, hospitals, schools, YMCA's, supermarkets, churches, synagogues, and fraternal organizations. To make it easier for prospective customers to remember your phone number, list it on small tabs cut so they can be torn off easily. Recheck your locations periodically to see whether tabs are being taken and whether they need replacing.

To make your notices look professional without paying for expensive typesetting, use press-on lettering. This lettering is available in a wide array of styles and sizes from your local office supply store, which will also have a variety of border tapes to outline and call attention to your message. If you already have a computer, small computer-printed posters can be printed out with software programs like Printshop.

Once you have your master copy prepared, you can take it to a quick-copy print shop and have a few hundred postcard-sized photocopies made for a small cash outlay. Post these on all the bulletin boards in your market area.

Whether you plan to distribute 10,000 flyers or post only a few bulletins, locations and visibility are prime considerations. A thousand home-improvement flyers passed out in a brand new community probably won't get nearly the response of half that many in an older community. But even if you choose the best locations, a four-page flyer won't do the job of a single-page notice. People usually don't take the time to read more than a few lines. So, keep your bulletins like your signs, simple and eye-catching. In addition to the locations already mentioned, consider posting signs in post offices, courthouses, libraries, grocery stores, community centers, boat clubs—any place that has fairly heavy foot traffic and where the proprietor will allow it. If your time and money limit you to just a few bulletins, choose the most strategic locations, those where your potential customers are most likely to go. Have business cards handy so that you can tack one up on every bulletin board you see.

When planning a large-scale flyer distribution, be very selective. Use your best judgment to match prospective customers to your business. Figure out where they live, work, and shop, then let those places be your target areas.

### Flyers

Keep them to a single page and keep them simple so they can be read at a glance. Have an artist friend help, use press-on letters as already described, or simply type the information. Then mail them, hand them out, tack them on bulletin boards, have kids distribute through neighborhoods, put them on auto windshields in parking lots—wherever "your" customers hang out.

Make sure such distribution is allowed by law in your area, and remember that it is illegal to put any kind of notice in people's mailboxes—only the post office is allowed to do that. However, you can place notices on or hanging from the mailbox.

### Product displays

If you're an artist, photographer, crafts person, plant grower, etc., you can lend your creations to banks, libraries, office buildings, and restaurants. This gives great visibility to your product in a professional setting. Have a supply of business cards handy, and place a sign with your name, address, and phone number in plain view.

### Free services

Offer a freebie related to your product or service. For example, a new lawn-care company might offer free soil testing. A newspaper write-up (free) can invite people to bring soil samples from their lawns in envelopes to you, the lawn care specialist, any day of the week between nine and five. Once the soil is tested, the potential customers are right there to discuss lawn problems, products, and services.

### Talk it up

Offer to talk about your specialty to area groups. They're always in need of speakers for meetings, luncheons, and social gatherings. A nursery owner might give talks on plant care: a florist could talk on flower arranging. Take some of your photocopied or quick-printed flyers and your business cards and leave them wherever you've been. You should be able to obtain a list of organizations from your local Chamber of Commerce.

## "Bird dog"

If your profit margin is high enough, offer family and friends a commission for every new customer they send your way. It will cost you a few dollars in profits, but at least you won't be spending money until you earn it. The increased volume will give you more actual earnings in the long run.

## Radio and TV talk shows and newspaper columns

Develop a free expert service for the local media. Write a column or tape a brief offer to answer questions, but don't commercialize the material by referring to your own specific business. Many radio talk shows have a local expert talk about his or her specialty for a few minutes and then answer phone-in questions from listeners. Call show hosts and newspaper editors and tell them you're available for a show or a column.

## Coupons

Work out deals with other businesses to include money-saver or free-gift coupons with customer purchases. They can pass out coupons from your business to their customers; you can hand out coupons from their business to your customers. Other new business owners should be especially cooperative. Look for businesses with mutual markets. For example, if your main market is a homeowner, work with another business whose major customers are homeowners.

## Trade-offs with radio stations or ad agencies

Most radio stations will let clients barter for commercial spots with services. If you're a janitorial service, for example, offer to clean their offices or windows for X number of spots each week. If you're a typing service, offer to handle a certain amount of overflow typing for an agreed-upon number of spots.

## Special events

Every community schedules holiday and local interest parades throughout the year, as well as anniversary celebrations, competitions, shows, and so on. Participate in these by building your own float, manning your own booth, or sponsoring a concession; or by helping some organization build or man its, with the agreement that your name and service/product will be given prominent attention. You'll be contributing your time for some publicity, so everyone will gain.

## Telephone

Develop a brief telephone questionnaire or sales pitch and make a specific number of calls per day to arouse interest, pick up leads, or make sales.

## Newspapers

For the small business newspapers are, of course, the standard form of advertising. Two categories are offered—display ads and classifieds. The displays are more noticeable and more expensive. If you decide on newspaper advertising, inquire about long-term commercial rates. Many papers also offer "specials" for short-term runs. So investigate all the possibilities.

Try to put your display ads in strategic parts of the paper. For example, instead of using the standard "services offered" column for your custom dressmaking ad, try a small display ad on the Special Announcements page. You'll probably make up the difference in cost with the extra orders for wedding gowns and designer originals you will receive.

### Free newspaper publicity

Whenever you attend a training school, achieve some special accomplishments, perform a civic service, or give a talk, write up a short article about it to mail or hand to the business editors of every newspaper and radio and TV station in your market area. If your business is unusual, call the feature editors and tell them about it. Someone may want to run a feature story about you and your work.

Subject material for news releases can include openings, expansion or special events, unusual products or services, instruction on how to make or do something, unusual orders filled, unusual autobiographical material, new personnel, anniversaries, charity gifts, product success stories, etc.

This kind of publicity is often more effective than paid advertising. In larger cities with greater competition for space and air time, you may have to come up with a new "angle," perhaps with some tie-in or celebrity involvement.

Study your local newspapers and note what is picked up in the local news on radio and television. Find out the business editors' deadlines and usual slow days. A press release dropped off at a small university radio station on a Friday afternoon might be broadcast over the weekend and Monday morning, too, if the news director takes the weekend off. Schedule events for the morning if you want coverage in an afternoon paper.

Usually, it's a good idea to deliver press releases later in the week.

## Magazines

You may need extra cash for this kind of advertising, though classified rates are modest. You'll want to be especially careful to match product to readership. Refer to *Standard Rate & Data* (available at your library) for a complete list of publications and information about their readers and circulations. Contact the publications of your choice for rate schedules.

In this medium it's vital to plan ahead. If you're going to advertise a Christmas product, start making inquiries in July.

## Miscellaneous forms of promotion

Here are some other ideas for low-cost promotion. Using all of them could end up costing you a fortune, so pick and choose those that appeal to you or seem especially applicable for your business.

- *Display the name of your company on any vehicles you own and ask generous friends to do the same.* Check with local authorities to avoid conflicts with "commercial vehicle" ordinances.
- *T-shirts are a great way to advertise.* They're fairly cheap when bought in quantity and can easily be silk-screened with your name. Give them away free if you can possibly afford it; otherwise, sell them at cost.
- *Giveaways.* People love to receive "free" items, especially items they can use to gain knowledge or improve their lives. You can base an entire promotional campaign on this trait. If you're running a furniture repair business, for instance, you could give away a furniture repair brochure, free furniture planning guides, or color swatches. Once you begin giving away authoritative information, customers will begin to perceive you as an expert in your field.
- *News creation.* Want to get names and news from your business in the local newspapers? It may be easier than you think. If you don't have any news to report to the local media, create some. Maybe you're selling an unusual product line. Or maybe you've opened a free advice center for the community. Or maybe you've received an award from a civic or professional group. Let the media know. Local *PennySavers* and weeklies are often quite interested in business news of this sort and can help you attract the attention of thousands of people.
- *Events.* Another effective way to get attention is to stage a special promotional event. If you run fitness classes, for instance, you could stage a celebrity instructor day. If you're promoting a new real estate business, you can offer tours of a model home in the area. If you're selling children's products and it's springtime, you can offer lunch with the Easter bunny. Get the idea?
- *Charity tie-ins.* Are you launching a new product? Trying to increase visibility among a particular segment of your community? Offer your product to one or more local charities as a raffle prize or for use at a fund-raising event. You'll receive lots of exposure

among people who buy tickets or attend the event.

■ *Contests.* Offer a desirable or unique item—or even several items—as contest prizes. First, find a contest theme that ties into your business. A caterer might offer a quiche-eating contest. A photographer might offer a young model contest. A mail-order craft firm might offer an "Early American" handicrafts contest. Invite contest submissions and offer prizes to the winners. Do contests attract attention? You bet. All it takes is a few signs and a small press announcement or two and the word will spread throughout the community grapevine.

■ *Community service.* Nothing brings you to the attention of people faster—or more favorably—than community service. Ask yourself how your enterprise can be a "good neighbor" to your community. If you're running a lawn care and gardening service, perhaps you can offer one season's services at no charge to a needy charitable organization or nursing home in your area. Hundreds of people will hear about your work in the process through word of mouth (or you could "leak" the information to the media). Volunteer for various community causes. If appropriate, you can step in during a community emergency, offering products and services to help an organization or individuals in need.

■ *Badges and novelties.* You can easily and inexpensively produce badges, bumper stickers, book covers, and other novelty items for distribution in your area. You can imprint your business name and first names of customers on many of these products at little cost and distribute them for free. Or you can tie your novelty program into a contest: once a month you can offer a prize to anyone you encounter and who happens to be sporting one of your badges, or to any person whose car happens to carry one of your bumper stickers or badges with peel-off coupons, redeemable at your place of business.

■ *Celebrity visits.* With a bit of persistence you may be able to arrange for a local media celebrity, public official, or entertainment personality—even a fictitious cartoon character or clown—to visit your service. The celebrity can sign autographs, read stories to children, perform a cooking demonstration, or perform any one of a hundred other traffic-building activities.

■ *Celebrate holidays.* You'll probably want to celebrate major public holidays with special sales. But celebrate some of the offbeat holidays as well. Almost every business can capitalize on a few of the lesser-known holidays. Ever hear of National Pickle Day, for instance? Or Cat Lovers Month? Once you find the "right" holiday you can sponsor a special sale or special product offer or arrange special media coverage of a holiday event.

■ *Go where the people are.* Can you open sales or information booths at community fairs and festivals? This promotional technique can work wonders for gift retailers, craftspeople, and personal service firms. If you have the people and the time, can you handle regional fairs or even trade shows?

■ *Mailing lists.* Once you begin establishing a committed clientele, keep a mailing list. Save the names from your mail orders and telephone inquiries. Eventually, you'll be able to send product circulars or even catalogs to the folks on your list and promote your products by mail.

■ *Scavenger hunts.* If you want people to buy *now*, offer them an unbeatable deal. If they bring you an old product—a small appliance, a book, whatever—you'll give them a worthwhile discount on a comparable new item. Or stage a general-purpose scavenger hunt. Customers who bring in three canned goods for your community's food bank will receive a discount on products purchased that day.

■ *Parties.* Everyone loves a party. Why not celebrate the anniversary of your business or some special holiday by offering baked goods and beverages? If you're running a service business, perhaps you can offer an open house or reserve a small banquet room in your community. Besides refreshments, be sure the place is brightly decorated. You might even want to offer simple gifts.

■ *Greeting Cards.* Do you send out greeting cards to major customers or clients? Holidays, birthdays, and anniversaries make nice greeting card occasions. Greeting cards create enormous goodwill and keep your name in front of people.

■ *Seminars.* In this information-hungry age, people love to receive advice, especially about their personal needs and hobbies. If you sell health foods or run fitness classes, perhaps you can offer "wellness" seminars during lunchtime to your area's business community. If you're an interior decorator, perhaps you can offer one-hour decorating workshops to any group of ten people who will gather in someone's home. If you're running a printing business, perhaps you can offer tours and layout seminars at your plant.

By all means, advertise in the media if you must. But don't neglect your greatest promotional asset—your mind. Ponder the products, services, and events you can offer the community and devise a creative promotional strategy around them. You'll have to invest a bit of time and energy in the project, but the payoff will be worth it. You'll save hundreds—or even thousands—of advertising dollars and, better yet, you'll travel a well-worn shortcut to profit.

# PART FOUR:

# 100 BUSINESSES TO START FOR $500 OR LESS

## ADULT EDUCATION

**Start-up Costs:** $0. **Potential Earnings:** Negotiable. Average $200 for four-week course. **Advertising:** Generally handled by employer, college or organization. **Special Qualifications:** Specialized knowledge or skill and the ability to teach it to others. **Best Advice for Success:** Start at the beginning; don't assume that your students have prior knowledge of your subject.

All over the country, ordinary people are being paid for sharing their skills. It doesn't matter where you live or how old you are—you can do it, too. As an adult education instructor, you'll have fun sharing your experiences and knowledge and it won't cost you a thing to start.

Adult education classes, or continuing education classes, as they are sometimes called, provide non-credit instruction on a wide variety of topics. Consider a person who wants to learn to speak French. He or she could learn to speak French from an adult education instructor at a cost far less than a college course. If the word "instructor" makes you wonder if you need a teaching degree, wonder no more. To be an adult education instructor all you need is a talent or skill and a willingness to share it.

### How to begin

Most adult education classes are given in the evening at community colleges or neighborhood recreation centers. Your area YMCA, YWCA, or other clubs may offer adult education classes. Check local newspapers for locations of current classes, or call the local junior college or recreation center for information.

To decide what to teach, think of what you love to do best. Is it woodworking, refinishing furniture, cooking, playing the flute, writing, or restoring old photographs? Are you especially adept at a foreign language, lawnmower or bicycle repair, computers, or oil painting? Choose a topic you would like to share.

Call the person in charge of your local adult education program to ask if he or she would be interested in an instructor with your particular skill. When you meet with the program director, take samples of your work, if possible—oil paintings you have done, samples of your writing, etc.

### What to charge; costs

The program director can help you decide what to charge. In most cases you can negotiate. If you feel the price is too low to be worth your time, say so. If you think the price is too high to be of interest to most people, let the program director know.

A course that runs four weeks (one night per week) can average $10 to $20 per person for the course. An eight-week course can run between $30 and $50. Specialized classes (such as acting or oil painting) can run $125 or higher per person. If you have ten students in a four-week course, and you charge $20 per student you will have earned $200, minus a percentage. (The college, or whoever is providing space for your class, will normally keep a percentage of your fees, often between 10 and 25 percent.)

You will probably want to set a minimum and maximum number of students for each class. Are five people enough to make it worth your while? Would thirty be too many?

As a rule, whoever is providing the classes will provide advertising. A catalog of classes is often published, or a listing of classes is printed in the local newspaper. However, don't underestimate the power of word-of-mouth advertising. Once you are hired to teach a class, tell your family, friends, neighbors, and coworkers. All this costs you nothing.

### Teaching methods

At first you may wonder if you "have what it takes." You do. Students appreciate adult education teachers because they offer skills at affordable prices. It may sound overly simplified, but when teaching others, start at the beginning. Don't assume your students have prior knowledge of your subject. If you are teaching bicycle repair, you may need to begin with explaining the names and uses of the different tools you will be using. Some students may not know a socket wrench from an air pump.

Make a schedule of the material you want to cover. During the beginning of the first class, talk to your students. Determine what they want to get out of it. If most of the students in a language class want to be able to speak only, they probably would not want to spend much time on writing or reading. Your main objective is to help them to learn to speak the language.

You are offering a service to your community. It's an added plus that you get paid for doing it.

— *Mary Glines*

## AEROBICS CLASSES

**Start-up Costs:** $500. **Potential Earnings:** $15,000 to $20,000. **Advertising:** Direct contact with business and community centers. **Special Qualifications:** First, train to be an instructor. **Equipment Needed:** None. **Best Advice for Success:** Search for skilled instructors and spend the necessary time in training so that you feel comfortable they are representing your company in the best possible way.

Music fills the large room as the instructor leads a class of leotard-clad women in a challenging workout. Small children enjoy supervised play in the room next door, while their mothers burn off calories and attempt to twist and bend their bodies into shape. This class is only one of forty weekly sessions that are conducted under the supervision of Linda Neason, the twenty-five- year-old owner of Linda's Aerobics. Linda's Aerobics has become an exciting and growing new business with sixteen instructors, a spa, and mobile aerobics classes.

A minimal start-up cost of $500, few expenses, rapid growth, and high profitability make Neason's success worthy of attention. At the age of fifteen, Neason taught aerobics in local spas. After high-school graduation she brought her expertise to the community centers and the YWCA. These organizations, eager to sponsor exercise classes in their own facilities, asked her to provide the instruction. In just a few months Neason had more opportunities than she could realistically handle. She hired her first instructor, then another, and another, and soon began marketing Linda's Aerobics to corporations.

Many companies eager to improve morale and physical fitness saw Linda's Aerobics as an economical way to bring exercise to the work place. Employees contributed a conference room and people flocked to the after-work program several times each week. As Linda's Aerobics grew it became crucial for Neason to focus on the quality of each instructor.

### Instructing instructors

Neason says, "I hire only the individual who wants to teach other people. My instructors should be aware of each person's needs and level of ability. Their attention focuses on the class at all times, watching for signs of fatigue, insuring that the exercises are done properly and that everyone is having fun." Instructors spend six weeks in training. In addition to an hourly salary, Neason pays her instructors cash incentives for increasing number of participants that attend each session. Sharing the profits encourages each instructor to give his or her best to every class.

Neason's largest class meets every Tuesday and Thursday night. One hundred and ten people, including teens, adults, and senior citizens, gather in a neighborhood community center to exercise. Everyone performs the same routines to the same music, so it is possible to rotate responsibilities as employees request time off or change schedules. Neason leads the sessions herself for at least the first two weeks. Then, gradually, she gives the leadership of the class to the instructor, but only when she has confidence in that person's ability.

Because her expenses are low, Neason can offer workouts for a nominal cost of $3 per session. For an additional dollar parents can take advantage of the on-premise baby-sitting service while they exercise. Participants pay only for the classes they attend, unlike health clubs and spas, which charge a monthly fee.

## Working out the details

Neason spends little on advertising or promotion, choosing instead to market her product directly by calling on businesses and community centers. Your marketing efforts should be equally energetic and persistent. Contact any business or community group you think might be interested in your services. Consider offering discount introductory sessions or live demonstrations at local malls and health fairs.

Before you begin teaching, consult your own attorney for additional insurance and liability information.

If you are interested in beginning an aerobics enterprise in your area, follow Neason's example and train to be an instructor first. Local universities, community centers, and the Red Cross offer courses in safety, first aid, and CPR. If you need aerobics training, consult your local gyms and fitness centers. These courses will give you the knowledge you need to start your own classes. After you have established your credentials, concentrate on insuring that your high standards are consistently demonstrated by your employees. Search for high-quality instructors and spend the necessary time in training so that you feel comfortable that they are representing your company in the best possible way. Frequent evaluations and instructor incentive programs will enable you to keep the best people as your employees.

*— Laurel T. Griffith*

## AIRPORT EXPRESS SERVICE

**Start-up Costs:** $500 (assuming you already own a passenger minivan). **Potential Earnings:** Up to $50,000. **Advertising:** Newspaper ads; Yellow Pages ad. **Special Qualifications:** None. **Equipment Needed:** Minivan. **Best Advice for Success:** Start slowly, but put your all into it.

Mark McConville's entrepreneurial instincts switched on when he overheard a person complaining about the high cost of air fare for shuttle flights between Montgomery, Alabama, and Atlanta, Georgia, plus the inconvenience of having to leave one's car parked at the airport for days at a time.

"It hit me that what we ought to do was offer a service in which we go and pick up people at their homes in Montgomery and drive them to the Atlanta airport," McConville says.

The service, called The Airport Express, features one round-trip drive to Atlanta's Hartsfield International Airport in a luxury van driven by a licensed chauffeur. The trip between the two cities takes about two and a half hours, and passengers are offered soft drinks and reading materials to help them pass the time.

It took McConville and his wife Libby between seven and eight months to put their idea together. The McConvilles had to purchase a van, a comprehensive auto insurance policy, and equipment and investigate local, state, and interstate ordinances before they could even think about going on the road. Since their business transports passengers and goes out of state, the McConvilles must meet the conditions of the Interstate Commerce Commission (ICC): proper licenses, insurance, and the ability of the business to fulfill its promise. In most states the agency to contact is the Public Utilities Commission, which regulates rates for interstate transportation, including the railroad and moving vans.

Once the paperwork was completed, the McConvilles bought a minivan at a cost of about $14,000; it was the single most expensive purchase needed to begin the business. If you already own a minivan, your start-up costs will be minimal.

"And then there was the insurance," says Mark McConville. "We had to be insured for at least a million dollars." You must have a policy that covers accidents and death, and the policy must come from a company that is familiar with all aspects of transportation.

Equipment was another expense. Since the McConvilles wanted to offer a luxury service, they added extra features to their van: such as velour seats, soft drinks, and snacks. The couple eventually invested in a computer to help run the business.

In the beginning, Mark did all the driving while Libby sat home managing the telephone. It was difficult, at first, answering the telephone in response to advertising and keeping written schedules and records, but now they are set up on computer and have four drivers driving between the two cities. Mark is able to concentrate on promoting the business while Libby runs the office at home.

Today the McConvilles have three minivans in their fleet. The small, luxuriously appointed vehicles hold seven passengers, but Mark tries to limit the number to five passengers per trip in order to provide roominess and comfort for his clients. Because Airport Express is aimed toward providing needed service, the McConvilles will run a van if only one person is booked, although the service does not break even on the trip.

## Profits and fees

Volume is the key to the McConvilles' profit picture. An estimated figure as to how much each van can earn in a year, would be roughly in the neighborhood of $50,000. This figure is tied directly to the number of passengers that are booked; it can vary up or down by several thousand dollars.

"A one-way trip to Atlanta airport with Airport Express is $35 a person," says Libby. "Round trip is $65. That's half price, or better than the least-expensive round-trip air ticket from Montgomery to Atlanta, and if you are part of a group, your round-trip fare is only $35."

In their first weeks of business the McConville's made runs to Atlanta based on customer demand. Now that the service is established and their future looks sound, they offer schedules that are compatible with many airline arrival and departure times.

## Advertising

Initially, they used newspaper advertising. They've been featured in local articles as well as on the radio, and local response has been very good. Now, very little advertising is used, except for occasional newspaper ads and a listing in the Yellow Pages. Other than that, it's mostly word of mouth.

Airport Express picks up customers right at their front doors and drops them off at the terminal entrance. Customers don't have to worry about a taxi from the bus station to the airport—and they don't have to fight the traffic. Airport Express does it all for them.

The McConvilles advise that if you want to make anything work, you must put your all into it. The shuttle service is only the beginning of what the McConvilles plan to offer.

*— Ed Chaffin*

# ALTERATIONS BUSINESS

**Start-up Costs:** Approximately $500 for business cards and notions, more if you must buy a sewing machine. **Potential Earnings:** $10,000 per year, part-time. **Marketing:** Leaving business card with specialty and retail stores, otherwise, word-of-mouth referrals. **Equipment Needed:** Sewing machine, hem and sewing machines optional, work table, fitting mirror and purchase notions and appliques as needed. **Best Advice for Success:** "Be able to listen and treat each person coming in [as] the most important customer."

Alice Garcia had been sewing cheerleader costumes for her daughter and classmates when a friend asked if she could fill in doing alterations for two weeks at her dry cleaning business. She did, and worked for them for seven years, learning the fastest ways to repair zippers and pockets and take up hems.

When the cleaning business was sold, Garcia decided to go out on her own operating "Alterations By Alice" from a room in her home.

At first Garcia did alterations part-time to give her six kids "nickels and dimes" until she became well established. One of the first accounts to provide her with steady business was a bridal and evening wear shop. She moved her sewing machines and fitting mirror into a bigger room in her house, which has a private entrance. Now Garcia works full-time (six- to eight-hour days per week in winter, and twelve- to fourteen-hour days in the summer) and has hired an assistant to help several days a week.

## Setting up shop

The first requirement is to get a city and state license and a resale number from the franchise board for sales tax payment. That number entitles you to buy fabrics and notions wholesale. Buy hooks and eyes and zippers by the gross, but only buy the fabric and notions you need for specific jobs.

Garcia suggests that you have a supply of business cards printed up and distribute them at local dry cleaners, specialty dress shops, and fabric stores. These stores may not be able to recommend you personally, but they often keep a binder of business cards for referral. You can ask to have your card placed in it for free advertising.

When you are just starting out, it's important to network—to share information and experiences and develop good business practices. Alice suggests joining a local chapter of the Association of Fashion Professionals (AFP). Quarterly meetings offer speakers, group discussions, and workshops for skill development. A newsletter is available by subscription. Another national organization you might join is the Professional Association of Custom Clothiers (PACC). (Check your phone book for local contact information for both groups.)

At one AFP meeting, Garcia met a rep for petticoats. This was a lucky stroke for Garcia, since she buys petticoats wholesale and rents from one to ten of them per weekend as a profitable sideline to her alterations business. Customers often do not realize until the fitting process that their formal dresses or bridal gowns may require a petticoat to complete the look.

"Take as many classes and seminars as you can afford," suggests Garcia. You should also pick up books (see sources below) and read sewing magazines articles for new ideas and techniques.

## Qualifications needed

According to Garcia, knowing the basics of sewing is certainly helpful in an alterations business, but having patience is equally important. You must be able to be professional and keep your cool to be in control in sometimes highly emotional fitting settings.

Garcia's company is not advertised in the phone book. Rather, she has built her business on word-of-mouth referrals. "If I do good work, that is my advertisement," says Garcia with pride.

Being able to listen is a quality that will serve you well, according to Garcia, because a bride-to-be often will bring pictures from magazines, but will turn to *you* to help her sort out what she has her heart set on and what will work best for her.

Since most of Garcia's clients bring her dresses off ready-to-wear racks, alterations often will entail adding gussets to a standard-size dress to make it fit a larger client, or rearranging lace appliques after a waist has been cinched to fit a petite woman.

Another helpful hint is not to overlook the potential repeat customer—especially the teenage customer—for continued business. That clientele has certainly has been a mainstay for Garcia. Sewing cheerleading outfits and prom dresses, with perhaps a bridesmaid's dress or wedding gown requiring customization. These all spell years of loyalty and referrals.

## Equipment and billing

Alterations is a year-round business, what with weddings and parties and people scouting for work. When she was doing general alterations, 90 percent of Garcia's business was altering business clothes. Sometimes a bride would request that Garcia alter her husband's suit pants after the wedding. She has made a couple of gowns but recommends straight alterations because of the short turnaround time.

It is possible to earn more than $10,000 annually for part-time work, according to Garcia. All you need to ply the trade is a good sewing machine that sews backwards and forwards, a sturdy table, and good lighting. A fitting room with a good mirror is necessary for dress and gown fittings. If your budget permits, a blind stitch hemming machine and sewing machine add convenience.

"You learn not to take out more than you need," says Garcia in describing how to save time, a skill that comes with practice. She recalls laboriously ripping out whole zippers when just starting out—and soon after being able to install ten zippers in one hour. Garcia recommends hiring an assistant when your business reaches the point where you don't want to disappoint or turn away a client, but "when you don't want to work fourteen-hour days."

For billing, Garcia uses an invoice that has triplicate copies, one for her files, one for the customer, and one for her daughter who acts as her bookkeeper. Previously, she used a binder ledger to record client names and phone numbers.

As for costs, you might charge $10 to hem a skirt, $4 to $7 to hem men's slacks, $19.50 for a circular skirt, and $25 for a party dress hem. When setting prices, research what other businesses charge in your area. Keep in mind that a person doing alterations from home may have less overhead than a person set up in a dry cleaning or dressmaking shop. You must also consider whether the pants, skirt, or cuffs have lining or lace hemming. if they require hand or machine sewing, and if you must purchase any supplies such as zippers or matching buttons. Before accepting a formal dress or wedding gown, consider asking the customer to bring the garment in person for an estimate. Again, prices vary; on circular hems, they may range from $25 to $75, depending on what the market will bear.

### Pricing examples for hems

|                | No. California | So. California | Arizona      |
|----------------|----------------|---------------|--------------|
| Men's slacks   | $4 to 10       | $4.50         | $4           |
| Jacket cuff    | $16            | $6.50         | $6           |
| Full skirt     | $12            | $12+          | $6 to $8     |
| Straight skirt | $12            | $8 to $12     | $6 to $8     |
| Zipper         | $7             | $6            | $5+ zipper   |
| Circular dresses | $25 to $75   | Estimated     | Estimated    |

Let the customer know verbally and on the invoice how much you are charging, and list what you will be doing so that she can agree and pay half by check up front and the remainder in cash when she picks up her order. That way you won't have checks coming back for insufficient funds later. With experience, she says, you learn to charge an appropriate price for the amount of time the work will take. Otherwise, she says, if it takes longer, you "eat" the overtime. Remember too, that follow-up is important for satisfied customers; be sure to give clients—especially brides—a fitting appointment date and a reminder call letting them know when they can expect to pick up the work.

Garcia says while she "can't please everyone," she loves the business. Whatever the occasion, bridal or dress-for-success, doing alterations offers the opportunity to earn as much as you want, to work and to set up shop from home as an independent operator, accepting referrals from dry-cleaners or specialty dress shops. However you conduct your business, Garcia suggests that, for maximum benefit you "treat everyone very, very special—treat each person as the most important customer you've ever had."

### For more information, see

*Sew to Success: How to Make Money in a Home-Based Sewing Business,* by Kathleen Spikes; *Threads and Sew News* magazines.

— *Paula Nichols*

## APARTMENT CLEANING

**Start-up Costs:** $500 or less. **Potential Earnings:** $25,000 to $40,000. **Advertising:** Shopper papers, word of mouth. **Special Qualifications:** None. **Equipment Needed:** Basic cleaning equipment. **Best Advice for Success:** Don't be afraid of long hours and hard work.

Mary Regis and Linda Winter are Mar-Lin Enterprises, a partnership that grew out of a long-term friendship. The two women originally started a vending business, but soon switched to offering house-cleaning services. The idea blossomed when Regis saw a television interview with a woman who became a millionaire in a year with her newly founded cleaning business. "We're not millionaires," Regis says, "but Lin and I have made money on this from the day we started."

Both women are meticulous housekeepers themselves and actually enjoy this kind of work. Both have business experience (Winter was an office manager and Regis was secretary to eight businesspeople), and they knew an orderly approach to this venture was the only way to successfully blend both areas of expertise.

The two women each drew up lists of the housekeeping tasks they regularly tackled at home, and combined them. Then they separated the jobs into two categories: general cleaning (weekly "musts" like vacuuming, dusting, and bathroom work), and heavy cleaning (moving furniture, washing baseboards). When they were satisfied with the list separations, they called friends and acquaintances and scheduled lots of free house cleaning sessions. From that experience they determined how long it took to clean homes of various sizes, and in this way were able to establish a team routine. "We knew when someone called, we had to look professional, whether it was our first house or our hundredth." By the time they took on their first customer a few months later, they were experienced professionals.

When Mar-Lin advertised in a local shopper paper, response was so good that they expanded operations quickly. They now have two full-time and three part-time workers to whom they subcontract work in teams of two. The same teams, trained by the pair, are assigned to "regulars," and Mar-Lin provides all the equipment, including vacuum cleaner, bags, and mops. The workers provide their own cleaning supplies, like window cleaner and bleach.

During the slower summer months, Regis and Winter relinquish some of their own assignments to keep their subcontractors working steadily. The people they depend on can also depend on Mar-Lin, a feature the pair feels is vital to a smooth operation. During the tourist months, when residents return, the pair do as many as five houses in a day to keep up with demand.

Although they advertise their service in the area shopper paper, much of their work comes from word-of-mouth referrals. The forty homes they service regularly in an exclusive resort area, for example, started with one job for one homeowner.

Regis and Winter feel that dependability is as important as offering quality service at competitive prices. "In all the time we've been in business, we've never stood a customer up."

Rescheduling is the sole difficulty these women face, and that's only when a team member calls in sick.

The women are not afraid of hard work and long hours; they feel it's an important support beam of an entrepreneurial platform. In return, they reap the benefits of self-employment, which for them include a flexible time schedule, control over future earnings, and satisfaction at a job well done. Regis adds, "Besides, we're making more money than we'd ever make as secretaries."

*— Phyllis Zauner*

# APARTMENT PREPARATION

**Start-up Costs:** $200. **Potential Earnings:** $25,000 and up. **Advertising:** Direct solicitation to apartment-owners. **Special Qualifications:** General handyman skills. **Equipment Needed:** Cleaning equipment, soaps. **Best Advice for Success:** Increase your maintenance skills to increase your potential income.

For the past two years Ron and Norell David have been preparing apartments for occupancy. For the amount of time they spend doing it, they make an excellent profit. They are so successful, in fact, that they now manage a large apartment complex. To prepare an apartment, the Davids' work together to clean the entire apartment, shampoo the rugs, clean the stove and oven, wash and paint the walls, repair coolers and heaters, and even rebuild cabinets and repair countertops. This may sound like a lot of work, and it is unusual for one couple to be able to do all of these things, but the David's have learned many skills and use these to cut the costs of hiring specialized help.

Ron David worked for many years as a maintenance man for a large company, where he acquired electrical and pipe-fitting experience; he also worked as a carpenter. As a result he has quite an inventory of tools for the different jobs he does.

David advises that, to get started, you will need basic cleaning products such as oven cleaners, window cleaners, a product to remove lime and soap deposits, and bleach to disinfect. Norell David adds that most important are the rubber gloves. All of these supplies can be bought in quantity at a wholesale dealer for great savings. You will also need to buy a good, heavy-duty vacuum cleaner and a rug shampooer, or you can rent the rug shampooer for a small cost.

Approximate total start-up cost is $200. Your income will vary according to the amount of time spent on the job and what you do. This amount will also vary from place to place.

An apartment preparation service can evolve into many other job opportunities, depending on your skills and dependability. You can offer a maintenance service to businesses and residences, or manage a mobile home park, hotel, motel, or resort. It is an easy line of work to break into, and if you have a variety of skills and necessary supplies you are well on your way to starting your own business.

*— Jo Ann M. Unger*

# APPLIANCE REPAIR

**Start-up Costs:** Under $200, if you already have a pickup or a trailer. **Potential Earnings:** $500 to $1,000 per week. **Advertising:** Classified ads. **Special Qualifications:** Nimble fingers and a strong back. **Equipment Needed:** Repair manual, general tool kit with voltage and temperature tester, and appliance dolly. **Best Advice for Success:** Avoid paying too much for used machines; provide written guarantees.

Mike Kilbane collects used washing machines and dryers, rebuilds them, and sells them for huge profits. Kilbane lives in a small town with a population of about 10,000 people, but still finds plenty of work to keep him busy.

There is a lot of competition in the field of home appliance repair, but Kilbane has found that he can edge out the competition by keeping costs low; he operates out of his home. He gets the appliances he fixes by running an occasional classified ad in the local newspaper: WANTED: WILL PAY FOR USED WASHING MACHINES AND ELECTRIC DRYERS IN NEED OF REPAIR. He only handles four major brands, which keeps his stock of different used parts to a minimum. If you're just starting out, you might only take one major brand, such as Whirlpool or Kenmore [the most popular ones], until you have learned these machines inside and out; then start including other brands.

Kilbane pays $5 for every washer and dryer he purchases. If the cabinets are in bad shape or the repair is going to be too costly, he'll remove all the parts he can use, then haul the rest to the junk yard and sell it by the pound.

In order to get the appliances, a pick-up truck or a small utility trailer is a must. Dryers are not too heavy, but washers can be back-breaking, so a vehicle that is low to the ground is helpful. Maneuvering washers and dryers in and out of homes requires strength, but with the aid of a good appliance dolly or hand truck, this task can be minimized.

To give an example of how much money can be made, let's say you pay $5 for a washing machine and find that the pump bearings are frozen and will not turn. You install a used pump from one of the washers that you have scrapped. You check the entire operation, replacing or repairing anything else that's wrong. With the cost of the ad, gas in your vehicle to pick it up, and the original $5 purchase price, you might have invested $15 to $20. (Keep in mind that many washers and dryers are purchased through the same ad, and that numerous parts are salvaged from the same machine.)

Now you run another ad in the local newspaper under "Used Appliances" and sell the new repaired machine for $150 or so, depending on the condition of the machine. You have just made about $135 profit in a very short time.

Sometimes the profits can be much higher. For example, Kilbane picked up a matched set of Whirlpools for which he paid a total of $10. Upon inspection he found that the only thing wrong with the dryer was a broken heating element, while the washer had nothing wrong with it at all. The previous owner had had the machines for about ten years and just decided when the dryer quit working to get a new set. Kilbane replaced the heating element with one from a dryer that he had scrapped, cleaned up both machines, and sold the set for $250.

In a larger city several washers and dryers can be picked up and repaired each day, so you can see the profit potential. There is a great demand for used appliances, and they usually sell quite fast.

Giving a thirty-day guarantee really helps the sale, and if you do a good job to start with, there should be very few call-backs. Kilbane guarantees operation only and states on his receipts that he is not responsible for any damages caused by the machine, such as water damage to the premises resulting from a broken hose. Customers are understanding, because these are used machines and anything can happen. If a problem arises within thirty days of sale, Kilbane will either repair the machine, replace it with another appliance, or refund the customer's money.

Anyone interested in this outstanding opportunity should check state and local laws pertaining to home business, sales tax, and any repair license that may be required. If you need a repair manual, Kilbane has compiled a two-part appliance repair course through twenty years of experience. The material in the manuals covers common problems he has encountered and how to repair them. In addition to washers and dryers, the manual covers repair to ranges, refrigerators, garbage disposals, dishwashers, and water heaters. The cost is $20 plus $2 shipping and handling, for a total of $22, and is available from M.A.S. Inc., 236 S. Third St., Dept. IO-9, Suite 300, Montrose, CO 81401.

### Correspondence courses:

Appliance Servicing. NRI Schools, McGraw-Hill Continuing Education Center, 4401 Connecticut Ave., Washington, DC 20008; free catalog.

# AQUARIUM MAINTENANCE

**Start-up Costs:** $500 (not including the van). **Potential Earnings:** $25,000 part-time. **Advertising:** Word of mouth works best. **Equipment Needed:** Buckets, hoses, sponge, siphon, chemicals. **Best Advice for Success:** "Buy a fish tank and practice. Read as much as possible about tropical fish and their tank environment. And try to locate a friendly tropical fish store owner whom you can watch in action and who will answer a lot of questions."

John Giacchi runs John's Aquarium Maintenance. During any given month, he visits approximately a hundred fish tank locations in doctors' waiting rooms, building lobbies, offices, restaurants, cocktail lounges, private residences, and, most frequently, dentists, who believe a fish tank in the waiting room can relax uptight patients. "It's my responsibility to make the fish tank look as good as possible and to keep the fish as healthy as possible," says Giacchi.

On an average day, Giacchi tends to as many as ten fish tanks or as few as three. Many are oversized and require as long as three hours each to be thoroughly cleaned. In some respects, Giacchi is not unlike a doctor himself. He often receives emergency calls that run the gamut from sick fish to broken filters, pumps, or heaters to accidental water spillage.

Leakage doesn't occur often, but when it does, says Giacci, it can be a disaster. There was the time, for example, when an exterminator accidentally sprayed the seam on a restaurant's 175-gallon fish tank, which sat behind the bar. "All of the water, some 250 pounds of gravel and about fifty African cichlids were flopping about on the floor," Giacchi remembers. Fortunately there were two other fish tanks in the restaurant, and Giacchi was able to scoop up the fish and toss them into the undamaged tanks. The rest of the cleanup was a matter of collecting the spilled gravel and supplying a new tank.

Giacchi's job includes changing the water, cleaning the tank and filter, replacing charcoal, and eliminating algae. He also repairs or replaces tank motors, pumps, and heater elements and checks on the well-being of the fish. Giacchi maintains that experience is the only way to recognize the difference between a healthy and an ailing fish. On occasion, he has cured sick fish with antibiotics.

Giacchi travels from client to client in a large service vehicle that he bought used for $7,000, plus a $150 charge for painting the name of his service on both sides of the truck. The vehicle is kept stocked with approximately $500 worth of cleaning equipment and supplies: hoses, siphons, buckets, and spare parts for tank accessories. He also pays $1,500 a year for general liability insurance geared to a small service business, workman's compensation, and vehicle insurance, which is a legal requirement in New Jersey. His major expense is driving back and forth to his many clients; he spends approximately $300 per month on gasoline.

Charges for the monthly aquarium maintenance visits range from as little as $40 to as much as $150 for an oversized tank located at a site that requires lengthy travel time. Giacchi also feeds fish on a regular basis for vacationing clients (for a special charge). Owners don't mind paying from $7 to $15 a visit because they know the fish are in good hands.

Giacchi doesn't ask clients to sign a contract, relying instead on verbal agreements. "I never thought about the need for a contract during the first three or four years I was in business," he says. "I don't think a signed agreement is necessary. If I do a miserable job, chances are you'll never see me again. But no one has ever told me I've done a poor job."

Giacchi always had a special fondness for fish and worked in tropical fish stores from time to time. "It suddenly occurred to me that when I worked at tropical fish stores, I sold a lot of tanks to a lot of people," Giacchi says. "The tanks needed cleaning, and not every owner has the time or the ability to tackle the job. And then I began to move."

Giacchi told everyone he knew about his business plan. One day the phone rang. "It was the owner of a nearby tavern who wanted me to clean his fish tank. He heard about my service from one of my friends." Since then the venture has continued to expand, always by word-of-mouth recommendations. For the first year or two, Giacchi used his own automobile and a supply of buckets, hoses and sponges that could be purchased at discount stores for under $100. A business telephone and an answering machine required a $200 expenditure. The cost of professionally printed business cards was roughly $75.

Fish tank maintenance is a service that is needed everywhere in the country. Giacchi recommends, "Buy a fish tank and practice. Read as much as possible about tropical fish and their tank environment. Try to locate a friendly tropical fish store owner whom you can watch in action and who will answer a lot of questions. If you wish, take a short-term job in a tropical fish store to gain hands-on experience."

*— Mildred Jailer*

# AUTO GLASS REPAIR

**Start-up Costs:** $200 for tools, advertising. (assumes you have a van or pickup.) **Potential Earnings:** $150,000 gross 2nd year. **Advertising:** Yellow Pages and coupon books. **Equipment Needed:** Truck or van and basic tools. **Best Advice for Success:** "Develop a good relationship of trust with your glass supplier and reinvest as much as possible in the business."

When Tim Geiger decided to start an automobile window glass replacement business called GlassTek (not to be confused with Glass Technology; see below), he started with $200 and a van. "Now," he says, "I have a shop, a mobile service, and four employees."

## Starting up

Geiger's GlassTek is a mobile auto glass replacement service, working at the home or office of the customer. Geiger charges the same rates for the "free" mobile service as he does for in-shop work, and underbids the big companies. He made certain his company name was general enough to include window tinting, installing business glass (such as store fronts), and other glass-related sources of income.

"The first thing I got was a mobile phone," Geiger says. "It got me ten or fifteen jobs a month, so it paid for itself quickly." Once the business grew big enough to create a very large mobile phone bill, it made sense to open a shop where he could work during the day and answer phone calls, having an employee run the mobile service.

## Advertising

During Geiger's first year of business, word-of-mouth advertising supplied $39,000 worth of sales. At the start of his second year, Geiger took out a $500-per-month, half-page Yellow Pages ad. His phone calls jumped from eighty per month to over four hundred. His second-year gross sales jumped to $160,000.

Realizing that the advertising was well worth its cost, he also bought space for $3,000 per year in local coupon books, delivered with the mail to local residents. "These coupons have been phenomenal, and sales are incredible," he says.

Repeat customers are an important part of GlassTek's business. "I would rather do one high-quality job at a higher price than many cheaper jobs," says Geiger. Not only does this attitude please customers, who are willing to pay for good work, but it reduces the wear and tear on GlassTek employees and equipment.

Glass replacement is a low- or no-inventory business. When Geiger successfully bids a job, he calls his glass supplier, who delivers glass on a twice-a-day schedule. A good relationship with his glass supplier has been fundamental.

## Operations

When a phone call comes in, Geiger opens the *National Auto Glass Specification* (NAGS) book for price information (the book is free from the glass supplier). In his second year, Geiger has invested in an IBM PS2 computer and a program called LePic Lite, available for about $1,000 from Classic Business software; it contains all the NAGS information, with billing, accounting, and other tasks built in. While greatly speeding up sales, updates to NAGS information will cost $600 per year, making computerization justified only when the business has begun taking in many calls.

There are basically four markets for a glass replacer: retail and insurance companies, retail customers, fleet deals (hard to get and they do not pay well) wholesale, which requires a large (expensive) inventory.

How much money does he take home? "As little as possible," says Geiger. Profit means taxes, so the more you reinvest in the business the better. Geiger tries to keep a minimum of $2,000 in the bank as a buffer against sudden expenses, such as the van breaking down.

## A typical job

Replacement of a car door window involves removing the broken glass, both by hand and with a vacuum from the inside of the car and from the interior of the door. The installer then pops off the door panel and loosens the raising mechanism. He slides the new glass down into the door, fits it onto the riser, and retightens the mechanism. Once the tracks are aligned and the glass goes up and down smoothly, he puts the gaskets back on and reinstalls the door panel. A few wipes with a cloth and some glass cleaner and the job is done.

In addition to the basic hand tools, GlassTek uses vacuums, glass-carrying racks (large vertical combs or aluminum tubing covered with rubber), a glass-cutting table covered with soft cloth, and a stock of basic nuts and bolts washers.

## Companies to get you started

There is an alternative to replacing auto windshields, and that is to repair them. Unless a windshield is shattered or has an unmendable crack, many with stone damage and scratches can be made to look like new. This is accomplished with technology available from a number of companies, which we have listed below. Each has its own method or repair and operations, and each can help get you started in your own glass repair business with training and materials. Information is free from each company.

Glass Mechanix, Inc., 10170 N.W. 47th St., Sunrise, FL 33351; or call toll-free 1-800-826-8523.

Glas-Weld Systems, 20578 Empire Blvd., Bend, OR 97701; or call toll-free 1-800-321-2597.

NVS Corporation, 48 Springvale Ave., Lynn, MA 01904; or call 617-595-6224.

Novus, 10425 Hampshire St., Minneapolis, MN 55438; or call toll-free 1-800-328-1117.

Ultra B-O-N-D Inc., 9249 Loquat Dr., Riverside, CA 92508; or call toll free 1-800-347-2820.

Clear*Star Products Inc., 102-39 Jamaica Ave., Richmond Hill, NY 11418; or call toll-free 1-800-848-8009.

Auto D-Tail Plus, 10541 Royal Club, Dallas, TX 75229; or call 214-351-4801.

Glass Technology, 434 Turner Dr., Durango, CO 81301; or call toll-free 1-800-441-4527.

Pit Stop, 700 Burbank St., Broomfield, CO; or call toll-free 1-800-937-7487.

*— Erik Hyypia*

# AUTO STRIPING

**Start-up Costs:** $500. **Potential Earnings:** $20 to $50 per job. **Advertising:** Direct contact with auto dealers; classified ads in local shopper papers. **Special Qualifications:** Training and practice. **Equipment Needed:** Striping tape, razor blades. **Best Advice for Success:** "Start by contacting a small number of dealers whom you can provide with good service."

Many auto-related businesses require special training, equipment, and a large investment of time and money to get them started. Auto striping, however, is one professional area of expertise that entrepreneurs often overlook. It's a business you can train yourself in after receiving a minimal amount of instruction.

When automobile manufacturers first started applying stripes and graphics to vehicles, they did so with paint. When technology enabled auto makers to create automotive striping out of vinyl, they quickly switched to this less expensive and more durable product. The idea caught on, and it wasn't long before people began to specialize in the design and installation of vinyl stripes and graphics for automobiles. A new car dealer can usually have a stripe applied by an auto detailer—like you, for example—for less money than an auto body shop would charge, and get a more professional job and a better product. You can also offer customers a custom-designed stripe or graphic so they don't have to settle for what happens to be available.

Putting a pinstripe on a car may sound like a difficult job, but with practice and determination you'll quickly master it.

When Troy Robinson first got into the striping business, his boss told him that he would have a one-week training period. It was more like a one-week *practice* period. After the basic instruction, Robinson learned the rest on the job, until he developed the proper skill and learned all of the tricks.

### Guidelines for striping a vehicle

First, thoroughly clean the area of the vehicle where you will place the strip using a wax and grease remover such as Prep-sol, Acry-sol, or TFX cleaner. Then make a continuous wipe from one end of the car to the other with a clean, soft, dry cloth. The continuous wipe is important, because if you lift the rag halfway down the side of the car, you'll leave a deposit of dirt.

Begin laying the stripe by tacking it down at one end of the car. Unroll a few feet of the tape at a time and apply each section as you go. When you have an entire side done, press the tape down to set it against the surface of the vehicle. Do this gently at first to prevent the tape from sliding around, then go over it to secure it. Use a sharp razor blade to make the cuts at the ends of the stripe, at the doors, and anywhere else on the surface where it might be necessary (door handles, mirrors, door locks, etc.). Remove the waste material and the carrier (the plastic covering the vinyl) as you make the cuts along the side of the vehicle.

The vinyl stripes will actually set on the finish of the car like paint. The stripes eventually harden so that they will not peel off.

### Pinstripe pricing

Prices for installing an accent stripe, or pinstripe, vary across the country. In some places installers give them away to promote other accessories. In other parts of the country, dealers are paying as much as $50 for them. A price range of between $20 and $30 would be a good place to start, until you settle on the going rate for your area.

Pricing for other kinds of stripes and for graphics is usually figured as $2\frac{1}{2}$ or 3 times your material cost for the stripe; more if the job required some detail work or elaborate craftsmanship. Never underprice your work.

Being dependable is very important to the success of your business. If the dealer sees that you can give him the best service, even if he's not giving you any work, you will eventually get the account. Do not call on more dealers than you can handle. This will endanger all of your accounts, especially if you have competition. Start by contacting a small number of dealers whom you can provide with good service.

There are as many used car dealers as there are new car dealers, but you are better off avoiding them. A used car dealer will often not want to pay a fair price for a striping job, and will frequently try to give you demeaning tasks like covering up rust spots, striping over old stripes, or removing old stripes.

### What you will need to start

Since one of the keys to running a successful striping business is regularly calling on new car dealerships, you will need dependable transportation. Whatever vehicle you choose will serve as your shop, warehouse, and transportation. You can use your home as a base of operations and an office, so your overhead will be very low.

Don't rush out and buy a few hundred dollars' worth of striping tape and then immediately start calling on new car dealers. Buy two or three rolls of $\frac{5}{16}$, double-pin tape and practice on friends' and relatives' cars for a few days. Get the hang of it first so that when you approach a dealership, you'll know what you're doing.

You can buy striping tape at any auto parts store and at department stores like K-Mart and Wal-Mart. There are several manufacturers of automotive striping vinyl in the United States. Sharpline Converting and Universal Products (addresses below) produce top-quality tape and will happily send you catalogs and ordering information.

You can run an automobile striping business as a full-time or part-time operation. It is possible to cultivate a full-time route, possibly branching out into other areas of the auto aftermarket industry. Create your own business and tailor it to fit your needs.

### Supplies

Universal Products, 521 Industrial St., Goddard, KS 67052

Sharpline Converting, 1520 S. Tyler Rd., P.O. Box 9608, Wichita, KS 67277-0608.

*— Troy Robinson*

# BALLOON DECORATING SERVICE

**Start-up Costs:** $150 to $200. **Potential Earnings:** $90 to $100 per booking. **Advertising:** Word of mouth, business cards and flyers, classified ads, direct mail. **Special Qualifications:** A flair for decorating. **Equipment Needed:** Balloons, mylars, a curling iron (to seal mylars), helium tanks, air/gas filler, streamers, netting, assorted colored marbles. **Best Advice for Success:** "Have patience and determination as your business grows. Try different methods of advertising, and concentrate on the ones that bring the most customer response."

Judi Wagner was looking for ways to earn some extra money when a friend asked her for help in decorating a hall for a wedding reception. Wagner agreed and decided to use balloons to decorate the hall. "I remembered seeing some creative uses of balloons when I was a waitress for some banquets," she says, "so I thought it would be fun to try them."

Wagner's friend and those attending the reception were so impressed with the job she did in decorating with the balloons that Wagner began to get word-of-mouth referrals to do decorating for other occasions. With so many requests, Wagner decided to start a decorating service from her home. In addition to weddings, "Balloons by Judi" will decorate for birthday, theme, and company parties as well as new baby, anniversary, graduation, and retirement celebrations and will make "clown" balloon deliveries where requested. Wagner also offers special balloon centerpieces for tables and will perform balloon releases for organizations.

## Finding supplies

At first Wagner bought her supplies from local gift shops and party-supply stores, until a man at a church fair lent her a balloon-supply catalog. The catalog, published by U.S. Balloon, has really helped Wagner. "It's been a great help in starting my business," she says. "The catalog has given me valuable information on new supplies and decorating ideas."

From a nearby welding supply company, Wagner rents a tank of helium for $5 a month, storing the tank in her basement. She uses approximately one tank of helium for an average wedding (which averages 250 to 300 balloons), with gas refills costing $30 to $45, depending on the size of the tank. Wagner advises, "I also recommend you have an air/gas filler with a gauge, so you know the amount of gas you use and how much is in the tank."

Not all of Wagner's balloons need helium, though, as she offers special balloon "drops." The air-filled balloons are held in large nets and are released in a colorful cascade at a special, predetermined time. She ties other air-filled balloons to a special trellis (designed by Wagner and built by her husband) which is placed behind the bride and groom at wedding receptions. It provides an attractive frame around the newly-weds as they sit at their table, according to Wagner.

Other supplies Wagner uses include mylars (foil-type balloons); streamers, ribbons, string, tape and scissors; drapery hooks (for attaching balloons to carpets); and colorful marbles enclosed in netting to "anchor" gas-filled balloons to tables. Wagner concludes with some helpful hints: "When I make my orders for supplies, I try to order for several bookings at one time. This saves shipping costs, and usually discounts are given for larger orders," she says.

It takes Wagner about three hours to decorate a hall for a large wedding reception. A typical wedding will include balloon bouquets on every table, a huge balloon arch around the hall entrance, Wagner's balloon trellis placed against the wall behind the newlyweds, and another arch with heart-shaped mylars to frame the band or D.J.

## Pricing; set-up

For a typical wedding, which includes the arches, trellis, and table balloons, Wagner will charge $225. "I learned some other pricing guidelines for a 'how-to' video I purchased through the balloon supply catalog," she says. "The video recommended charging $3 to $5 per lineal foot for balloon arches." After expenses, including paying her helpers, Wagner clears about $90 to $100 for a wedding. Wagner saves part of the money she earns to buy more equipment.

When customers inquire about prices, Wagner arranges a meeting and fills in two sheets to help her give an estimate. One is a Customer Sheet, which records information about the event—room dimensions (including a space to sketch the placement of doors, windows, electrical outlets, and any unusual features), and a contact person. The other is an Estimation and Placement Planning Sheet, which Wagner and her customers fill out together, detailing the kinds of balloon decorations needed, including the estimated number of hours needed to set up.

Wagner asks for a non-refundable $50 deposit. "I use this deposit to purchase needed supplies; it insures I will at least have my costs covered if the customer cancels," she says. Sixty to ninety days prior to the event, Wagner asks for $50 more, with the balance due the Wednesday before the actual date.

"I have fixed prices for certain events, plus an *a la carte* price list of extras, like my table centerpieces or extra arches," says Wagner.

## Advertising

Wagner uses a variety of advertising methods. At first she used one-page flyers with tear-away tabs that listed her telephone number, posting them on public bulletin boards in banks, grocery stores, and other locations. A freelance graphic artist designed a special business card and flyer. "These flyers were professional-looking and contained a better description of my business services. Recently I began to send out both the flyers and business cards to newly engaged couples, and I've received almost a 75-percent response rate from these mailings," says Wagner.

Wagner also places ads in her local paper's business directory at a special, six-month low rate. Yet Wagner still gets customers from word-of-mouth referrals and from those who have attended celebrations where she did the decorating. Wagner's customers can also look through a photo album of her decorating displays to decide what kind of decorating to choose.

Where does she get her ideas? Trade magazines like *Balloons Today Magazine* (Festivities Publications) give advice and display photos of creative uses for balloons. The video "Balloon Arches and Decorating" showed some unique ways to form balloon "numbers" for graduation parties.

With the steady growth of her business, Wagner has every reason to be proud of what she can do with ordinary balloons in some not-so-ordinary ways!

## For further information

Judi Wagner offers a set of her balloon trellis plans, plus one copy each of her "Customer Sheet" and "Estimation and Placement Sheet" for $9.95. To order, send a check or money order to: Judi Wagner, 44 Walnut Street, Sellersville, PA 18960.

*Balloons Today Magazine.* A monthly international trade journal for professional party decorators and for gift delivery businesses. Festivities Publications, 1205 West Forsyth Street, Jacksonville, FL 32204.

National Association of Balloon Artists, 1205 West Forsyth Street, Jacksonville, FL 32204.

— *Priscilla Y. Huff*

# BIKE REPAIR

**Start-up Costs:** $200 to $300. **Potential Earnings:** $20,000 a year, part-time. **Advertising:** Flyers, business cards, word of mouth. **Special Qualifications:** Mechanical skills. **Equipment Needed:** Standard and special bicycle tools, greases and oils, air pump, repair manuals. **Best Advice for Success:** "Emphasize quality workmanship: a little polish, chrome cleaner—these extra touches will make your business shine amid the competition."

If you like working with your hands, don't mind getting a bit dirty, and have an interest in getting paid while you learn a mechanical skill, then the bicycle business is the road to good part-time profits. Part-time mechanics command $25 per hour for their labor. It's not uncommon to earn over $20,000 a year working twenty hours a week. Bicycle riding is becoming increasingly popular with young and old alike, so ace mechanics will be in demand far into the next century.

If you are mechanically inclined or have a good working knowledge of bicycles, then you're all set. If you need to learn how to repair bicycles, your local library or bookstore is sure to have several books on the subject.

## The working environment

Repairs on bicycles range from greasing the chain and wheel bearings to modifying front and rear gear sets. You may also have to do some leather repair, installation of new equipment, and the removal of old parts. A lot of the work deals with tire repair, spoke adjustment and replacement, and cable adjustment and replacement. With all of this in mind, the typical home-based bicycle repair business involves simple tools that you can buy for less than $30, some repair manuals ($30), some chain and bearing grease (less than $10), and special bicycle tools (less than $20). One other well-used piece of equipment is the air pump. You can purchase a hand air pump for less than $15 or you can purchase a mini-air compressor from your local department store for less than $150.

The work area can be a 12 by 15-foot basement or den, or half of a two-car garage that isn't being used. Simple lighting, a home-made work bench, and a bicycle stand complete the work area.

## Practice makes perfect

If you are too unsure of your repair skill to open up shop, practice on your family's and friends' bikes. Take the bicycle apart piece by piece. See how each mechanical piece works. Try putting the bicycle back together. Ask a local mechanic about the parts of the bicycle most prone to mechanical servicing. Ask him or her what manuals to use. Ask where you can acquire parts and supplies wholesale.

Establish a rapport with your local bicycle dealers. If they know of your service, they will start asking you to take some of their mechanical work off their hands. As you go along, the amount of work you acquire will depend on your business skills as well as your mechanical ones.

## The business

According to successful bicycle repair people, the four primary elements of success are customer rapport, customer satisfaction, integrity in workmanship, and dependability. Commercial advertising, although important, wasn't as crucial to these dealers' success. Most agreed that word-of-mouth advertising was the best method.

Let's take a look at each of the above elements for success, and then add some inexpensive methods of advertising.

*Customer Rapport.* Sometimes it is the chemistry between you and your customer that will make or break the relationship. Be pleasant, show enthusiasm, and handle the customer in a way that shows respect for personality and equipment.

*Customer Satisfaction.* Concern yourself with the art of fine workmanship at affordable prices. Don't reduce the cost of your labor to get more work through; you'll wind up with a bunch of bicycles no one else would work on. Instead, emphasize quality workmanship, standard rates—and that something extra: a little polish, a little chrome cleaner, and a little glass cleaner on those mirrors. These will give your bicycle repair business that extra touch necessary to make your business shine amid the competition. This extra effort will have customers talking up your business to friends and neighbors.

*Integrity and Dependability.* These work hand-in-hand. If you tell a customer that his or her bicycle will be ready by that afternoon, it should be repaired and gleaming when he or she arrives to pick it up.

## Advertising

First, invest in business cards. Place them on your customer counter, put them on bulletin boards around your community, and drop them off with other businesses in the locale. Have a customized rubber stamp made to fit the back of your card, saying, "I was referred to your repair shop by _____." Your satisfied customer places his or her name on the blank line and gives the card to another potential customer. When the new customer comes into your bicycle repair shop with work for you, the first customer gets a discount on the next service or maintenance job.

Flyers are another inexpensive way to advertise. These are more visible than your business cards, and when they are placed where there is a lot of traffic—your local supermarkets and the convenience stores—they are apt to be seen by the right potential customers.

After you make a repair, follow it up a month later with a phone call or letter. This is an effective way to establish customer satisfaction and create more business. Talk to the customer about any problems he might be experiencing, if any, and offer—free of charge—to tighten or adjust the work you've done. This lets the customer know you care about the work you've done as well as reminding him or her of your existence.

It's also important to target your advertising. Local college newspapers, thrift papers like *PennySaver*, and local outdoor specialty publications are all likely to give good returns on your advertising dollar.

When you have all of this working for you, you could have a bicycle repair business that you operate in your spare time to the tune of over $20,000 a year.

*—R.T. Edwards*

## CAKE DECORATING

**Start-up Costs:** $200. **Potential Earnings:** $7,000 to $20,000 part-time. **Advertising:** Local papers. **Special Qualifications:** Cooking and baking skills. **Equipment Needed:** Basic cooking equipment. **Best Advice for Success:** Buy supplies when you need them. Create custom cakes, giving customers exactly what they want.

Patty Edwards' business, Patty Cakes, has become a phenomenal success. Edwards and her husband are busy raising four sons, so she thought that owning her own business was just a dream. She had been baking decorative cakes for friends and family, and was commended on how beautiful, creative, and delicious they were. Then a friend suggested she take up cake decorating full-time. Deciding to go ahead and try it, she placed one small newspaper ad and was on her way.

Edwards works out of her home and bakes special occasion cakes, rum cakes, checkerboard cakes, and a variety of pies, eclairs, cream puffs, and napoleons. She offers these to the public by special order and receives regular weekly orders from restaurants. Her cakes are always fresh, baked the same day she sells them. She also delivers in her community.

When Edwards was starting, she went to the library and hobby shops for books on decorating. From these she taught herself the many skills and techniques she needed to know. One book, by Wilton Enterprises, offers a home-study course in cake decorating. From Wilton you can get cake pans in a variety of shapes, including Superman, Pink Panther, and Wonder Woman, along with a complete instruction kit. Each year Wilton publishes a yearbook with the latest ideas in decorating (Wilton Enterprises, 2240 W. 75th, Woodridge, IL 60517).

Edwards suggests asking around for tips and short cuts from friends and relatives. You might come up with some good recipes for cake or frosting that have been sitting in grandma's drawer for years. Most of all, however, keep reading and experimenting with different mixes and icings.

While learning the basics you must acquire a few tools: icing bags, decorating tips, spatulas, separation plates, a whole-sheet cake pan, a half-sheet cake pan, a set of round pans sizes 16", 14", 10", 8", and 6", and basic square pans. Edwards says the maximum start-up cost is around $200, but she didn't go right out and buy everything at once. When someone would ask for a certain size or type of cake, she would get the supplies needed and add them to her collection. She buys boxed cake mixes in quantity at wholesale to cut costs.

Edwards got started by advertising in the local newspaper, but she also goes around to the local restaurants and markets with samples of her baked goods. Who could resist? She shows customers pictures of different cake styles, but she is flexible and will create any style. Many customers will bring a picture or drawing of what they want. Edwards claims her prices are competitive but not out of sight, knowing that people are willing to pay more for fresh baked goods.

Other opportunities available to a cake decorator include catering for hotels that hold wedding receptions and parties and displaying pictures of your wedding cakes at bridal shops.

*— Jo Ann M. Unger*

# CALLIGRAPHY SERVICE

**Start-up Costs:** $200 or less. **Potential Earnings:** $10,000 a year part-time. **Advertising:** Shopper's paper; bulletin boards. **Special Qualifications:** Good calligraphy skills. **Equipment Needed:** Calligraphy pens; practice books. **Best Advice for Success:** Provide quick, accurate, top-quality work.

Calligraphy, the art of beautiful writing, can also be a way to write yourself a spare-time income. It's an ideal way for anyone with no formal art experience, training, or talent to make extra money at home. Beginners at this easy-to-learn craft can start making money by addressing envelopes, filling in certificates, and making place cards for formal dinners. With some experience you can create publicity flyers for schools and churches, and design invitations, birth announcements, and signs for businesses.

First, of course, you must learn the art of calligraphy. Learning the basics is easy; check with your local junior college, park districts, or continuing education center. If you can't find a class in your area, there are several fine books available at your local library. The important thing is to practice. Even the best teacher in the world can't give you the polished, consistent look practice provides.

## Beginning

Let's say you decide to start with one of the many calligraphy books on the market. Your next purchase is a calligraphy pen. If you take a class, the instructor may recommend a brand and size. If you're learning from a book, chances are the author will suggest a pen. Most students start with a standard calligraphy marker, available at art supply stores, stationery, and office supply stores, or by mail order. The least expensive choice is a marker with a limited lifetime (unlike a pen that can be refilled), but its point tends to lose the necessary sharpness after a while. For the investment of about a dollar, though, markers let you "play around" with calligraphy and see if you'd really like to perfect this craft.

Slightly more expensive, but still available for under $10, are No-Nonsense Calligraphy pens made by Shaeffer. These pens come with three different nibs (points), ranging from broad to fine, and use standard Shaeffer ink cartridges. If you really want to get fancy, there are other pens with gold-plated and solid gold nibs, but the Shaeffer pens are affordable.

Next you'll need good-quality paper, a sturdy writing surface, and time to practice. Read the book you've chosen, practice one alphabet until you master it, and *use* your calligraphy. There's no comparison between writing endless rows of letters and actually addressing an envelope with your new skill. As soon as you've learned one alphabet, start practicing a second. Most clients need one of three standard types: italic, uncial, and black letter (similar to Old English).

## Finding clients

As a freelancer, you'll need business cards. Provide the printer with camera-ready copy you can create yourself—in calligraphy, of course. A calligraphed business card instantly provides potential clients with a sample of your work. Keep the information on the card simple: your name, address, and telephone number is enough.

You must also advertise. A local shoppers' paper, which offers low rates for a display ad, is a good place to begin. Design a small flyer in calligraphy and leave copies of it on bulletin boards and at the supermarket. The calligraphy alone is an attention getter. Printers are also approached by people who need calligraphy, so leave some business cards with your printer.

Who are your potential clients? Anyone sending out wedding invitations will consider paying a calligrapher to address the envelopes and fill in the place cards for the dinner. You address the envelopes from a list of the guests (request that it be printed or typed) and then return them to the client for stuffing and sealing. Rates for this vary but you get $1 per envelope on average, with an extra 25¢ per place card. With some experience you should be able to address eight to twelve envelopes an hours.

Businesses need freelance calligraphers to letter signs, to prepare camera-ready copy for flyers and even to design special greeting cards. Schools and organizations will contact you to fill in or even create award certificates. The fees for these kinds of tasks are harder to gauge, but you can set your goal for a certain amount per hour and charge with that rate in mind. Contact wedding consultants and party planners to reach a wider audience. They usually charge a commission, but the exposure may be worth it.

If you don't mind sitting at art fairs, this is a good way to exhibit your calligraphy. It takes a big investment: you'll have to pay an entry fee, create a display, mat and frame your work, and perhaps pay a percentage of your sales to the promoter. However, there are advantages to the art fair circuit in terms of increased exposure and future commissions.

### Dealing with clients

Let's say someone contacts you about possibly addressing her wedding invitations. You agree to meet with her and show samples of your work (have a prepared portfolio of your work to show). Once the client settles on a style of lettering, discuss ink color. Black is standard, but ink is available in many different colors. If you use a cartridge pen, you'll need to know which colors are available for your particular pen.

Insist on legible copy to work from, especially if you're addressing envelopes. Don't agree to look up zip codes or check your client's spelling—that's her job (unless she'll pay you extra to do it). Remember, the more accurate the copy, the easier and better your job will be. Be sure you know how names should be prefaced—(Mr., Mrs., Miss, Ms., or Master)—and how the client wants names of states to be written—spelled out, or the Post Office's preferred two-letter abbreviation. Finally, agree on a price and a delivery date.

Go home with the envelopes, your pen, and ink—and write! If you pre-line each piece, be sure to let the ink dry before erasing. Work carefully and in private. Pay close attention to your copy and check often for errors. Break when you're tired and don't eat or drink while working (a poorly placed drip can ruin an otherwise perfect piece). If possible, have someone else check your work for accuracy after you finish.

When you deliver the calligraphy, include a business card or two along with the bill. Word of mouth is a powerful advertising tool for calligraphers.

— *Deborah Stern Harris*

# CANDLE MAKING

**Start-up Costs:** $200. **Potential Earnings:** $50,000 and more. **Advertising:** Home parties, catalogs. **Special Qualifications:** Candle-making skills, which are easily learned. **Equipment Needed:** Wax, molds. **Best Advice for Success:** Create unique candles of a kind not readily found in local stores.

If any business was ever started with a lack of planning and projections, it was Lund's Lites—a company that began when Joyce Lund decided to raise a little extra money making candles. She knew a little about candles because her parents owned a candle shop. About business she knew nothing. She had never heard about "knowing your market." She hired family and friends (no-no's in the business world); she didn't worry about five-year plans. She was concerned only about getting from one day to the next.

Today her gross sales are $5 million annually. Lund founded the company almost by accident. Her immediate goal at the time was to find a way to buy Christmas presents for her six children. When a friend dropped by for coffee and suggested she make candles and sell them, it seemed like a good idea. So, melting wax on her kitchen stove, Lund started turning out candles. She put up a display shelf in her living room and pretty soon, recalls Lund, "People started coming to the house, buying candles as fast as I could make them."

Then there was another coffee-hour suggestion: hold candle parties and take orders. After nine parties, each ringing up more than $300 in orders, Lund spent $200 on candle molds and devised a hostess plan. She figured she'd make candles for next Christmas and start selling them in September. "But in January the phone started ringing off the hook," says Lund.

"By the end of February we were completely booked with parties, six nights a week through December. By the end of spring I knew I needed help."

Lund called every friend she could think of—from church, from the kids' soccer teams, from school. Friends responded and candle production went into full swing. The kitchen stove was the manufacturing plant. Finishing was done in the dining room. The living room fell to wrapping, and the bedroom was a warehouse. "There wasn't a room in the house except the nursery that wasn't being used for candle manufacturing," she says. "When my husband came home from work, he'd feed the kids and make candles while I was out giving a party. When I got back from the party, we'd work two-hour shifts through the night, melting wax and pouring candles. We took turns sleeping on the couch. The Lunds earned $23,000 a month in candle orders in the three months preceding Christmas.

A year later, Joyce Lund moved her business to a small warehouse. By then she had fifty dealers in three states. She negotiated to build her own factory. Before it was finished, however, the warehouse lease ran out; there was nowhere to go. That's when Lund fell apart. She woke up in a hospital, prostrate from nervous exhaustion. "Is it all over?" she asked her husband. It wasn't, by any means. Her neighbors had moved the equipment into basements and garages and had kept the business going.

Today, Lund's Lites is the tenth-largest candlemaking company in the country. Apart from size, however, things haven't changed much. Joyce still sells on the party plan and through a catalog. Even now the operation is only a step away from the kitchen stove. Candles are finished with ordinary hand irons, and electric mixers are used to make froth. Most of her managers are the friends she started with. To them she gives the credit for the success of Lund's Lites.

"These women came from dishes and diapers to the business world. We made up and learned the jobs and our systems as we went along. It was a group of friends working together, and we've made it work."

To start your own candle-making business, you can learn all the how-tos of candle production from books available at your library; molds and other supplies are available at hobby stores. For more information, contact the National Candle Association, 2045 North 15th St., #1000, Arlington, VA 22201.

— *Phyllis Zauner*

## CAR OPENING SERVICE

**Start-up Costs:** $500. **Potential Earnings:** $10,000 and up. **Advertising:** Yellow Pages; police referrals. **Special Qualifications:** Some locksmithing knowledge. **Equipment Needed:** "Tools of the trade." **Best Advice for Success:** Get there quickly, and underprice the locksmiths.

Take a day's aggravation, add a touch of imagination, and you have Judy

Newton's recipe for success. "When I came out of the bookstore and saw those keys still in the ignition," she says, "I knew the locksmith a block away was going to charge $25 to come unlock the car, although the whole operation would take less than five minutes. I'd already spent more than I intended, and I didn't need the extra expense—or the aggravation."

Instead of getting mad, Newton got inspired. "Right then and there," she says, "I decided I'd pay no more locksmith's fees. I knew I could open cars as well as he could, if I had the tools and the training. I knew I could do it for less, and the more I thought about it, the more determined I became."

First thing next morning, Newton met with the local police chief and discussed her idea with him. That afternoon she bought her tools from a police supply store and started practicing, first on wrecked cards at a local junk yard, then on her car and those of family and friends. For the fine points on using the tools, she called the manufacturer. To learn more about lock mechanisms, she visited local body shops and car dealers, eliciting their cooperation.

When she felt confident and competent, Newton got a business license, was bonded, had a business phone installed at home, and got an answering service and pager. Then she began contacting local businesses, passing out the cards she'd had printed. She got her service listed with the police, who rotate calls on locked vehicles among area locksmiths. She also arranged an interview with the local paper and purchased some advertising, and The Car Opener began operations. Newton says the "tools of the trade" aren't expensive—$25 to $65.

Nearly all her first calls were police referrals, but business has steadily increased since she began. One reason is her Yellow Pages advertisement stressing fast, economical service. Newton charges $13 for daytime calls and $18 for night calls, as compared to the standard $25 locksmith fee. Another reason is word-of-mouth advertising.

"I enjoy not being tied to a routine," Newton says. "I enjoy the extra money and the extra time I spend with my children. I like being my own boss, and I like helping people. There's not much glamour in it—but I love it."

There are "tricks of the trade," but Newton says they are things picked up with practice. "Different cars do have different locking mechanisms, and it helps to know the trick to the lock. For instance," she explains, "there's a trick to opening Fords, and I'd been in business four months before I figured it out, though I opened a lot of Fords during that first four months. Mostly it's a matter of patience. I know I have the tool and I know the lock's in the door, so it's just a question of taking the time to find it. Usually I'm there and gone in ten minutes, but some cars take thirty or forty minutes to open." When that happens, she says, "I just tell the customer to get comfortable and relax, reassuring them that I have opened cars like theirs before and that it's just going to take some time."

"If you lock your keys in the car," she explains, "you don't want to hear from me two hours later. You want me there in ten minutes or less, so the answering service and pager are essential, and they're my biggest business expense." One thing is certain: as long as there are cars, keys and careless people, there'll be work for people like Judy Newton, wherever their business may happen to be.

*— Sanna Fortson*

## COMMUNITY MAPS

**Start-up Costs:** $500 or less. **Potential Earnings:** $11,000 or more. **Advertising:** Door-to-door sales. **Special Qualifications:** Sales skills. **Equipment Needed:** None. **Best Advice for Success:** Try to get the local businesses as enthusiastic about the map project as you are.

Community maps are a popular new advertising program that local promoters can easily profit from. The cartoon-style maps depict individual businesses in full color on an almost-accurate map. Hot air balloons and planes fly in the map's sky towing advertising banners. Trucks, vans, or ambulances scoot along map streets advertising on-the-go businesses like TV news and emergency medical services. Lakes, trees, parks, and landmarks are shown. Although the maps are not to scale, businesses are in the correct places and main streets are drawn in.

Several companies are already lining up the big cities, producing large color posters, and now they are sending representatives into the medium-sized towns. However, there are still opportunities for the local entrepreneur.

While the production of a two-foot by three-foot, four-color poster of a town may be a bit too ambitious a project for the beginner, some entrepreneurs are having considerable success putting together small-town community souvenir maps printed on 11-inch by 17-inch textured paper. Business people in these communities love to have their establishments spotlighted on the maps, and they use them as promotional items in a number of ways. Restaurants, for example, like to participate in the maps because the size makes them just right for use as place mats.

While you can specialize in drawing small-town maps—areas where community pride is a strong force—you can also create pictorial maps for downtown business districts of larger cities, residential neighborhoods, and even commercial parks where it's hard to find specific offices. The list of possibilities for the pictorial maps is endless. The best thing is that because businesses move, open, and close with such frequency, one can update the same map every two or three years, charging the same fee again and again. Businesses are usually anxious to be on the new version.

### Designing the map

To produce a map, decide first what the boundaries will be. Get a regular street map of the area and draw a line around the part you plan to depict. You might want to get a sample pictorial map from another area to show the business people what you are planning to do. Contact everyone whose business is within the proposed boundaries and explain that the map is a "community promotional piece," one that will be enjoyed as a souvenir by everyone who sees it.

Once you have a complete list of—and a check from—everyone who wants to be identified on the map, hire a local or regional artist to produce the map in two-point perspective. The artist could work from photographs or by actually walking around the area.

When the maps are printed, have one framed and get the local newspaper to photograph you as you ceremoniously present it to the mayor. Distribute the rest of the maps to the businesses in the area to sell, or sell them yourself.

How much you charge for a business to be identified on the map depends, of course, on your printing expenses and how much your artist charges you. You can generally ask each business to share in the production cost of this community promotional piece at a cost of $35 to $40 per business, although some have charged as much as $50. If you charge $35, for example, give the business owner thirty-five of the maps when printed. If the owner chooses, he can sell the maps for $1 each and get his money back. (Some business people love that aspect.) Maps have sold for between $1 and $15 each, some of the higher-priced ones being "signed and number" copies, which collectors seem to prefer.

If you have fifty businesses each paying $36, that's $1,800 gross. One map maker sold 450 ads to businesses at $25 each, for a total of $11,250, and other business people were disappointed when he had to turn them down because there wasn't any space left. In addition, he's selling the signed and numbered copies for $5 to $10 each.

Companies selling large color-poster pictorial maps are charging business anywhere from $75 to $250 each to be on the map. So there is plenty of room for leeway in the advertising pricing.

### Hiring an artist

Where can you find an artist to do the drawing? Contact your local art league for possibilities, or check with your local high school. Some aspiring young student artist might have just the right blend of cartooning and perspective drawing skills. If that fails, check the mechanical drawing classes at the area vocational-mechanical school. Producing the pictorial maps really only takes basic two-point perspective drawing skills, and they don't have to be perfectly accurate, so the artist can exaggerate a little and give the drawing "character." You can also check with local architects' offices; they usually have a young architect who might have time to use his architectural drawing skills in a venture such as this.

Try to include a little local historical information on the map, as well as some information on local tourist attractions. This gives the maps not only commercial advertising value but historical and tourist value as well, adding to their souvenir status.

*— Ron Barthet*

# CONSULTING

**Start-up Costs:** Less than $200. **Potential Earnings:** Up to $500 a day. **Special Qualifications:** In-depth knowledge about a specific subject. **Advertising:** Create an image as an expert. **Best Advice for Success:** Don't be vague about what you do as a consultant; be specific about your service and its benefits to the client.

If friends and relatives respect your knowledge of a certain subject—perhaps computers, interior decorating, hairdressing, or gardening—and constantly ask for your opinion and advice, you are engaged in the practice of consulting. Although you are not getting paid for your special talents and services, it is quite likely that you could be making a profitable career of helping others in the area of your specialty.

Consulting is a pleasurable occupation. Who is not flattered to be asked for his or her expert opinion and advice? And if the joy of being "the respected authority" is not motivating enough, add to it the bonus of actually getting paid for providing that advice, and you begin to understand the lure of consulting as a career.

Professional consulting is a field open to all. There are no state boards or licensing examinations for consultants, although a few of the professions in which consultants practice are licensed (medicine, law, and professional engineering, for example). Otherwise, there are no legal requirements that do not apply to business ventures of all kinds.

## A few misconceptions

The classic view of a consultant is that of the professional who is called upon by others to solve difficult problems or provide second opinions. In most consulting work, being retained and paid for counsel alone is much more the exception than the rule. Most assignments require something more than study, analysis, and advice. Clients may retain you to offer your advice on some problem—how to decorate a new suite of offices, for example—but they will usually require that you design the layout, write a set of specifications, suggest suppliers, and even select and order furniture and oversee the work done on the suite.

The client normally presumes that you are an expert. At the same time, you do not have to know everything there is to know about whatever field you specialize in. Most professions have grown too complex and diverse for one person to master their entirety, so most consultants specialize within their field.

Consulting is a flexible term and a flexible idea. It includes freelance or fee-paid services of many kinds of specialists. There are consultants who design a client's office procedures, write newsletters, plan political campaigns, advise on security systems, run a public relations campaign, manage a merger, or accommodate almost any special need.

## Earnings

Independent consulting is both a career and a business. Earnings vary, but in most cases competent consultants today command a minimum of $500 per day (plus expenses). With few exceptions, consultants' overhead costs are relatively small, primarily for marketing and administration. In many cases, you can set up an office in your own home, and probably will not spend a lot of your time there, depending on the nature of the business.

## How to get started

Many consultants start by helping friends and casual acquaintances. Soon after the demand for help becomes so great that they must either refuse offers or get paid for their time. Others start when they accept temporary jobs, moonlight after regular working hours, or seek part-time jobs after early retirement. Few, it seems, deliberately set out to become consultants; they are propelled into the field almost by chance or circumstance.

Consulting today can be approached in two ways. Some consulting services cater to the client in need of advice and guidance, others to the client who needs a specialist to serve as a temporary or quasi-employee. In the latter case the consultant need only report every day and do the work competently. In the former, however, the client may require you to do detailed and time-consuming work. Many consultants recoil from these duties, preferring to restrict their role to that of the professional temporary.

Those who choose this kind of consulting often start by becoming the employees of consulting companies who supply professional temporaries as their main activity. In this way they serve a kind of apprenticeship, learning how such arrangements work, which kinds of organizations are most frequently in need of such help, what to charge, and other important details. Veterans of such work arrangements can later strike out on their own, selling their services directly to clients.

The consulting market is predominantly one for specialists in high-tech fields. Clients are generally defense and other high-tech contractors, although many government agencies employ such consultant specialists directly on government premises. Government agencies, especially those of the federal government, are therefore, excellent prospects for consulting services.

Conventional advertising does not usually work very well in winning consulting assignments. The typical route is a more indirect one: marketing by creating an image for yourself as a professional while you gain visibility. You may choose to speak publicly, conduct seminars, write articles, or become active in the right associations.

Another route you can take in marketing your services is having your name added to bidders' lists in government agencies, companies, and associations who have need for such services and who then invite bids and proposals. Those organizations have standard forms (in the federal government it is Form 129), and it is necessary to provide one to each agency with whom you want to do business. When dealing with state and local governments, you will need to furnish an application only to the central purchasing organization of the state, county, or city.

## A few guidelines

Don't be vague about what you do as a consultant; be specific about your service and its benefits to the client. It is essential that your image be clearly defined and that you are firmly identified with what you have to offer.

Another way to expand, a way that reinforces your image and supplements your income base, is to add products and services. Here are several suggestions:

- A newsletter, published monthly or twice a month.
- Special reports, published intermittently.
- A mail-order bookstore. Many newsletter publishers find this a useful and profitable service.
- Seminars and paid public addresses to groups.

*— Herman Holtz*

# COOKBOOK PUBLISHING

**Start-up Costs:** $500. **Potential Earnings:** Up to $20,000 per book published. **Advertising:** Letters of solicitation to contributors. **Special Qualifications:** Sales experience helpful. **Equipment Needed:** Rented copy machine. **Best Advice for Success:** Solicit advertising from local merchants to boost profits.

You can profit from a cookbook that contains the best recipes of the best cooks in your area. Ideally, the cookbook will contain about four hundred recipes, each one by a local resident, offering what he/she considers his/her best recipe. It will also contain hundreds of little tips and household hints, handyman tips, and items about local stores and shopping by the local merchants on how to save money on daily needs. With such a book you can make a quick $10,000 about six times a year, and you do not need a large capital layout to do it.

Sales of the book are made before you print it. The contributors are your major buyers, your equipment costs you very little, and the material for the book costs you nothing. You can create different books in neighboring cities and towns and have several "best sellers" on the market at the same time.

Begin by choosing a town or city with a population of about 30,000, and obtain a list of all the local residents. The town hall will have a voters list, or you could simply consult the telephone directory. Your cookbook will contain 200 pages, printed on both sides, so you'll need 400 contributors. Choose the best areas and keep the addresses you pick (400 of them) several houses apart. The letter you send to each should read as follows (you may change the wording, but we give you this example because we know from experience that it works):

---

NEIGHBORHOOD COOKBOOK PUBLISHERS
Phone 555-3131
123 Main Street
Anytown, Kansas
H.K. King, *Editor*

Dear Mrs. Jones,

The NEIGHBORHOOD COOKBOOK PUBLISHERS has chosen this area to publish a cookbook of favorite recipes for the resident homemakers.

We take the liberty of writing you to ask if you will favor us with your favorite recipe. Since we would like to devote a whole page to your contribution, we would appreciate any tips you may wish to pass along to the less experienced homemaker.

We are going to have four hundred contributors for the complete publication, and it will be a valued addition to any homemaker's library.

If we could also be favored with a snapshot, we would appreciate it.

Our assistant editor will be calling you in a few days—that is, within two weeks—to see if it is convenient to call on you.

Yours truly,

H.K. King, *Editor*

---

Most homemakers will not receive a letter like this in a lifetime, and you will be swamped with phone calls even before you call them. This gives you a chance to tell them you are not necessarily looking for an original recipe, just their favorite one, and that it won't cost them anything to contribute, nor will they be under any obligation of any kind.

Hire three salespeople (perhaps family can help). Equip each one with notebooks, a sample cookbook as it will look when published, and a good instant-picture camera. This is no cold-canvas-type of sales work: each call is made on the invitation of the homemaker. When the salesperson calls, the homemaker will usually have the material ready.

The contributor will want one or more of the books herself, priced to her as a contributor at only $15 each. The actual selling price is not set until after publication, as we are not able to forecast the production cost exactly. She may order as many as she wishes at this low price, with a $5 deposit on each to be delivered in approximately ninety days. Your buyer is very anxious to receive the finished book, with a full page devoted to her contribution and her name and photo there for all her friends and relations to see. The average purchase is four books.

It will take a month for you and your crew to work an area, secure 400 contributors, and gather at least a thousand orders for books. One test area yielded 1,750 orders.

Now check the Yellow Pages and visit the dealers of duplicating machines and equipment. The kind you need would cost between $4,000 and $5,000 to buy, but the dealer will rent you a beautiful new machine for about $200 per month on a 36 month lease. The machine will copy almost anything, so you can lay out each sheet neatly typewritten, with a snapshot in place, and if possible a little art work to make each sheet as attractive as possible.

Use paper of 20 lb. bond, punched for a vinyl cover with three rings.

Print on both sides of 200 sheets. Design an attractive label to fit the vinyl cover. This is important to make the finished product attractive, so spend time and money on this step—it will pay big dividends.

Printing and putting these books together requires a rather large space—at least 400 square feet. You need three tables made from 4 ft. x 8 ft. sheets of ¾" plywood and equipped with metal legs; (they're available at building supply stores for about $20. This gives you 96 square feet of table space. Lay out your printed sheets in piles of 100 each and put together 100 books at a time. The finished product will reflect the care and thought you put into it, so shop around for an attractive cover (three- ring vinyl). As you need 1,000 copies or more, shop the wholesalers and your cost should be around $1 each, or about 50 percent of retail.

Your books are now ready to deliver and you have one last harvest to reap. Load your car with sample books and start the promotional campaign. Merchants will probably be glad to order a dozen or more cookbooks at $10 each to retail at $20, and equally glad to pay $50 for a full-page of advertising to be inserted in the book. You may be able to collect at least $5,000 in sales and advertising from this effort.

When you finally make your deliveries, you will find many requests for additional books. One area showed a net profit of more than $13,900 on the sale of 1,000 books. Much depends on the quality of the finished product and the skill of the sales force, but the beauty of this promotion is that once you have successfully promoted a cookbook, you are established. You have very impressive samples to show, and you have experienced salespeople. You will be getting repeat calls for books from every area you work, and the books never go out of date.

You will notice that the figures given have been based on the sale of 1,000 books. In fact if the true figures are taken, the net proceeds from a successful promotion, done by a professional sales team with an attractive product, are well up to $20,000. This is indeed a small business that can make it big.

*—H.K. King*

# CRAFTS—LOCAL SHOWS

**Start-up Costs:** $500 to $1,000. **Potential Earnings:** $8,000 a year or more depending on how often and where you display. **Advertising:** Done for you through show promoters; also word of mouth. **Equipment Needed:** Sewing machine, work table; whatever materials pertain to the project you're working on. **Best Advice for Success:** Take a

few craft courses, watch for popular colors and use them, but
most of all use your imagination and be as creative as you
want to be.

It can be done while watching your favorite television program or listening
to your favorite music in the comfort of home. Craft making requires little
training, and you choose the time you want to spend doing it. Then you
choose how to spend the money you make.

Viola Edwards strolled on the beach in the mornings picking up
shells on the way, not knowing those shells would be the start of a profitable business. A next-door neighbor showed her how to arrange those
shells on plaques with dried flowers and sell them to other neighbors. Edwards soon decided that she could do this on her own.

Edwards wanted to take the time and create high-quality products
people could use and enjoy. Word of mouth was her only advertising at
first, but that word quickly spread. She put together shows out of her
home, setting up tables and offering snacks and coffee for her customers.
People often commented on how much they enjoyed shopping for gifts
there instead of hassling with the crowds at department stores.

Edwards learned that she could purchase shells, dried flowers, and
all the materials she needed at local craft stores and flea markets. "I cannot
stress enough how many ideas you can come up with while visiting your
local flea market or dropping by garage sales," she says. "It saves time and
money."

## What you'll need

Edwards's initial set-up cost was $500, and she paid for that from
the items she sold in her first show. She says, "It would have been perfect
to have $1,000 to start with, but you can make it work with $500." As her
crafts became more popular, she began to receive invitations to participate
in local craft shows. These invitations allowed her to expand into a wider
variety of crafts and to make more money without the worry of increasing
overhead.

According to Edwards, the following supplies are essential: assorted
scissors, a glue gun and glue sticks, a small work table, paint, and thread.
She explains, "Dried flowers and pine cones can be found in parks and
along walking trails. All you have to do is keep an eye out." So, those long
walks on the beach or in the park that you love can become material-gath-
ering expeditions. There is the possibility of virtually no cost on what you
feature in your crafts.

If you don't have one, your main expense will be a sewing machine.
Edwards bought hers at a flea market for $15. To this day she does all of her

sewing on it, selling some of the pieces she makes with it for $25 or more.

The only other start-up expenses are the craft books that contain various sewing patterns. There is also the cost of renting tables at shows, which run anywhere from $15 to $30, depending on the size of the show. The advertising of these shows is done for you, which saves you the time and expense of taking out your own ads.

## Pricing and operations

Pricing largely depends on where you live and who you're selling to. Edwards considers the time she puts in on a project and the cost of material she used, then doubles it to come up with the selling price. She doesn't want to price things beyond people's wallets, so this is when you consider where you live. Edwards lives in a small foothills community where much of the population is retired and there are no big-salary businesses, so her prices are lower. On the other hand, when she visits her son in an upscale community where the people are able to pay more, her prices go up.

The location of crafts shows is also very important to Edwards. She says it isn't worth her time to go to little shows with low turnout. Instead, she finds shows put on by local boosters clubs that put out good money for advertising. The turnout is tremendous and she gets people from all over the surrounding areas.

Another selling option that works well is setting up in the lobbies of local businesses. With the help of a friend at the local telephone company, Edwards sets up a table and can easily make a good day's wages during a lunch hour.

There are no universal techniques in the craft business. Craft making is up to individual taste and an eye for what is being created. Unless you have an artistic background, Edwards recommends taking a couple of floral arrangement classes from your local community college. Craft books are also a great help during and after the learning process.

When Edwards puts on a craft show at home, she always serves food and drink along with friendly conversation. She suggests that you have your customers sign in with name and address so you can drop them a card letting them know about your next show. When displaying her creations, she takes the time to arrange the items so that the right objects catch the eye. With each show she learns how to display them better the next time.

If you like working your own hours and working at home, crafts offers both. The enjoyment of creating things with your own hands and making money doing it can be very fulfilling. You decide how much time and effort you want to spend. Allow yourself time and a little start-up money, and you will be on your way to fun and profit.

**For more information**

*How to Profit from Your Crafts.* A complete crafts marketing manual from the editors of *Income Opportunities.* Income Opportunities Manuals, P.O. Box 40, Vernon, NJ 07462; $43.90 ppd.

*— Tom Edwards*

# CRAFTS—HOME PARTIES

**Start-up Costs:** About $500. **Potential Earnings:** $200 to $300 per average party. **Advertising:** Word-of-mouth. **Special Qualifications:** "The skill and love of making crafts." **Equipment Needed:** Electric saws; sewing machine; paints and other craft supplies; wood scraps. **Best Advice for Success:** "Hire and work with the right people, people who can help you with business matters. Offer quality items at reasonable prices."

Sandy Thomas and Charlene Minor ran a small business selling dried and silk flower arrangements, but they were not getting the profits they had expected. They did, however, enjoy making the arrangements and other crafts and country products. When friends repeatedly asked Thomas and Minor to make crafts to give as gifts or to decorate their homes, they decided to sell their crafts through home parties. Since then, they have developed a thriving home party business called Gram's Country Cupboard, featuring one hundred different gift items along with fifty items in their Christmas line.

Friends as well as business partners, Thomas and Minor work as many as ten or twelve hours a day creating items for their business in a third-floor room in Minor's house. When they decided on the home-party route, Minor and Thomas attended several other kinds of home parties to see how they were conducted and what incentives were offered to the hostesses and the customers. After doing this informal survey, the women felt confident they could offer their own line of quality craft items at very reasonable prices.

## Finding suppliers

Thomas and Minor first bought supplies retail, never having bought from a wholesale supplier before. Most suppliers would not even talk to them in fact, because they didn't have a tax number. So one of the first steps was registering their business name and obtaining the tax number.

A friend who owns a small shop gave the women suggestions as to the kinds of gifts that sell best, and also lent them her business directory of wholesalers. The two learned other ways to obtain supplies and names of suppliers. To find the address or telephone number of a wholesaler, they took the bar code from the back of a package and then called the Mercantile Library (they called directory assistance for the number in Philadelphia), who will give out the supplier's name and address listed for that code.

In their search for new suppliers, Thomas and Minor attend local trade shows. Thomas says, "It gives us opportunities to talk to representatives and to see if we can afford their minimum order. We've picked up several good suppliers at these shows, many with 800 numbers to call in our orders." To get wood for their crafts, Thomas and Minor visit local lumberyards, where they pick up scrap wood for free. Minor says, "Usually, they burn the wood anyway, so they let us have all we can use."

## Getting help

The women say the best move for their business was to hire an accountant. Minor says, "We brought the accountant our notebook with all our receipts, etc., and asked him to start us from the beginning because we really knew little about running a business." Thomas adds, "He guided us step by step and referred us to another man who sold us an easy-to-manage bookkeeping system." "Now," says Minor, "with this system, we send our accountant our quarterly statements, and he tells us how much money we are making."

Others who work with Thomas's and Minor's business are those who do piece work for them: they're demonstrators and the consignors who make crafts and sell them to Thomas and Minor, who then add on their markup. Whatever item they offer, though, must be top quality. Minor says, "We do our own quality-control, because everything we offer [for sale] reflects back on us."

## Profitable parties

The average party brings in $200 to $300, of which the demonstrators receive 25 percent. When Thomas and Minor started, they were running the parties *and* making the crafts themselves. Now that they have several demonstrators, Thomas and Minor have more time to create their gifts and run their business. Demonstrators help fill in the lull periods of the year because they are out looking for more parties to book.

When Thomas and Minor hire a demonstrator, she is given a "kit" of the items to be displayed at the parties. The demonstrator must buy the kit (it usually takes only two parties until a demonstrator has earned enough to buy her kit), and must book at least five parties. Demonstrators take better care of the kit items if they own them. Besides the 25 percent earned on each party, the demonstrators get 50 percent off any item they might want to buy. Thomas and Minor supply them with order blanks, door prizes and invitations.

Thomas and Minor have discovered other ways to keep customers happy. They do not require the customer to make a deposit on an order, because they feel that limits what people will order. Minor says, "People will order more things if they can pay later. We get bigger orders, and so far everyone has paid."

### Pricing

To set their prices, Thomas and Minor first added 20 percent to their costs and have since gone to a 50 to 75 percent mark-up. Thomas says, "Even with that price increase, our customers have told us how reasonable our prices are."

Reasonable prices, hostess incentives, and good quality have made their business grow faster than they ever expected. Thomas and Minor have decided, though, not to have any parties in January, February, July, or August. They say they need this time to take stock of the business, get new ideas for spring and the Christmas season, and to reorganize their business goals.

The women have found their best advertising has been through word of mouth. Minor says, "Classified and display ads did not work for us. Our items sell best when seen. Even though each of our demonstrators carries an album with photos of other decorative items, Sandy and I have found that customers will buy more from the items at the party than those offered in the album."

Thomas and Minor offer these pertinent tips to other craftmakers/sellers:

- Be creative with the crafts by offering variety. Try to be one step ahead; know what items are most in demand.
- Keep organized. Don't offer more items than can be made.
- When updating your current line, shop carefully.
- Be flexible. If a customer wants a special order, a different color, for example, try to do it. That little extra may pay off in a booking later on.
- Never back out of a party once it is scheduled.
- Learn all you can about merchandising and marketing to keep your business growing.

*— Priscilla Y. Huff*

# CRAFTS—PARTY-PLAN CLASSES

**Start-up Costs:** $200 to $500. **Potential Earnings:** $120+ per party. **Advertising:** Referrals through hostesses and party attendants. **Special Qualifications:** Knowledge of crafts. **Equipment Needed:** Crafts supplies and products. **Best Advice for Success:** Purchase supplies wholesale to keep overhead low.

Kathleen Gleaves began teaching craft classes in her small handicraft/gift shop. During that time she made an interesting observation: people achieved better results and had more fun in her classes when they came with a friend. That one tiny thought became the basis for the popularity and success of Gleaves's Home-Party Craft Classes.

After two years as a shop owner, Gleaves realized she wasn't cut out for the stress and pressure of the business world. She sold her shop but wanted to continue teaching, both for the pleasure and for the extra income it provided. However, she was unsure about where to ply her trade.

One evening, at the closing of a Tupperware Party, the hostess, a friend of Gleaves's, brought out a craft project she was having problems with and asked her "expert" advice. The ensuing conversation attracted everyone's attention, and what had been a subdued affair blossomed into a unique evening of swapped advice, helpful hints, and the answer to Gleaves's own dilemma. She began offering classes on a home party plan. The plan was simple: the hostess receives her instructions and supplies free of charge if she can get a minimum of ten friends and neighbors together in her home for the class.

To ensure that everyone will have the proper supplies, and to eliminate time-consuming shopping trips for busy students, Gleaves provides the materials needed to complete the project and sets her class fees accordingly.

The classes last from two to four hours, depending on the project and how well members of the group know each other. Trading gossip sometimes slows down the class, but no one seems to mind, and Gleaves lets her students dictate the speed of their progress, to a reasonable extent. Everyone leaves the class with her project completed, or far enough along that she is able to finish it on her own. A printed instruction sheet for the project is included for future reference, along with Gleaves's phone number, should they have any problems or questions.

Gleaves teaches a wide variety of crafts so that people have a number of classes to choose from, and she always brings examples of other projects to each party. This "show and tell" style of advertising usually guarantees additional bookings.

## Craft demonstration parties

In a similar vein, Joanne, an acquaintance of Gleaves, pursues the home craft parties idea by giving demonstrations rather than actual "hands-on"-type classes. She and her sister demonstrate several silk- and dried-flower projects: vine-wreath wallhangings, willow-basket arrangements, and seasonal centerpieces. All the supplies necessary to complete those projects are available for immediate sale at the party.

Customers select flowers, ribbons, and containers to coordinate with their own particular color schemes and receive expert advice on arranging and displaying their choices. Additional materials are also available for sale. Party guests go home with the supplies and the know-how to complete their own versions of the project, and, of course, information about the bonus incentive offer of free merchandise if they book a party of their own.

## Operating fundamentals

Neither of these approaches requires an exorbitant amount of capital investment, and since there are no employees, overhead expenses are minimal. Gleaves's plan requires less money because she purchases supplies only as needed for a known quantity of students. Joanne, on the other hand, must stock and transport a larger volume and variety of merchandise. She will take orders for any item that sells out at a party, but has discovered that customers, inspired by her demonstration, want to be able to go and begin working on their own projects immediately. They don't want to wait for an order to arrive. So maintaining an adequate inventory is important to her ultimate profitability.

The price of Gleaves's classes averages about $30, so her income range for any one evening is $300 to a maximum of $360, minus the cost of the supplies, which amounts to roughly one-third of the cost of the class. Joanne, because she can accommodate a larger party and spends less time at each engagement, stands to produce a greater income.

Securing the supplies and inventory is basically the same with both jobs. Obtain a state business license, if required in your area, which will enable you to shop in wholesale establishments. Check the Yellow Pages of your phone book under "Floral" or "Craft Supplies, Wholesale" for the nearest warehouse. Spend an afternoon inspecting as many establishments as possible. Make notes of the inventory available, prices, minimum purchase amounts, and quantity discounts. Use this information in planning your class offerings.

Once you have established yourself as a regular customer, you should be able to set up a charge account that will enable you to obtain the merchandise you need and pay for it after you receive the party income.

That can be a helpful convenience as long as you are prudent and don't let your credit account outstrip your ability to pay it. In the beginning it may not be feasible to purchase everything wholesale, especially items you only need in small quantities.

The real beauty of a job like this is the flexibility. You can tailor the plan to any project that suits your talents and to any schedule that suits your lifestyle.

*— Kathleen Gleaves*

# CREDIT REPAIR

**Start-up Costs:** $500. **Potential Earnings:** $100,000 or more. **Advertising:** Community newspapers. **Special Qualifications:** None. **Equipment Needed:** Small office space, phone. **Best Advice for Success:** Guarantee an overall improvement in the client's credit condition.

When Deborah McNaughton first took an interest in credit repair, her goal was to boost sales for the real estate company she co-partnered with her husband. Increasingly frustrated over the number of clients who were disqualified for home loans because of long-since-resolved credit problems, McNaughton decided to do something about it. Months of research into the ins and outs of credit record keeping and reporting laws, however, convinced her that there was far greater potential in credit repair than just helping her own clients. So she launched her own one-person credit repair venture: Professional Credit Counselors. Here is your opportunity to learn from McNaughton's experience how to set up a part- or full-time system with as little as a phone and some well-placed advertisements.

Today, McNaughton's still-blossoming business includes a credit repair service, a mail-order/consulting how-to operation, and a line of "all about credit" books. Her gross yearly income approaches the $100,000 mark. McNaughton's credit service now requires the help of a full-time secretary and two field reps. What's more, McNaughton insists that she spends no more than twenty to twenty-five hours a week in the office so that she can devote time to her family.

## Building the business

In spite of McNaughton's phenomenal success, building Professional Credit Counselors into a thriving business has not been easy. To begin with, she says, "This had been a scam business. I heard lots of complaints about people who took money and left town. I also heard of companies that charged $1,200 for credit counseling. Because seeking credit repair is an action that's usually precipitated by an emotional incident, like being rejected for a home or car loan, it's easy for unscrupulous companies to play on customers' emotions. When I started, I found that lots of people were skeptical. I had to overcome their mistrust with personal contact. I also decided right away that clients should work with me, so that they could see what was being done in their behalf. It cuts costs, too."

McNaughton is licensed, insured, bonded, and registered with the Better Business Bureau. She works only by written contract agreement, and in initial contacts with potential clients, she encourages them to check her references and BBB ratings.

## How it works

McNaughton's system of credit repair is simple. First, she screens applicants by phone to determine whether they are eligible for credit repair. Clients' problem accounts must have been solved and paid off for at least one year, preferably three or four. The telephone session also allows McNaughton to explain her services, contract, and fee ($195 for a couple working with two reporting agencies; $175 for an individual). If everything is "go" from there, the next step is to set up an office appointment, during which clients learn the credit repair process, including their own role. They review documents and worksheets and sign a contract.

Under McNaughton's supervision, clients then obtain their own credit records, identify problems, decide on the best approach, and send the appropriate documents and correspondence to the appropriate agencies. When updated credit records are returned to clients, they check back with McNaughton to determine whether further action is called for. If it is, additional technical correspondence can be filed that will either remove or clarify any blemishes which remain on the record.

"No reputable company should guarantee 100 percent that a specific item can be erased. If they do," McNaughton warns, "it's a bad sign. What I do guarantee is that there will be an overall improvement or the client's money will be refunded. And I have never had to return anyone's money."

## You can do it, too

"Actually," McNaughton says, "credit repair is a service that anybody can do, like selling a house. However, it's something that most people feel they don't have the know-how or the time to follow through on. I even offer a $39.95 do-it-yourself kit to all applicants, but nine out of ten want us to do it for them."

From the time she first decided to go into the credit repair business, McNaughton believed it was a service industry just waiting to happen.

"When I got my idea together," McNaughton recalls, "I rented a phone and ran an ad in a local newspaper for three or four days. I was overwhelmed by the response: forty-five calls. I knew from the beginning that I wanted to help other people get started in this business. So I documented everything and worked out the bugs as I went along." Unlike a franchise operation, McNaughton provides only how-to materials and six months of consulting service. There is an initial fee of $695, but new business owes her no additional fees or percentage of profits.

For additional information, write to: Professional Credit Counselors, 18912 Brookhurst, Fountain Valley, CA 92708.

— *Yvonne Emerson*

## CROSSWORD PUZZLES

**Start-up Costs:** Under $50 if you already own a typewriter or personal computer. **Potential Earnings:** From $10 to $350 per puzzle. **Advertising:** Directly soliciting potential employers/markets. **Special Qualifications:** Enjoyment of trivia, attention to detail. **Equipment Needed:** A typewriter or personal computer, pens and pencils, and paper. Reference books can help. **Best Advice for Success:** Submit your work regularly, follow each potential employer's guidelines closely.

Do you love crosswords? Are you a whiz at word-search puzzles? If you're already a solver, the transition to puzzlemaking will probably be a snap. Like the hundreds of other constructors (trade lingo for puzzle-maker) now managing their own low-overhead cottage industries, you'll learn that making puzzles yields a pleasure very similar to solving. Many have found the challenge even more satisfying—and it pays.

Even if you've never bought a puzzle magazine or been tempted to fill in the little white squares in your daily newspaper's crossword, you can quickly learn the basics of puzzle constructing and earn money in your spare time.

Many kinds of piecework are suitable for a home-based sideline, from quiltmaking to calligraphy, but making puzzles and word games is the ideal piecework for busy people and those seeking a manageable low-investment second income. Here's why:

- The pieces are small. You can construct and type many puzzles in less than a half-hour.
- The work is portable. Some busy freelancers do all their con-

structing while commuting to and from their regular jobs, leaving only some typing and fact-checking and mailing to be done at home.

■ The work is adaptable to your schedule because, with the rare exception of a commissioned puzzle, there are no deadlines. Publishers select from what they have on file; your new submissions go into a pool of available material that is paid for when used. Thus, you may spend as many or as few hours on your sideline as your schedule permits.

## Getting started

The largest and most accessible markets for freelance puzzle constructors are newsstand magazines, which also depend on subscription sales for a large part of their circulations. The big three puzzle magazine publishers alone—Official, Penny Press, and Dell—publish a total of more than thirty issues a month, with an average of at least seventy puzzles in each issue. That's over 2,000 puzzles every month, and only one fraction of the booming puzzle industry. Nearly all the puzzles are constructed by freelancers working out of their homes.

Because of this dependence on freelancers, most of the puzzle markets are happy to provide guidelines for potential constructors. A brief visit to your local newsstand or bookstore will provide you with a starting list of potential markets. Do a little phone research and address your request to a middle-level editor or editorial assistant and include a self-addressed stamped envelope. (Always include a self-addressed, stamped envelope with every submission or correspondence with editors.)

Begin a log; you will use this for recording submissions as well as guideline requests. A periodic check of your local newsstand or bookstore will allow you to keep abreast of new markets. Your log will allow you to keep track of your responses to guideline requests. It will also help you to track your submissions and guarantee that you neither oversupply nor neglect markets that have expressed a willingness to accept your work. Finally, if you have trouble placing a particular puzzle, your log will tell you who has already rejected it and who is still a potential buyer.

## Constructing your first puzzles

Publisher's guidelines are specific as to content, style, and submission preferences. Nevertheless, new freelancers continually skirt or ignore the carefully crafted rules altogether. This tendency of newcomers can work in your favor. Follow the guidelines and use published puzzles from the magazines to which you submit as your models, and you'll start with more than a leg up. The editor will remember that your puzzle required little extra editorial time and will be more likely to select your work in the future. The differences in guidelines from one publisher to another are slight but significant: you should heed them. The guidelines relate to clue writing style and presentation when typing the puzzles.

There's a single golden rule that applies to all puzzle constructing: solving in reverse. When you solve a puzzle, you usually deduce the shortest and easiest answers first, and work your way to the hardest and longest. When you construct, however, you tackle the hardest and longest first (which often provides you with a strong framework within which to continue), then work your way through to the shortest and easiest. When you encounter an unsolvable constructing problem, it is usually because you have jumped into the middle of your puzzle rather than started with the longest and most difficult element.

Similarly, you will use solving tools in reverse to help you construct. Specialized dictionaries and encyclopedias will help you write spiffy definitions and come up with offbeat puzzle ideas. Word-finders and anagram dictionaries will help you select the right word to fit into your half-completed grid. For the uninitiated, a word-finder is a book that lists all possible words, by length, that have chosen letters in given positions. For example, you'll find fifty words of five letters with the pattern — O — L —, from BOILS to YOWLS. Special encyclopedias also help in this way if you're willing to scour a little bit. The index of the *World Atlas*, for example, is packed with unusual place names that may fit the letter pattern you need.

For ideas, you can also consult published puzzles. Puzzle editors are just like their colleagues in other areas of publishing: they want material that is old but new; that is, familiar enough to be accessible, but fresh enough to engage interest. For example, a puzzle on the circus might spark an idea for a puzzle on the rodeo or on the names of movies set at a circus. Every time you solve a newspaper puzzle or buy a puzzle magazine, write down (in the back of your log) the ideas that it triggers.

As to the nuts and bolts of making puzzles, there are very few trade secrets, and the best education is practice. Remember to start with the hardest and longest, and to use published puzzles and the guidelines you have solicited as your blueprints.

## Basic puzzle types

There are three basic types of puzzles. Here are simple methods and additional tips for constructing each.

*Word Searches and Other List-Based Puzzles.* Begin with a list of about fifty possible entries (more if your puzzle will be a jumbo-sized one). Figure an ideal grid size and number of entries by consulting the magazine to which you will be sending your work. Use graph paper and define with a pen the perimeter of your grid. (For submission, you will only have to type the grid letters with space in between.) Remember the golden rule and start with a few long entries that radiate from a single letter in multiple directions. Add entries from your list that connect. Your finished grid should be equally dense in all areas and should feature roughly equal amounts of across, down, and diagonal entries. (If it is a crosspatch puzzle, there are no diagonals, but the other guidelines apply.)

Other list-based puzzles include cryptofamilies and quizzes; both are easier to make because they require no grid. Or perhaps you can invent your own.

*Double-Crostics and Other Quotation-Based Puzzles.* The double-crostic is one of the easiest and most enjoyable puzzles to construct, because it requires no solving expertise or understanding of crosswords. It essentially involves coming up with interesting words based on a pool of letters.

Briefly, a double-crostic features a list of clues, letters from the answers to which fit into a grid, which in turn spells out a quotation. Additionally, the first letters of each answer spell out the name of the author and source of the quotation.

To construct, check the length of the quotation you have chosen against published puzzles to make sure it's appropriate in length and subject. Some publishers require that you send quotes in first for approval. On a piece of lined notebook paper, break the quote down by letters (all the A's on one line, and so on). This will be your letter pool for determining the clue answers.

On another piece of lined paper, write in two separate columns the name of the author and the title of the source. Remember that these also will be the first letters of your answers. Cross out the used letters from the pool. Compute an average answer length by dividing the number of letters in the pool by the number of answers. The first answers you come up with should be a couple of letters longer than the average, which will get progressively smaller as the pool diminishes and you find words for all the initial letters in your list.

When looking for quotations to use in double-crostics, you will come across many that are clever but too short. These might be suitable for other easy-to-put-together quotation-based puzzles like cryptograms or quotefalls.

*Crosswords and Other Grid-Based Puzzles.* As the *pièce de résistance* of word puzzles, and as the bread and butter of most puzzle magazines, crosswords merit an entire book for discussion, not the scant few paragraphs here. However, a few pointers can easily get you started. You will find that, like many crafts, the best education for crossword constructing is practice. And there are several books available to provide additional instruction and remind you of the basics.

First, don't try to devise original grids on your initial crossword constructions. Use grids from magazines or newspapers that appeal to you. The most promising grids for beginners have a few long theme answers (ten letters or more) and no other answers over six letters long. Fifteen squares across by fifteen down is the standard size for "regular" crosswords, covering most puzzles in the newspaper. Most magazine puzzles are twenty-one across by twenty-one down.

Notice that once you fill in the long theme answers (remember that in constructing you tackle the hardest and longest first) you can divide your grid into manageable isolated quadrants; nine quadrants in a fifteen by fifteen puzzle and sixteen quadrants (usually) in a twenty-one by twenty-one. A puzzle that has very long theme entries and non-theme entries of six letters or less divides into quadrants best, because there are no longish (seven to nine letters) answers that spill into multiple quadrants.

Some other tips: A word finder will help with thorny letter combinations, but trial and error and a long eraser on your pencil are the only constants in filling in the quadrants. Sometimes the first word that pops into your head fits perfectly into the grid and never gets changed, and sometimes it's a new word time and again . . . and again.

Try to think in terms of words that alternate consonants and vowels; they create a natural interlock. When you read the newspaper or watch television or if you solve puzzles, list interesting offbeat words that you might use in a tight corner. I'm talking about contemporary acronyms (like MADD) and celebrity names (Mia) and fictional characters (Aleta, wife of Prince Valiant) that you won't find in standard dictionaries and word finders.

Other tricky examples include *Uh-Oh* (the new best seller by Robert Fulghum), EMF and Color Me Badd (two hot contemporary rock groups), and Rhee (former President of South Korea). These offbeat words will not only help you in a pinch, they may also make your puzzles more interesting and marketable.

The bottom line: The best way to learn how to construct puzzles is to construct puzzles. Make the small investment in a few magazines and a few queries, and you may discover a sideline that rewards you both intellectually and financially.

*— D.J. DeChristopher*

# SPECIALIZED DATING SERVICE

**Start-up Costs:** $500. **Potential Earnings:** $50,000 or more. **Advertising:** Local newspapers, magazines; Yellow Pages. **Special Qualifications:** None. **Equipment Needed:** Home office space, phone, stationery. **Best Advice for Success:** Cater to a specific category of singles.

As the divorce rate continues to climb and as the number of single people multiplies, the need for unmarried people to meet grows. First all-purpose dating services blossomed, then video dating services, but the two entrepreneurs profiled here felt that these businesses were too general. Specialized dating services are proving to be lucrative businesses nationwide. Plump Pals appeals to overweight people and average-sized people as well; Gentlepeople will accept only "achievers" as their clients.

Starting one of these specialized dating services usually involves a minimal investment of home office space, a telephone, stationary, and some advertising money.

## Gentlepeople

Zelda Fischer realized that she had numerous highly educated friends who were successful in their careers but not so successful trying to meet mates. With money raised from friends, she opened a dating service named Gentlepeople, aimed at pairing up culturally minded achievers.

Gentlepeople has proven such a success that Fischer has taken on a partner, Dana Wechsler. "There's an enormous need for single people who are well-educated, culturally active, and accomplished to find one another," Wechsler says. There are ways for people to meet who feel comfortable in bars and through personal ads, but Gentlepeople was the first business that targeted the highly educated. Over 75 percent of Gentlepeople's members, Wechsler notes, possess advanced degrees. Many are doctors, lawyers, and architects, but almost all of them are "achievers who are attracted to the arts."

Unlike many generalized dating services, which accept all candidates, Gentlepeople is highly selective. Wechsler contends that nearly half of the people who apply are rejected. Nonetheless, she doesn't consider the organization snobbish, viewing Gentlepeople as selective and realistic. "We give people honest assessments. If we don't have the right man for a certain woman, we say so," Wechsler says. There are no rigid criteria as to who is rejected, who is accepted. Finances are only one factor in determining acceptance; since Gentlepeople attracts the culturally minded, "starving poets are welcome," Wechsler asserts.

A candidate who is accepted is asked myriad questions in order to best ascertain who his/her right mate will be. What the person seeks in a member of the opposite sex, their values, lifestyles, likes and dislikes are recorded in this personal interview.

Gentlepeople members meet each other in one of two ways. First, a member is given a highly personalized recommendation of someone to meet. Gentlepeople prides itself on personalized arranging, knowing every member and calling each member for feedback on their dates to help in arranging the next date. Arrangements are constantly refined until someone finds the right person.

Members are also invited to bimonthly private parties, more like cocktail parties. Often these parties include chamber music or a lecture. "People can meet there," declares Wechsler, "and select their own mate." Through both of these ways, chemistry, that all-important ingredient, has a chance to work.

The most difficult stage in starting a specialized dating service is the beginning period. People are often suspicious at first. Getting through the first two years involves having enough capital on hand to weather the hard times. Start-up costs include a telephone system and stationery. The other major cost is advertising. Gentlepeople has run ads in the *New York Times*, *New York*, and more specialized publications like *The Law Journal* and a *United Nations* newsletter.

To generate membership at the outset, Gentlepeople offered reduced membership when it first opened. "This business can't work until you have a large enough amount of people to deal from," Wechsler says.

Yearly membership costs $950 a year in New York, slightly less in other cities, and there's a special trial membership fee of $250 for a two-month period. Members are guaranteed one date a month plus invitations to all parties. By establishing a selective singles dating service, Wechsler says the service can be more useful to people than a more generalized approach.

## Plump pals

Rita Kenny, herself a slim 125 pounds on her five foot two-inch frame, learned something from her daughter that changed her life. Her daughter, who weighed over 350 pounds and worked at an Atlantic City hotel, told her mother that European tourists, unlike many Americans, were attracted to her and didn't care whether she was overweight. Kenny started thinking about how difficult it was for an overweight person in suburbia or anywhere to meet someone. With a limited amount of capital, she opened a tiny one-person office near her home.

She placed a small ad in the local newspaper about Plump Pals, the name she gave her specialized dating service. The day the ad ran, Kenny received over twenty-five calls from eager overweight people, desperate to meet a mate. "Is this a joke? Is this for real? Are you legitimate?" Kenny says were the questions that were asked at the outset. Kenny's phone continued to ring.

"Three out of five Americans, at one time in their life, are overweight," Kenny says. "There is a lot of money to be made." Kenny has also learned one surprising fact about human nature: many slim men are attracted to plump women. "Over 95 percent of my male clients are average-sized men looking for big women."

There are no limits on who can join Plump Pals. Clients range anywhere from 100 pounds to over 450 pounds, from ages twenty to sixty-eight. Dates are arranged in a personalized way by Kenny and her assistant. Each client, who pays $250 for a year's membership or $125 for a four-month trial membership, is asked what he/she is looking for in a mate, whether they're attracted to slim or plump people, whether they smoke, what their religious preferences are, and so on.

"The most difficult task in running Plump Pals is maintaining quality control," says Kenny, who knows every one of her over a thousand clients. She arranges these dates like a personal matchmaker. If her business continues to grow, she worries about how she will handle the increased number and still offer personalized service.

*— Gary Stern*

# DAY CARE

**Start-up Costs:** $100 to $300. Cost may be higher if you require smoke detectors, fire extinguishers, furnace inspection, etc. **Potential Earnings:** $75 per week per child, or whatever your going rate may be. **Special Qualifications:** None. **Advertising:** Word of mouth. **Equipment Needed:** Toys, games, and anything that makes your home child-proof and safe. **Best Advice for Success:** Provide a loving environment for the children; if they have a good beginning, it will carry through their lives.

The house is full of kids. Play-Doh and poster paints tumble from closets. Blocks and puzzles spread themselves like peanut butter across the floor. The woman in the middle looks frazzled, but cheerfully speaks above the din, one child on a hip and one at her feet. Gail Parker isn't the neighborhood babysitter. She's a professional running a small business from her home and providing a vitally needed service. She's licensed, educated, and meets the regulations of her state. She's also earning a great income.

Demand for high-quality home day-care is extremely high. And it's just the freedom many women have been looking for. They can earn a respectable income while staying home to raise their children. Depending on location, the age of the child (rates for infants are sometimes higher), and the program offered, weekly rates per child range from $50 to $150.

## Forethought and preparation

Starting a home day-care service requires significant forethought and preparation. The question to answer before you buy one box of graham crackers is, do you really want to do this? Can you spend ten hours a day in the company of toddlers, retain your sanity, and your good humor, and make their day happy and creative?

Joanne Sweedyk worked for eight years at an engineering firm before beginning day care. "I love it," she says. "It really fits me and I fit the job. I wake up in the morning with a smile on my face to greet my families. The kids are glad to come here."

Begin by viewing yourself as a professional offering an important service. Providers all agree that they aren't babysitters; they are running a small business from their homes. Be assured that the IRS and state regulatory agencies will view you that way. Get a list of your state's regulations for day care through the Department of Social Service. These vary considerably from state to state; no licensing is required for up to five children in Nevada, while Minnesota requires both CPR and child development training within the first year of caring for any children. Complying with state rules may account for a portion of your start-up costs, estimated as $100 to $300, along with toys and equipment. You may need smoke detectors, fire extinguishers, electric outlet covers, and a furnace inspection.

Line up your resource and support system. There are local Family Day Care Associations and child-care coordinating centers or resource and referral services. These agencies offer advice and support and sometimes run a referral service and library. Look under "Child Care" in the Yellow Pages, or call the National Family Day Care Association (1-800-359-3817) for resource catalogs, lists of state regulations, and useful information for new and established day care businesses. Also ask about the child-care food program, a federally funded financial aid program to day care providers that will reimburse you a certain amount per child for a daily breakfast, lunch, and two snacks. Minimum nutritional levels are required, and field workers sometimes inspect homes for compliance.

Visit several family day-care businesses. Each is unique. Ask yourself specific questions: What ages will I take? Will I charge more for infants? What kind of program do I want to run? Most providers plan regular projects and have varieties of materials and supplies on hand.

Gail Parker discovered, after opening her home, that the program she wanted to run didn't work with children under three. Now she limits her children to ages three and over. Sharon Straight doesn't accept children before 7:00 A.M.

### How to start

Compile a policy sheet for your families—and yourself. Set your limits and know what's important to you. Consider sticky areas like discipline, emergency procedures, and how you'll handle illnesses and communicable diseases. Will your fee schedule be weekly or hourly? How will you handle late payments and overtime charges? What if a child misses a day, or several days?

Sweedyk charges a straight $75 per week for her full-time charges, a competitive fee in her area. Parker has a more elaborate, sliding scale of hourly rates for her two dozen part-timers.

Kids and all their paraphernalia take considerable space. Review your home and figure out where it will all go. An outdoor play area should be safe, fenced, and sturdily equipped. Straight lets the children have the run of her house except for the upstairs, which is reserved for her own children. Sweedyk uses her large family room with a small table in the kitchen for the little ones, plus an upstairs bedroom with four cribs for the nursery. The remainder of the downstairs and bedrooms are for her family. Parker has completely remodeled her garage, creating a light, airy, well-stocked play space with a separate entrance and bathroom, and electric outlets four feet above the floor for her group home.

However you arrange your space, keep in mind the privacy needs of your family. Their support is crucial to the success of your business. Your children need a place of their own and the reassurance that it is respected. Your spouse must stand behind you as you launch a fifty-hour a week business that will consume most of your energy and the home you share.

### Finding clients

Where do the kids come from? If neighbors and acquaintances haven't beaten down the door, continue to spread the word. Call the school secretary, talk to bus drivers, get on child-care referral lists. Providers agree that quality day care sells itself best by word of mouth. Once you've got the group you want, the same children will probably be with you for several years.

Choose your families carefully. You'll be intimately involved in their lives for a long time. Interview them once or twice. give them your policy sheet, fee schedule, and a contract. Set up a one- or two-week trial period. Compare your basic approaches to child care and don't avoid anything that is unclear or unpleasant.

Insurance is a nettlesome area to providers. Ideally, you should carry liability and accident insurance for your day-care children, but most companies will cancel even your homeowner's policy if you begin day care. You'll have to shop around for carriers who will cover you, and a few even have a liability rider available through the National Family Day Care Association.

The hours are long and the work demanding, but invariably providers express a deep satisfaction with their contribution. "The kids need a loving environment," says Sweedyk. "If they have a good beginning, it will carry all through their lives."

### For more information

National Association For Family Day Care, 815 Fifteenth St. NW, Ste. 928, Washington, DC 20005; 1-800-359-3817, 202-347-3356.

National Academy of Early Childhood Programs, 1834 Connecticut Ave. NW, Washington, DC 20009; 202-232-8777.

*— Kate Convissor*

# DELIVERY SERVICES

**Start-up Costs:** $500 or less. **Potential Earnings:** $10,000 and up. **Advertising:** Flyers, word of mouth. **Special Qualifications:** None. **Equipment Needed:** Varies. **Best Advice for Success:** Provide convenience and quality service.

Several specialized delivery services have sprung up over the last few years aimed at one of the strongest buying segments in America: the college student.

Recent studies show that the average college student has over $4,000 in disposable income (above and beyond tuition, fees, books and basic room and board) per year. Add another well-off buying segment, university employees, and the college market becomes a boon to anyone with good entrepreneurial skills. Here are some delivery businesses you can start that capitalize on this market.

### Survival kits

One of the first major delivery ventures to target the college market was the so-called "survival" or "final exam kits." These kits are now available from several small firms at many of the larger campuses, but most smaller campuses and junior colleges are untapped. The kits usually contain food, flowers, soda, candy, a trendy toy or two, and a humorous card.

Actually, you will not sell the kits to the students directly, but to their parents. The parents then send the kits to their sons and daughters during finals week, their birthdays, or other special occasions. The best way to market the kits is to obtain a student directory that lists the students' home address. Most college directories now list that information. Send a direct mailer, consisting of a color brochure with a picture of two or three kit choices, to the parents. Pricing is simple: pre-price your goods and delivery costs and add in the margin for profit.

### Party service

What would college life be without parties? With such a service available, all the would-be party holder has to do is call the service, and all of the necessities of the party are delivered for one price. It saves the party holder time and, in some cases, even money.

One instant party firm is Peter Siegel's Party Helpers. Siegel began the company with the help of several other college students as a way of making a little extra money. Party Helpers started slowly, working a few small parties around campus until the firm's reputation grew. To spread the word about his service, Siegel made sure that all party goers knew he catered the party. Siegel's on-campus business grew.

"We started with the idea that if we were good, we would expand by doing more parties," says Siegel. "We soon developed such a reputation for delivering complete parties that we began to host private parties for people outside the university. It just took off."

Party Helpers quickly expanded its operation to the point where it hosted over 1,000 parties a year. Success gave Siegel another idea: a yearly party guide for Southern California and a subscription-based newsletter. The party guide and newsletter are doing so well that Siegel has now moved out of the instant party business to pursue the publications alone.

"*The L.A. Party Guide* sold all 10,000 copies last year," says Siegel, "so this year's book will be an even bigger hit. We now have 5,000 regular subscribers to the Host Helpers newsletters."

### Laundry pick-up and delivery

Michael Stein offers a laundry delivery service. "I really inherited the company and the idea," says Stein. "a senior and fellow tennis team member came up with the idea. Within a year after he graduated, I bought the company."

Under Stein, the company has seen impressive expansion. Each year since he started running Tucker's Laundry, the company has shown a 40-percent growth rate. "Our business plan is simple," says Stein. "We have a drop box right on campus where students can deposit their dirty clothes. We guarantee to have the clothes delivered to the student's room within a day."

Stein also employs three students to pick up laundry at the residences. Tucker's has done so well within the student community that the business is now serving university staff and customers off campus. Tucker's Laundry now picks up, washes, and delivers about 700 pounds of laundry a day.

The key to the firm's rapid growth, according to Stein, is the care they take with the clothes. "Trust and reputation are the most important thing about this business. People are very particular about their clothes," Stein explains.

To assure quality and careful washing, Stein contracted with several local homemakers, whom he has thoroughly tested. The core crew that does the washing has a profit-sharing option, as do the delivery people; this gives them the incentive to do quality work.

## Grocery delivery

Connie Long, a student at Wichita State, the home of the Association of Collegiate Entrepreneurs, owns and operates a grocery delivery service called Grocery Express. "I had the idea for two years before I acted on it," Long explains. "I finally put the plan together and started the business."

The grocery delivery service is a fairly easy one to operate. Long has accounts at three of the larger supermarkets in Wichita to assure that she gets the best prices for her clients. She takes the orders by phone, buys the goods, and then delivers them to the customer's door. "The major market is two-earner families. Most of them are employees of the university. University employees are very busy and need this kind of help," Long says.

Grocery Express depends on promotion to get new clients. Long has appeared on local TV and has been featured in several local publications. She also circulates flyers at grocery stores.

The college delivery service market is as diverse as the college scene. A smart entrepreneur living near a college or university campus can exploit the lack of transportation and free time common in that market. Wise campus marketers say that if there is a regular need for an item, a delivery service for that item is possible and profitable.

*— William and Wendy Ball*

# DEFENSIVE DRIVING INSTRUCTOR

**Start-up Costs:** Minimum $300, plus equipment costs. **Potential Earnings:** Variable; depends on location and class size. **Advertising:** Flyers, classifieds; media publicity. **Special Qualifications:** Certified license. **Equipment Needed:** TV and VCR; textbooks. **Best Advice for Success:** "Make your presence known to justices of the peace and municipal judges; they may refer (or order) customers to you."

If you like talking before groups, being a full- or part-time self-employed defensive driving instructor may be the field for you. It's relatively easy to learn, because you will be teaching people who already know how to drive, and the class material doesn't change much as time passes. You don't have to sell the idea since people will be coming to you.

You will need a special license. Contact an insurance broker or your state trooper headquarters. Or try the Department of Public Safety or the Department of Motor Vehicles. They can tell you how to become certified.

## The work

You will give classes to people who want to learn safe driving methods, who have been ordered to the classes by a judge for driving while intoxicated, or who just want to lower their insurance rates. Classes may last as long as eight hours and can be conducted on a Saturday or in two four-hour evening sessions during the week. Since many people who take these classes work during the day, they'll want classes to be after hours. These hours may also benefit you if you have another job.

To supplement your talk you'll need a television and VCR on which to play several safe-driving video tapes. Your state may require you to follow a specific book outline, in which case you may have to supply textbooks as well.

You can conduct classes at work sites or in the community rooms of banks or churches. A local business or public building may let you use its conference room. In many cases, you won't be charged a fee because your class is a public service. You must, of course, reserve the meeting places and make sure there will be enough seating for your students. Your class size could vary from ten students in small towns to fifty in cities, but you'll want to determine your optimum class size and aim for that. When there are too many students, they may find it hard to see the video unless you have several televisions stationed around the room.

You may need to drive to the place where the class is held. If you live in a large city, you may want to hold the classes in a different part of the city each time, or you may be successful always having the class in the same place. In small towns you will find it more appropriate to hop from community to community to be near the students, eventually making your rounds back to the first town to start all over.

## Advertising and publicity

Make flyers listing your phone number and the class dates, times, and places. These can be typed or created with press-on letters (available at an office or art supply store), or you can use computer software designed to make such flyers. Ask businesses, especially those with lots of foot traffic, to let you put up the flyers. In small towns, this works especially well. In large cities, however, you may not want to go to the businesses each time you put on a class.

Run a classified ad in the newspaper about two weeks prior to the class. If you have a daily newspaper, you may want to run the ad more often. For continuously held classes in one area, run a display ad and schedule the students for specific classes as they call in. The display ad should feature a cut-out box for the students to fill in and mail to you. Classifieds are cheaper, but displays could work better.

Publicity is a good complement to advertising. Because this business is a public service, the local newspaper editor should be happy to run a short item about the class for free. Write up a couple of paragraphs and inquire. Even a radio station may do this; it doesn't hurt to ask. Make your presence known to justices of the peace and municipal judges. They may refer people guilty of drunken driving to your classes (or even order them to attend).

## Costs

Figure a cost that will cover your meeting room fee (if any) and your travel cost, depending on the estimated number of students. Your Department of Public Safety office or your local courthouse may know the going rate for such classes in your area. If the class is too expensive, people who are merely trying to save insurance costs will shy away. Feel this out in your community to see what's best.

The initial cost to you is the certification fee and whatever classes are involved to learn how to teach defensive driving (somewhere around $300), as well as the purchase of the TV and VCR if you don't have them; one option is to rent them. Each class will have the additional cost of the room rental, travel, and your time. If books are required, you may have to purchase them.

Some people make careers of teaching this class. Other just do it as a permanent sideline. While it is a rewarding and certainly a needed service, one instructor comments that he is glad he does it part-time, because it gets tiring giving the same class repeatedly eight hours a day. He needs a break of a few days each week. Nevertheless, this is an often-overlooked specialty where you won't have much competition.

*— Sandra G. Holland*

## DROP SHIPPING

**Start-up Costs:** $50 to $250. **Potential Earnings:** $3,000+ per year, on a part-time basis. **Advertising:** Newspapers, magazines, direct mail, fairs, trade shows, club meeting, in-home shows. Obtain as much free promotion as possible. **Special Qualifications:** None. **Equipment Needed:** None. **Best Advice for Success:** Don't try to compete against already-established direct mail businesses. Narrow in on specialized, niche markets.

Five years ago Michael Sedge decided he wanted to be a publisher. He had established a name, Strawberry Media, had printed some letterhead stationery and business cards, and had even opened a business bank account. There was only one problem: he had no books to publish or sell.

Having worked as a publicist (one who promotes products through newspapers, magazines, and radio) for publishers and computer software manufacturers, Sedge knew that the most difficult part of a direct sale was getting a product known. So rather than put his efforts into someone else's success, Sedge decided to build his own. That was when he learned of a unique selling technique called drop shipment. Basically, drop shipment refers to a sales practice used by hundreds of thousands of manufacturers throughout the world. Under this system, people use their business to sell products without actually buying or stocking any items. In return, the manufacturers offer commissions from 15 to 50 percent, depending on the product.

To begin his "publishing" business, Sedge contacted Hunter Publishing and offered to promote Hunter's books on a drop- shipment basis. The conditions were fairly simple:

1. Sedge would cover any cost of promotion and publicity.

2. Orders and full payment would go to Strawberry Media.

3. Sedge would forward the orders to Hunter, with his shipping label and a check for 50 percent of the cover price, plus postage. Hunter, in return, would ship the orders immediately upon receipt using Sedge's shipping label. In effect, the buyer would think that the book had been shipped by Strawberry Media. That's drop shipping.

Strawberry Media physically had no books, yet had a list of over 400 titles to sell. Sedge also obtained 300 full-color catalogs from Hunter. He merely attached a Strawberry Media label over the order form and, without spending a single penny—other than for stationary—he was a "big-time" publisher. Soon Strawberry Media had a drop-ship with several publishing houses.

### Finding products

Finding products for your drop-shipment business is easier than you might think. Where you begin your search will depend a great deal on what you want to sell. If, for instance, you wanted to handle holiday flower arrangements, you might contact a local florist. If, on the other hand, you are interested in children's items, you might contact D & K Enterprises, which produces personalized children's books. Once you get into the drop shipment frame of mind, you'll be finding new products everywhere. You might begin selling garden tools, then include books on gardening, gloves, seeds, and other items commonly used by gardeners.

It's best to work with small manufacturers, where a one-on-one relationship is possible. Many business publications mention people who offer unique products. Another option would be to join organizations like the Direct Marketing Association (6 East 43rd Street, New York, NY 10017) and contact members who produce goods. There are also associations, like The Mellinger Company, that brings manufacturers and drop-shipment operators together. Members receive several benefits, including a color catalog of products from around the world, most of which can be sold through drop shipment.

### Getting publicity

Like any business, the key to drop-shipment success is getting people to purchase your goods. There are several ways to "spread the word." Sedge decided his best bet was publicity. Contrary to advertising, where you pay to have a product appear in a particular media, publicity is free. In addition, it is often more successful than advertising. No matter what your product is, you must "think" promotion to get free publicity successfully. Ask yourself these questions:

- Who would be interested?
- What magazines and newspapers does this market read?
- What is unique about my product that would make writers, editors, broadcasters, or producers "want" to talk about it?

Armed with the answers to these questions, contact media people by letter, phone, or in person. Send them samples. Let them know the benefits their readers, listeners, and viewers will obtain by knowing your product exists. Local media contacts are the best place to start. Sedge sent photos, brief descriptions, and ordering information on three items to a women's club after learning that they planned to review Christmas gifts in their newsletter. The results? Thirty-seven sales for a profit of over $920!

In addition to promotion, some drop-shipment businesses produce catalogs (or use the catalogs of manufacturers). However, this can become very expensive, considering one must not only produce and print the catalog but also purchase lists and pay for postage.

Beginners might better spend their money with small ads in local newspapers and club newsletters. In most cases these can be placed for a few dollars. Other very profitable ways to sell drop-shipment products is to hold house parties—much like Avon or Amway. In this case you pass around display items, then simply take orders. At one point Sedge had several family members selling items to friends in this fashion.

While drop shipment may not be for everyone, it offers a unique opportunity for people with little capital who want to increase their income with a home business. What's more, it lets you operate in any field that interest you. It lets you become as large, or remain as small, as you like. All that is really required are organization skills, a little marketing know-how, and time.

## Drop shipping tips

- When considering a product line, stay in a field that interests you.
- Know your market and how to reach it. Make a list of the clubs, fairs, and trade shows that cater to that market. Then become involved in these activities.
- Join clubs—both professional and those that involve the market in which you hope to sell.
- Make a two-year marketing plan, including how you will reach customers—fairs, open-house shows, promotion, advertising, and direct mail.
- Get all drop-shipment agreements in writing. Be sure you know who pays postage and how returns will be handled.
- Try to get promotional materials—photos, brochures, catalogs— from the manufacturer free of charge.
- Drop shipment is basically a mail-order business, so obtain a copy of "Mail Order Rules" (Superintendent of Documents, U.S. Government Printing Office, Washington, DC 20402) and follow them.
- Keep adding new products to your line. This will insure the continued interest of your market.
- Visit your local library and read about marketing and promotion techniques. Look for titles such as: *Free Press: A Do-it-Yourself*

*Guide to Promote Your Interests, Organizations, or Business; Practical Publicity*; and *The Publicity Manual.*

■ Because time is required to get orders filled under a drop-shipment system, be sure all ads, catalogs, and order forms clearly state: "Allow 30 days for delivery," In some cases, up to 45 days may be needed.

### Selected drop shippers:

The Mellinger Co., 6100 Variel Ave., Woodland Hills, CA 91367-3779. Novelty and imported items.

Mail Order Associates, 120 Chestnut Ridge Rd., Montvale, NJ 07645. Household and novelty products.

Wilshire Mail Order Books, 12015 Sherman Rd., No. Hollywood, CA 91605. How-to books.

Selective Publishers, Box 1140, Clearwater, FL 34617. Books, manuals, directories.

Premier Publishers, P.O. Box 330309, Fort Worth, TX 76163. How-to books.

*— Micheal H. Sedge*

# ELECTRONICS CONSULTANT

**Start-up Costs:** $100 or less (chief costs: tools, gas). **Potential Earnings:** $35 to $150 per call. **Advertising:** Word of mouth, human interest stories in newspaper and radio. **Special Qualifications:** Interest in electronics, ability to enjoy what you do, patience and imagination. **Equipment Needed:** Telephone, tools, various screw drivers, wire crimper, various adapters, clamps. **Best Advice for Success:** Be interested in what you do. Offer a hotline for additional questions. Keep careful records of type of work done and customer's equipment, so that future questions can be answered over the phone.

Oliver Reed's marriage was in trouble, but he knew just what to do. He phoned The O'Neal Solution. Technobuff Cindy O'Neal, age forty-two, rushed over, walked Reed's wife through their new state-of-the-art TV/VCR system and restored marital accord. The "solution" that quells many a family crisis is not a counseling center, but Memphis, Tennessee's only in-home electronics installation and training service.

"There's nothing better than having a job where you get constant

positive reinforcement," says O'Neal. According to her, teaching somebody to record one program on the VCR while watching the other, when
that same somebody previously only knew how to play a videotape, is exciting. The former Circuit City manager enjoyed her job, but found it frus-
trating to have customers slam newly-purchased equipment on the counter
and demand a refund, only because they were overwhelmed by all the bells
and whistles. She decided to do something about it.

In April 1991, she founded the electronics consulting firm which de-
mystifies people's TVs, VCRs, sound systems, and satellite dishes. Instruction averages $1\frac{1}{2}$ hours and the basic fee for training on one TV/VCR
combination is $35. Costs vary with the sophistication of the equipment
and customer's needs.

O'Neal is finding new job satisfaction and independence in her business. "There are no complaints or dissatisfied customers," says O'Neal,
who sees her task as reducing anxiety about entertainment centers. The in-
home consultant doesn't just do hook-ups, she teaches people how to program their equipment as well. "I don't make it a big mystery," she says, "I
tell them what gets what to work, not just how to push buttons. I am doing
my job when the fear disappears from owners' faces as they make friends
with their equipment," she says.

O'Neal developed electronics expertise by playing with home
equipment, heading off customer complaints, and learning installation and
programming procedures from a senior manager. She developed a knack
for coordinating various sound system features and translating them for
people in a non-intimidating way. Her supervisor then began sending her
into homes to familiarize customers with recent purchases. Soon, she was
packing a small gray tool chest containing assorted screwdrivers, adapters,
clamps, and wire crimpers. The kit, which still bears the handwritten disclaimer, "This is not my make-up kit!", accompanies the consultant on
runs to adjust any of over 150 types of sound equipment.

## Personal qualities are the main investment

Tools and household and transportation expenses represent total
start-up costs for the mobile consulting firm. Other equipment includes
home and car phones, a pocket computer for storing addresses, and office furniture. Equipment costs are minimal. The initial investment is more time than
money. And since it's a service, O'Neal notes, it's virtually all profit.

Personal qualities are what is needed most. "You have to be a people
person," says O'Neal. The electronics specialist has to have the patience to
answer dozens of questions. After the initial consultation, O'Neal provides
a hotline. Customers usually phone several times for two or three days un-

til they get most of their questions answered. Then, they may call again eight or ten months later.

O'Neal retains records listing equipment types and everything she did for a given client. Careful notes enable her to instruct on programming procedures over the phone even months later.

An electronics consultant must be part teacher, part psychologist. O'Neal uses humor to help people overcome sound system phobia. After listening to stories about other people's snafus, clients are ready to ask all their "silly" questions. "Actually, I don't think any question is silly," says the consultant, "Anything that's necessary to make them feel comfortable operating their components is valid." The customer is the boss. "They tell me what they want to be able to do and I explain the systems and teach them how to get the performance they want," says O'Neal.

Seventy percent of O'Neal's clients are women who feel more comfortable asking another woman about programming procedures. Yet she still gets surprised looks when the client discovers the electronics expert is a woman.

O'Neal recalls one man who asked hesitantly: "Are you the lady who comes to people's homes and teaches these dumb women who don't know a thing about VCRs which button to push?" "I wasn't sure I wanted to continue the conversation, let alone answer the service call," says O'Neal. But then he said: "Well, I've got this wife who wants to learn to program our VCR. And if by some chance this woman's husband is in the room at the same time, is it possible that he might understand how to program it, too?"

Runaway technology has people of all ages too rattled to ask for help. They fear appearing incompetent. They fear the instructions are beyond their ability to comprehend. O'Neal's customers range in age from twenty to eighty-nine. Many are professionals—doctors, lawyers, and executives who simply haven't the time to spend two or three days studying manuals poorly translated from German or Japanese. O'Neal admits the first time she sat down with a manual, it took her four days to decipher it. The O'Neal Solution provides a real human being who can take the client step-by-step through the techno-jargon.

Technicians, salesmen, and the industry in general do not offer assistance with programming. Delivery men don't know how to install equipment; too often, they just dump it in the consumer's lap. Technicians simply attach wires, push buttons, and leave without conveying knowledge of the wide range of capabilities available.

## The service sells itself

Getting the word out involves maintaining a business listing in the telephone book, serving customers who refer you to others, and winning free publicity through radio plugs and newspaper human interest stories.

A repair shop referred Oliver Reed to the service. The radio announcer was so pleased with the results he plugged the new firm on the air. Newspaper coverage has also boosted business. Months later O'Neal hears from people who have tracked her down through LINC—Library Information Center—which keeps a file on local businesses. "There's such a need for the service," she says, "that a lot of people call up and say, 'Where have you been all this time?'"

Many of her referrals come from small electronics shops as well as chain department stores such as Circuit City, Silo, and McDuff. "They send new electronics purchasers to me to provide them with that something extra they can't get from stores," says O'Neal. Indirectly, this benefits their business, since people feel more confident purchasing more advanced and more expensive equipment when they know there's someone to call on for knowledge and assistance.

### Planning for growth

Future plans for the business include hiring and training assistants and adding a new line—computers. O'Neal gets frequent requests to assist with PCs. She is just now adding an IBM-PC to her office inventory. "I'll be going through the same frustrations," she says, "but when I'm ready I'll be in people's homes helping them go through things I've gone through."

O'Neal's best advice is to do what you do best and do it better than anybody else. What you enjoy doing, you'll do ten times better than anyone else. "Playing with electronic equipment is the most fun for me," she says.

The demands of an increasingly sophisticated technology are leaving the average consumer short-circuited. O'Neal is plugged into the need of the '90s and her solution is proving the means to her own independent business.

— *Cheryl Rodgers*

# ESTATE SALES

**Start-up Costs:** $200 to $300. **Potential Earnings:** 25 percent of all sales. **Advertising:** Ads in daily and shopper papers. **Special Qualifications:** Organizational skills. **Equipment Needed:** None. **Best Advice for Success:** Let the client know that you are taking complete charge.

Verna Clayborne has discovered a part-time business that's fun, is growth-oriented, and can earn extra income. The business is estate sales. Clayborne outlines nine major steps that helped her establish her thriving estate sales business, along with some "special" tips that she has found especially helpful in running her business. Perhaps her advice can help you start your own estate sales business.

Clayborne was inspired to start this kind of business after she held her first yard sale to unload a "white elephant"—a red velvet sofa. Along with the couch, she sold several other unwanted items from her home as well as goods her neighbors no longer wanted. The yard sale took place over a Saturday and Sunday—regarded as the best sales days—and netted $200.

As much as she liked running garage sales, Clayborne felt she would like estate sales even more. Her second step was to study what has been written about estate sales. "Visit any good library and you'll find help," says Clayborne. Two books she has found helpful are *Warman's Antiques and Their Prices*, and *Kovel's Antiques and Collectibles Price List*.

Attend and watch others run estate sales. Get to know other estate sales agents and talk to them about the business. Clayborne suggests that you ask pointed questions, take notes, and then study them. "Get to know others in estate sales in order to exchange information," says Clayborne.

## Once you feel prepared: advertise

"I take out ads in the daily papers, but I've found the smaller papers excellent for attracting business," says Clayborne. Write a simple ad stating that you are available to handle estate sales, and place it in the estate sales section of your local paper. Run your ad as often as possible. Post notices on church and campus bulletin boards, or anywhere else you think a potential client might look. Talk with people who might know of others who have estate items, people who are going into nursing homes, moving out of town, or moving from houses into apartments. It doesn't take long for word to get around if you're well prepared.

Your reputation and expertise will grow with each sale, so you should organize sales as often as possible. If you really study and get deeply involved, you'll be surprised at the number of clients you'll get by word-of-mouth advertising.

In the beginning it's important to take the time to plan your business. Draw up a contract before you begin to work with a client. The contract can verify your fee and responsibilities and your customer's responsibilities to you. Your local library will have sample contracts that you can use for a model.

Clayborne says she has gotten a "world of satisfaction" from the items she has found for herself. "I am constantly amazed at how many people simply don't know the worth of items in their homes." She once found an old Italian musical tea kettle in a sale she gave for a neighbor.

"I've found Tiffany lamps I'd never have been able to afford," says Clayborne. "You'll become a collector before you know it."

## Clayborne's nine steps

1. Once you're set to do a sale, get to know the people you're giving the sale for.
2. Get someone else to help you keep an eye on objects to prevent pilfering of small articles.
3. Handle merchandise carefully.
4. Price your items fairly, referring to your catalogs, and, above all, price them realistically. Reduce prices as the sale nears the end.
5. The best time for sales is on the weekends, preferably on both Saturday and Sunday between the hours of 10 a.m. and 5 p.m.
6. Arrange your objects attractively and price tag them.
7. Your average share of the sales is 25 percent. Make it clear to your client that you're in charge of the sale. People can interfere by deciding at the last minute that certain items are too precious to sell after all. Try to get assurance that this won't happen at your sales.
8. Customers pay for advertising.
9. Get acquainted with a couple of good, small movers who can provide customers with a way to get their larger items home. Choose movers who will charge a reasonable fee and give careful, friendly service. Having a business relationship with a mover will be an asset to your estate sale business.

In addition to these nine basic steps, Clayborne gives the following additional tips she feels have furthered her success and will further yours.

- Be honest to a fault. Be the kind of person people know they can trust and count on.
- Cut your losses early. Not all sales work out. "I was once hired to do a sale by a man who kept sneaking items out of the collection until I confronted him with it. He wouldn't promise to stop, so I refused to go through with the sale," says Clayborne.
- Cultivate zest for your sales.
- Don't be satisfied with anything less than excellence.
- Never stop learning about estate sales.
- Take trips to other cities and communities to find out how sales are organized there.
- Ask members of your family and friends whether they'd like to assist you. Clayborne's nine- and fourteen-year-old daughters help her with the sales, and they're enthusiastic about it, too.

Running estate sales is not only advantageous for collectors but is also a great family undertaking, although you can do it by yourself with friends or hired help. "All in all, in spite of the hard work, I've found estate sales satisfying, rewarding, and so much fun," says Clayborne.

## Resources

*Warman's Antiques And Their Prices.* Warman Publishing Company, P.O. Box 1112, Willow Grove, PA 19090; $11.95 ($2 P&H).

*Warman's Americana And Collectibles.* Warman Publishing Company, P.O. Box 1112, Willow Grove, PA 19090; $13.95 ($2 P&H).

*The Kovel's Antiques And Collectibles Price List.* Crown Publishers, Inc., 225 Park Avenue South, New York, NY 10003; $10.95.

— *Marjorie Holtzclaw*

# FARM-SITTING

**Start-up Costs:** Minimal, since equipment is provided; advertising expenses. **Potential Earnings:** $100 a day per person; $125 on weekends. **Advertising:** Agricultural publications; booths at farm shows; word of mouth. **Special Qualifications:** Extensive farm experience; knowledge of dairy equipment. **Equipment Needed:** None. **Best Advice for Success:** "Every farmer has his own routine. Follow that routine to the letter."

After an intestinal bacteria practically wiped out Ed and Pauline Drexler's entire herd of dairy cows, they found a way to stay in farming without the headaches and overhead. They became professional farm-sitters. They don't have any cows now, and the only animals at their house are a few dogs and cats. Their business is called Farm Sitter Service, Inc.

When Ron and Susan Carr of Albion, New York, decided to take a vacation in Niagara Falls last year, they worried about entrusting their 100-head dairy farm to strangers. Like many family farmers, they fretted about the thousand things that could go wrong and how a "hired hand" might react to a crisis. They noticed an ad in *Country Folks* newspaper about a farm-sitting service that would allow them to take their first vacation since their honeymoon. After meeting the Drexlers, they left confident that their farm was in competent hands and they could enjoy their vacation without worry. "Once we met them, we knew that they knew what they were doing," Susan Carr says.

## Filling a need

The idea that there might be a demand for farm-sitting services occurred to the Drexlers when they won a trip. On the Saturday before they were to leave, their hired hand became ill and couldn't tend the herd while they were gone. The Drexler's figured their trip was off. "I got on the phone and must have called half the county," Pauline says. Just when it seemed fate was against them, Pauline found someone to take care of the farm and they were able to make the trip.

"When we got home, we said if there was someone who would do farm-sitting, we would snap them up in a minute," Pauline says. "For five years we remembered that. So when we got off the farm, we said we're going to run this business up the flagpole."

## The right background

Ed grew up on a farm in Smyrna, New York, and Pauline came from Hudson, Massachusetts, a small town between Worcester and Boston. After a brief time selling real estate, they bought their first farm, a sixty-two-head dairy farm where they increased milk production 22 percent in eighteen months. Then their herd was struck by a devastating sickness that turned their healthy cows to skeletons in a matter of weeks. They reluctantly sold their farm, bought forty-five acres of wooded land, and decided to start a Christmas tree business. It paid the basic bills, but dairy farming was still in their blood.

At last they rented a booth at a farm show and began advertising their farm-sitting service in agricultural publications. "We advertised at the end of February, we had a job at the end of March, and by the end of June we were off and running," Pauline says. They now have to turn down some jobs and book at least three months in advance. They have tended more than fifty farms all over New York and New England since they began the farm- sitting service.

## A profitable service

The Drexlers' service doesn't come cheap—$100 a day for each of them and $125 a day for Saturday and Sunday. In addition, they charge 50 cents per mile for travel expenses one way. The Drexlers' brochure promises: "We enable you, the farm owner, to enjoy time off without worrying about slipshod substitutes or minor breakdowns that could confuse inexperienced temporaries. Our goal is to have the farm never even realize you were gone."

Although most chores on modern dairy farms are similar, Ed says every farmer follows his own routine. The Drexlers send the farm owner a form ahead of time soliciting details of the owner's exact routine. The routine is followed to the letter, Ed says. The Drexlers pride themselves on being able to handle any unusual situation.

## Publicity

People learn about their service mainly by word of mouth, and many of their jobs are referred by former customers. Many farmers who didn't think they could leave their farm for any extended period find that the Drexlers are just what the doctor ordered. The time off rejuvenates them. "A lot of people who are considering getting out of farming are doing so because they can't get any time for themselves, so they become discouraged," Pauline says.

As good a pair of dairy farmers as the Drexlers are, they don't expect to be back on their own farm any time soon. "I like the challenge and variety of working on so many different farms," Ed says. They have the pleasure of doing what they love without the headaches.

*— Carmen Cambareri*

# FIREWOOD: APARTMENT DELIVERY

**Start-up Costs:** $500 or less. **Potential Earnings:** As much as $500 per cord. **Advertising:** Handbills. **Special Qualifications:** None. **Equipment Needed:** Firewood racks; pickup or other large truck. **Best Advice for Success:** Add specialized services to boost profits and assure customer satisfaction.

Firewood sells for $80 to $125 a cord, depending on location. Splitting, hauling, and stacking wood for an apartment delivery service business may seem like a lot of work for the return, but now it is possible to earn four times that amount with the new marketing techniques detailed here.

You're not the "lumberjack" type? You don't need to be. You don't even own a chain saw? You don't need one. You merely provide the delivery service and let someone else supply the wood—and the back-breaking labor that goes with it.

Fireplaces and wood stoves have shaken off the homestead image and are now seen in every conceivable type of dwelling, from mobile homes to plush condominiums. Apartment owners are finding it difficult to rent units without fireplaces. The concept of a customized firewood delivery service for apartment dwellers is so new, competition is practically non-existent. In the few isolated areas where this service is available, customers have responded eagerly, regardless of the cost.

This is a seasonal business, running from about mid-September to mid-March. You can earn extra income making deliveries on weekends only, or earn a substantial amount by operating full-time during the busy season.

Here's how it works. You buy from one to ten cords at a time (usually at a volume discount) from a big distributor. You then arrange to deliver a small quantity—say one-twelfth of a cord—of dry firewood to your customers on a regular basis. The wood is neatly stacked in a 20" x 24" x 4' rack provided by you for a minimal deposit. You can easily make such racks from 2 x 4s.

For each delivery you charge a minimum of $25. Customers can arrange for delivery once a month, but most choose twice a month when an empty rack is exchanged for a full one. With a weekend business you could service about eighty customers a month, for an average of twenty deliveries per weekend. A full-time operation can mean servicing up to three hundred customers a month for the busy six-month season.

## Locating your market

When searching for customers, the various apartment guide books, usually available free at supermarkets and magazine racks, will be an invaluable reference. Stick to the "high-rent" neighborhoods and concentrate on saturating a small area at a time. To help in this effort, encourage existing customers to tell their neighbors about your service by offering a small discount on their next order for every new customer they bring you.

Keeping delivery time to a minimum is an important consideration. A truck large enough to carry several loads at once is mandatory; a lift-gate is a great time and back saver. Racks can be loaded in advance and wheeled straight to the door. If such a truck is out of your price range in the beginning, carry the wood loose and load each rack prior to delivery. Set up a specific delivery schedule and stick to it. Divide your delivery area and make all deliveries to one area at the same time.

Cleanliness is another point to consider: wheeling a load of wood through a carpeted apartment to the back deck can leave quite a mess, particularly when it's raining or snowing outside. Laying a path of old sheets will help keep the floors clean, and a hand-held, rechargeable vacuum comes in handy should any debris fall.

On all "first orders," leave a printed card with specific instructions on firebuilding. Most apartment dwellers have little experience in this area, and you will save yourself many evening calls from cranky customers claiming ". . . there's something wrong with this wood, it won't burn."

Ease in starting the fire is the primary concern of the apartment dweller, not burning time. Selling wood that meets this criterion is most important. Thin-barked, porous woods such as alder and maple are ideal and must be bone dry! Apartment fireplaces are notoriously small and, as such, require smaller, drier logs than necessary for regular-sized stoves. Most bulk dealers do not split their wood small enough to accommodate the specialized market you are serving. If you opt not to cut the wood yourself, locate a source of cut wood early in the season. Unless you can make special arrangements with your supplier, you will probably have to split the wood once more before delivering it.

Adding a small bundle of kindling with each order is a nice touch and greatly appreciated by your customers. The above-mentioned rack is not just a nice added benefit for the customer, it also solves the major headaches of this business: how to get the wood from the truck to the porch and how to give an equal measure of wood to every customer.

## Advertising

Two methods of direct advertising are used. The first and most effective is the use of handbills, specially cut at a print shop to hang on door knobs. With the apartment owner or manager's permission, a notice is left on every door and extras are posted in the laundry, recreation, and lobby areas. Many apartment complexes offer "Welcome" packets for their new tenants and will include one of your flyers in these packets if you leave a supply of them with the main office. Whenever a delivery is made, take a few minutes to leave additional flyers at surrounding apartments. This business runs most efficiently when you locate a substantial number of customers in the same complex.

The second method of advertising is by direct mail. Because of the expense, use it only when you've been denied permission to leave the handbills. Address a postcard printed with the pertinent information to "Resident." The address information is occasionally available through the management office, but most often you will have to copy it from the mailboxes. This can be time-consuming at first, but your mailing list is a valuable asset that will be useful year after year. Above all, follow the rules of the complex concerning canvasing and advertising policies; having the complex managers angry with you will do more to hurt your business than any other single factor.

Mid-day, mid-week deliveries often necessitate the manager's unlocking the door to allow you to leave wood on a customer's deck or patio. Consider offering the manager a discount on wood deliveries as a thank you for his or her help and cooperation. A good working relationship with the management office will make your job easier and cut down on your advertising expenses; there's nothing like a recommendation from the office to bring you new customers.

A written receipt should be given with every order. This is your primary method of accounting and conveys a professional attitude to your customers. A weekly tally of sales and expenses, complete with receipts and invoices, can be presented to your accountant at tax time.

Though this business is a seasonal one, usually running from late September to late March, it can provide a significant income during that time and will leave you free during the summer months to pursue other interests or money-making enterprises.

*— Kathleen Gleaves*

# FLEA MARKET—CONSIGNMENT

**Start-up Costs:** $500. **Potential Earnings:** $30,000, for smaller communities, to $100,000 or more for larger communities. **Advertising:** Word of mouth. **Special Qualifications:** General knowledge of what things are worth. **Equipment Needed:** None. **Best Advice for Success:** Buy low and sell high.

When most people hear "flea market" (or swap meet, as they're called in some parts of the country), they immediately get the impression of a local mall parking lot crammed with people at tables selling everything under the sun. There is a new kind of flea market, though, and it may be the business opportunity for you: the consignment flea market.

In this new twist on a great pastime, you sell on consignment the remnants of other people's spring-cleaning chores. This saves busy people the hassle of spending an afternoon a week hawking their wares at garage sales, and gives them exposure six days a week with you doing all the work—and taking the lion's share of profits. Another advantage for you is that you expend very little capital on your flea-market inventory. If you are a little handy, repairing some of the broken-down items you receive can be a further source of revenue.

Mel Peterson started L & M Flea Market after the car dealership he worked for moved out of town. Peterson didn't want to move to another town to sell cars, so he looked around for another line of work. He opened the doors of the L & M Flea Market, intending to rent tables to vendors—the traditional way—but it quickly became evident that in a town of 5,473 or so it wasn't going to work. So, he began taking the customer's wares on consignment or buying them outright.

"It took only six months to fill the building I rent," Peterson says. His only investment in the business is the rent, his time, and a little bit of advertising. "We started out with basically nothing," Peterson explains, "and we put very little into it." Because very little is spent on stocking the flea market, the company's expenses are kept low. Rent, light, and wages are the main expenses, and since the business requires the supervision of only one person, wages are kept to a minimum.

"You're never going to get rich at it," Peterson says, but his flea market has turned out to be a pretty successful business. L & M usually brings in over $30,000 a year, but profits vary from year to year. Considering the size of the town, Peterson is not doing badly at all.

Word of mouth is the most effective way to advertise, although Peterson runs a small ad in the local paper.

### Stocking a flea market

Operating a flea market isn't really very difficult. "If you buy right," Peterson says, "you can make a dollar." He figures that 85 percent of his stock sells at the price he or the customer suggests, and his stock completely turns over in a year.

Peterson doesn't trash or replace the stock that doesn't sell right away, because he never knows when there's suddenly going to be a need for a particular item. There are a few things, however, that rarely sell. "Big old hair dryers," Peterson laments. "No one uses them anymore. I also stay away from auto parts and larger items because I don't have the room."

Although most of his stock is consigned, Peterson occasionally runs into people who want to sell items outright rather than consign. In these cases he's careful to purchase items that he knows will sell and are priced right. As an example of how he prices and evaluates stock, Peterson figures that an item that is clean and in good shape should be able to sell at one-third its original shelf price. When he buys it, he doesn't want to pay too much and wipe out his profit margin.

### The secret of success

The secret to being successful? "I think just a general knowledge of what things are worth," Peterson says. And that, to a great extent, comes from experience. Operating a successful consignment flea market doesn't seem to be too hard, and it isn't, Peterson admits. "Buy low and sell high."

Once you start, it's simply a matter of sticking with it and having a sense of adventure.

### For further information

*American Flea Market Journal.* Quarterly publication. M.H. Sparks, 1911 Avenue D, Brownwood, TX 76801; $10 per year; $3 for a sample.

*The USA Flea Market Directory.* Forum Publishing Co., 383 E. Main St., Centerport, NY 11721; $10.29.

— *Ken Larkman*

# FLEA MARKET STAND

**Start-up Costs:** $500. **Potential Earnings:** Varies. **Advertising:** Word of mouth. **Special Qualifications:** None. **Equipment Needed:** None. **Best Advice for Success:** Great customer service.

They shopped carefully through wholesalers' and distributors' catalogs. They converted sheets of wooden lattice into display panels. They rented a flea market stall, hung their merchandise on the panels, and spread it out on a long table. Then Debbie and Mark Stephenson waited for customers—and looked forward to success.

Flea markets have come a long way since the days when they consisted of low-quality merchandise spread over rough wooden tables set up in vacant lots. That kind of flea market still exists, of course, but today's flea markets may have up to 500 booths in an air-conditioned building, or several hundred booths in specially designed buildings sprawled over several acres.

## Who are the vendors?

Most vendors are part-timers who work flea markets two or three days a week to supplement their incomes. Others are full-timers who are trying to make a living from their efforts. Jim Bickel started selling fishing tackle at flea markets two days a week. He now operates three retail stores. Vern and Arlene Wright began selling an automotive metal treatment compound on weekends from an outdoor stall. Today they sell bicycles six days a week from an 1,800-square-foot-store.

Mildred Bishop began selling sweatshirts and other sportswear from a single booth. Today she operates from three flea market booths plus a full-time store, and wholesales to other vendors.

Today's vendors range from homemakers cleaning out the garage, attic, and basement to serious business people earning a living from their stalls and stores. In between are craftspeople who are selling their own handiwork, retirees keeping busy while they supplement their incomes, and even corporations for which flea markets represent an additional outlet for their goods.

## A few of the advantages

Flea markets offer significant advantages to beginners because capital requirements are low and customer traffic—all-important to a retailer—already exists. In addition, since most markets operate only two or three days a week, it is easy to start a business part-time while paying the bills through other employment.

Even for a small store, rents can be as high as several hundred dollars a month. In contrast, a stall in an air-conditioned flea market costs about $200 a month, with a month-to-month lease and no additional costs or assessments. The market itself attracts the customers. The vendor needs low-cost signs and displays in the individual booth but rarely needs costly outdoor signs and newspaper or shopper advertising.

It may also cost far less to stock a flea market stall than a regular store. This is a good thing, since vendors report that outside financing is nearly impossible to find. Most vendors must finance themselves, usually from savings and outside jobs. However, skimping on inventory can be fatal. The vendor must have enough inventory to make it worthwhile for the customer to stop and look.

### Become a success

The vendor, the market, and the merchandise are all important. Vern Wright, who parlayed a two-day-a-week outside stand into a successful bicycle store says, "The people who fail are those who come in for four hours with a hundred dollars worth of stock and expect to have a thousand-dollar day." In flea markets, as in any other business, you have to work for success.

Lois Ploegstra, manager of the Red Barn Flea Market, says, "The successful vendors operate like a business, with regular hours and good customer service." Ploegstra, for example, stands behind her merchandise with refunds or exchanges. Vendors concur that customer service is the key to success.

Successful vendors agree that people go to flea markets looking for bargains. That means you must price merchandise below other retail outlets. Look for merchandise in the directories of manufacturers, available at the public library, then try the Yellow Pages and the various state and local Chamber of Commerce publications. You can locate other sources through a variety of publications serving the field (see list at the end of the chapter). Many of these publications are available in the rental office of your nearest flea market.

In some cases, vendors go directly to manufacturers for closeouts, overstock, and irregulars. Making these contacts is often difficult, but worthwhile. Usually you must travel to the manufacturers' plants or offices to meet with representatives. However, you don't have to stock inexpensive items. Vendors at the Red Barn and other successful flea markets sell merchandise ranging from novelties priced at under a dollar to high-ticket items like hot tubs and power boats.

Vendors caution that the merchandise must fit the market. The criterion, vendors say, is the kind of customer the market attracts. Ploegstra urges vendors to be flexible in their choice of merchandise. "If one line doesn't provide the sales you want, change to another," she says.

## Choosing a flea market

Some sources say the flea market itself is nearly as important as the vendor and the merchandise. Customers are attracted to flea markets that are clean and convenient and offer a wide variety of merchandise. If the market doesn't have those traits, the customers won't be there and neither should you!

In some areas markets may operate on staggered schedules. For example, you can base your stand in one market for Saturday and Sunday, move to another on Monday, and so on for the rest of the week. One husband-wife team operates booths in two different markets on the weekends, then joins forces in booths during the week. Some vendors operate in the northern markets during the summer and move to the Sun Belt during the winter.

Most established markets do little advertising, since word of mouth keeps their aisles filled with shoppers. In fact, substantial advertising by a market may be a warning to the potential vendor: the market may be trying to build traffic. That's fine if you can wait for the traffic to be built. However, it's better for you if the traffic is already there.

Flea markets offer novice entrepreneurs a low-investment entry into retailing. Many vendors have found flea markets to be a profitable source of supplemental income. For even more people, however, they are a route to independence.

## For further information

*American Flea Market Journal.* Quarterly publication. M.H. Sparks, 1911 Avenue D, Brownwood, TX 76801; $10 per year; $3 for a sample.

*Closeout Merchandise Moneymaking Manual.* E.A. Morgan Publishing, P.O. Box 1375, Huntington, NY 11743; $9.

*USA Closeout Directory.* Forum Publishing Co., 383 E. Main St., Centerport, NY 11721; $10.29.

*The USA Flea Market Directory.* Forum Publishing Co., 383 E. Main St., Centerport, NY 11721; $10.29.

*— Bill Stephenson*

# FLYER DELIVERY SERVICE

**Start-up Costs:** $500 or less. **Potential Earnings:** $6 to $8 per hour, part-time. **Advertising:** Your own flyers, door-to-door. **Special Qualifications:** None. **Equipment Needed:** None. **Best Advice for Success:** Broker flyer design and printing services to boost your income.

There is a demand for people to deliver advertising flyers door-to-door for various small businesses, supermarkets, and shopping centers. With this business you can set your own hours and work in a stress-free environment (no telephones, no angry customers, no bosses staring over your shoulder while you work).

Although this is an ideal part-time enterprise, it need not be limited in scope. You are limited only by the number of clients you can acquire. In many areas there is potential for building a flyer-delivery service into a lucrative full-time business.

The competition you may encounter will come primarily from large distribution companies, local newspapers, and direct-mail firms in your area. In most cases they can offer your prospects a lower price per piece for delivery, but they usually require a minimum delivery of 5,000 flyers or more. Your advantage lies in your ability and willingness to handle smaller quantities. Most of your customers will be very small retailers and services with businesses who only wish to deliver 500 to 1,000 flyers at a time. Because of the minimum delivery requirements of your competitors, your overall price will be lower. Most of these small businesses don't actually need a distribution of 5,000 flyers, since, in many instances, their trade area involves only the local neighborhood. So your service is tailored to their needs.

## How to start

Begin by investigating local requirements for a business license. For example, Burbank, California, requires that you have a city business license as a Distributor of Advertising Materials (cost: $100 per year), a state resale license (which allows the purchase of services and goods for resale without paying state sales tax), and Workman's Compensation Insurance for employees hired. Costs and licensing requirements do vary from one locale to another.

Once you have your license, you need to deliver your own flyer announcing your service to local businessmen. An effective method is to make deliveries when businesses are closed, such as early mornings or on Sundays. This way, you will not have to take time to go inside each building, locate the owner or manager, and deliver a sales pitch to each person you approach. Instead, you can simply deliver your flyer to their door and move on. Those who are interested will call you, and from that point your sales pitch is easy. You can probably expect a response rate of about 1 percent from the flyers you deliver. You will find more success if you limit your deliveries to small businesses, as opposed to large chain stores.

Some of the customers who call you will already have a flyer prepared. Others will need to have their flyer printed. Still others will need a flyer designed. You should line up the services of a printer and a commercial artist ahead of time. These will be sources of additional income for you, since you can mark up your services.

### Making the deliveries

When scheduling deliveries for your customers, estimate that you can deliver 100 flyers per hour by foot in the average neighborhood; more by car. In hilly terrain or areas where houses are larger and more widely spaced, the number will be less.

Most businesses will be in a hurry to get their flyers delivered. Allow at least one week in scheduling deliveries to allow for unforeseen circumstances, such as the weather, heavy work load, failure of employees to report for work, and other difficulties. You may need to allow a little longer delivery time in cases where you need to design the customer's flyer for them!

It's not practical to hire outside help unless you build your business to more than 4,000 flyers per week. If you do choose to hire outside help, pay a per-piece rate as opposed to an hourly rate.

Supervise your employees closely. A common problem is dumping—when an employee simply throws large amounts of your flyers into a convenient trash can instead of delivering them. Another trick pulled by a dishonest employee is doubling up or tripling up on deliveries—he delivers to every third house on the route, leaving three flyers at that house saving several steps while convincing you he is doing an honest job. Such an employee is usually caught, because a homeowner who receives several flyers calls your client and complains. Obviously, this doesn't help your business reputation.

To counter dumping, spot-check behind employees frequently by looking for flyers on the doors of homes shortly after your carrier has passed through a neighborhood. Some homeowners will already have taken them inside, but you'll soon be able to tell whether or not an employee is doing his job. If you catch an employee dumping, be prepared to make good to your customer.

## Finding good help

There are several sources for good employees. Most employment offices have provisions for the hire of day workers (although they may want you to pay by the hour or guarantee a minimum wage). High school job placement offices can provide students willing to work part-time. Senior citizens make responsible employees; seek them through local senior citizen's organizations.

Whenever possible, pay employees by the piece instead of by the hour. If you must pay by the hour, consider a per-piece rate against a guaranteed minimum wage. If you pay an employee 3.5 cents per flyer, by the time you add fringes to the cost, your actual cost is more like 4.2 cents. If you pay 4 cents per flyer, your actual cost is about 4.8 cents each. The same principle applies to the payment of an hourly wage.

You can make from $6 to $8 per hour by delivering all the flyers yourself. In some instances you can deliver flyers for two separate customers simultaneously and almost double those hourly figures. You'll find this service an easy one to start, and your income in limited only by the amount of hard work you are prepared to put forth.

*— Ron Coleman*

# GARAGE CLEANING SERVICE

**Start-up Costs:** Under $500 (not including vehicle). **Potential Earnings:** Variable; depends on your fee and quantity of jobs. **Advertising:** Flyers, business cards, word of mouth. **Special Qualifications:** None. **Equipment Needed:** Cleaning supplies and equipment. **Best Advice for Success:** Work hard to please your customer. Pay attention to detail.

There are maid services to clean inside the home, lawn care services to clean up the yard, but few services that will clean out the garage, basement, attic, or shed—until you start such a business, of course. With a good business plan, market research, a truck or van, a small amount of equipment and cleaning supplies, and advertising you can get started.

If you work hard to please your customers, they'll have you come back when their garage, basement, or shed gets cluttered again—usually every three to six months. One-time cleanings will also be money-makers: people need garages cleaned for special occasions like the sale of a home, formal parties, graduations, or any other occasion for which they want their homes to look their best.

Some of the tools of your trade will be a wet and dry shop-type vacuum cleaner, a push broom and straight broom, a commercial mop and bucket, rags for wiping and cleaning, a water hose, and a dust pan or flat shovel to clean up piles of dirt after you sweep. You can buy all these items at almost all home centers for well under $300.

You'll also need good commercial cleaners to clean up oil and stubborn grime you'll find in the average garage. You'll need a grease- and oil-cutting agent, liquid detergent, stain remover, and glass cleaner. These supplies can be found at any janitorial supply house or home center. Check your area Yellow Pages, and shop around before you buy. These items should not cost more than $20 to start and should last through three medium garages.

As for advertising, flyers and business cards are best. A good flyer will list all of your services. For a professional look without spending a lot of money, ask the print shop to help you design your flyer; most offer that service. If you have a van or truck, painting your logo and phone number on the door panels will be valuable advertising. A professional paint job on your truck or van can be costly, however. If you want to go to that expense, shop around; if you can find a qualified person to do it for $1,000 you're in luck. Most professional shops will charge twice that amount. An alternative is a magnetic sign that attaches right to the van door. Check area sign shops.

The best kind of advertising you can get, however, is free—word of mouth from your satisfied customers about a job well done.

After you've served a few customers, you'll find yourself with another source of income. When you clean the garage, basement, or shed, you may be asked to dispose of a lot of unwanted items. Most of your customers will pay you to haul that "junk" off. You can take the usable items and sell them to second-hand shops, flea markets, or scrap dealers. A truck or van becomes necessary if you are planning to haul a lot of junk. Otherwise, a good-sized car or station wagon will be enough to start off with.

— *Charles Hayes*

# GARDEN CONSULTING

**Start-up Costs:** Less than $200. **Potential Earnings:** $150 to $200 a week. **Special Qualifications:** Solid background in horticulture through education (formal or informal) or personal experience. **Equipment Needed:** Basic gardening tools. **Advertising:** Business cards, signs placed in appropriate shop windows (garden centers, hardware stores, etc.),

word of mouth. **Best Advice for Success:** Keep up with
new plant varieties, and experiment in your own garden.

When Elizabeth Rose Dickerson gave birth to her second child two years
ago, she knew she would not be able to afford child care for two children.
Dickerson is a trained horticulturist who worked for the Burpee Seed
Company answering customers' questions about gardening. "I really enjoyed the challenge of the customers' varied questions," explains Dickerson, "so I decided to advertise myself as a gardening consultant and to set
up my own business." What she thought would be a part-time venture has
turned into a full-time business. She charges customers a one-time $50
consulting fee and $25 to $30 an hour teaching courses to various community groups.

Environmental concerns and recent housing trends have increased
the need for her services. "Many homeowners want to know how to garden organically," Dickerson says, "so their families and pets will not be ex-
posed to potentially harmful pesticides. I show them how to grow
vegetables and flowers with natural controls."

With the increase in housing costs across the United States, many
builders are constructing smaller houses on smaller building lots. Dickerson advises homeowners how to use medium-growing plants and shrubs
that will not outgrow the property in a few years, how to economize garden space using raised beds and patio containers, how to plant for much-
needed privacy, and how to create recreational space.

Dickerson will also design annual and perennial gardens, plus special "theme" gardens: butterfly, colonial, fragrance, tea, moonlight, or
whatever combination the homeowner decides on. She will test the soil,
advise how to improve it, and give general gardening advice.

There is one drawback to this part of Dickerson's business, however.
"I usually do such a good job of instructing that most people opt to learn
more about gardening on their own. Thus, I seldom have repeat customers!" Dickerson had to look for other ways to expand her business, and she
decided to teach gardening classes. She has found that teaching provides a
stable income for her business.

The local high school had an adult-education program, and they
hired her to teach a basic gardening course. Many schools will start their
instructors with $15 an hour; more in the succeeding years if the course be-
comes a popular one. Dickerson says, "Many of the adults who enrolled in
my course had prior gardening experience, so it was easy to teach them.
We shared information, and it turned out to be a lot of fun. Each class dictates what you need to teach based on students' gardening knowledge and
what they want to learn from the course."

Dickerson also teaches nursing home residents on a regular basis. She gives these sessions several times a week, charging $25 an hour. Dickerson says, "It is the most rewarding experience I have ever had! Even people with physical disabilities were able to join in." She had the nursing home construct raised beds so that those in wheelchairs would have an easier time participating.

## How to start

People interested in starting a similar business don't need a degree in horticulture. "All a person needs is the love of growing plants, and with it, an understanding of the cultural requirements of the varieties of plants used by most home gardeners and the ability to work with other people." She says many adult-education programs, vocational/technical schools, and community colleges can help you acquire the knowledge to teach gardening to others.

She also recommends the following:

- Visit your local library. "You can find information on any gardening topic."
- Experiment with horticultural techniques. "A person who best qualifies for this kind of work most likely gardens at home extensively, trying new varieties of plants and gardening methods."
- Volunteer to help others in their gardens. "The most valuable training a budding horticulturist can get is not only in their own garden but also in the gardens of their families, friends, and neighbors."
- Invest in basic gardening tools, but not the most expensive. Dickerson bought most of what she needed at her local chain department store.

Dickerson recommends a solid background in horticulture for anyone seriously interested in pursuing this line of work. She had seven years experience and her B.S. degree when she started in this field. "All this experience and education gave me the confidence to offer horticultural advice and instruction to others, yet personally I realize how much there is yet to learn. When I plan new gardens, I have the knowledge and experience that puts me ahead of an amateur. I highly recommend that anyone thinking of going into this business do the same."

If you persist, you can earn up to $75 an hour (during the busiest seasons). However, the intangible rewards can be even greater, as you see your students become as enthusiastic about gardening as you are!

*— Priscilla Y. Huff*

# GENEALOGICAL SERVICE

**Start-up Costs:** $200 to $300. **Potential Earnings:** As much as $35 an hour. **Advertising:** Classified ads; word of mouth. **Special Qualifications:** The patience for research. **Equipment Needed:** None. **Best Advice for Success:** Start by tracing your own family history and those of your friends. This will give you the experience you need to be able to charge for your services.

As a child you must have heard your parents declare, "Money doesn't grow on trees." Well, maybe they were wrong after all. The family tree that everyone has may indeed be the money tree you've been looking for, and genealogical research may be the means to harvest the cash crop! You can charge fees as high as $35 an hour plus a retainer fee as high as $500.

One personal quality helpful for success in the field of genealogy is curiosity. If curiosity is one of your vices (or virtues) why not put it to work? Alvira Herbert of Fairfax, Virginia, did. Herbert, like most genealogical researchers, started the research as a post-retirement hobby, beginning with her own family's history. The initial steps are talking to relatives, scouting out the family Bible, rummaging through salvaged birth or death certificates and wills, and locating everything possible from family sources. After that the dedicated researcher has to broaden the search.

One definitive source of information is the National Archives in Washington, D.C. Covering an entire city block, the National Archives contains 1.3 million cubic feet of historical records dating back to the Revolutionary War. But the Washington main branch is only one of many Archives facilities throughout the country. Eleven field offices in Boston, New York, Philadelphia, Atlanta, Chicago, Kansas City, Fort Worth, Denver, Los Angeles, San Francisco, and Seattle serve people who cannot conveniently get to Washington. Like the main Archives, each field office offers research assistance along with many microfilm publications, research rooms, a basic reference library, and microfilm reading equipment. The main archives and most regional branches provide trained volunteers and staffers who offer research assistance.

Another excellent source of genealogical information is available in Utah. The Church of Jesus Christ of Latter-Day Saints (also known as The Mormons) has the largest genealogical library in the world. The library's information is considered so valuable that some genealogists who specialize in areas as distant as France and Lebanon reside in Utah to be closer to their informational gold mine.

## Sticking with it

If curiosity is the first quality of a successful genealogical researcher, tenacity is the second. Dogged perseverance is required to go through hundreds—perhaps thousands of records before chancing upon the one magic name or the specifically desired information. Seasoned researchers advise neophytes to come prepared to spend hours in seemingly endless and fruitless searching. "Be patient. Keep looking," suggests one expert in the field. "If you get really discouraged, give it a break and come back later after you've recouped your enthusiasm. Sooner or later you'll find what you're looking for."

After completing your family research, you may feel ready for a bigger challenge. Once you have demonstrable results—documentable evidence of your efforts—you can apply for certification or accreditation as a bona fide genealogical researcher. Accreditation or certification programs verify your "business credentials" as a genealogist while raising the hourly fee and retainer. There are two professional certification programs: The Mormon Church in Salt Lake City, Utah, and The Board for the Certification of Genealogists in Washington, D.C. Both confer professional status on genealogists who can substantiate their expertise.

Several courses of study provide additional information before you seek certification. Brigham Young University in Provo, Utah, offers a four-year program leading to a bachelor's degree in genealogy. And The American Society of Genealogists in Arlington, Virginia, offers a sixteen-session home study course. (Addresses at the end of the chapter).

What you can expect to earn varies with your certification or accreditation, research specialty, and area of residence. Availability of information and experience in using that information to locate desired facts seems to determine the going rate. Small-town researchers may find themselves in the $4- to $5-per-hour category for their services; metropolitan area researchers can expect to collect $25 to $35 per hour. Most genealogists charge an hourly rate in addition to a retainer fee. Retainers can run between $50 and $500, depending upon certification credentials, research specialty, information availability, and amount of information sought.

You can locate prospective clients through a variety of media. Alvira Herbert advertises in her local and regional newspapers in the classified ads under "Services." Other researchers use ads in genealogical magazines or magazines targeted to potential clients. Still other researchers post notices in their libraries and leave pertinent information with local historical, preservationist, or genealogical societies.

Successful researchers find that word-of-mouth referrals from satisfied customers are an important part of their reputation and business.

## For further information

Home study course: The National Genealogical Society, 4527 17th Street, N., Arlington, VA 22207; for $300. According to Marion Beasley, librarian, "the course puts you through the paces doing your own genealogical research."

Trade journals: *National Genealogical Society Quarterly*, published by The National Genealogical Society, 4527 17th Street N., Arlington, VA 22207.

*New England Historic Genealogical Register*, published by The New England Historical Society, 101 Newbury St., Boston, MA 02116.

*American Genealogist*, 128 Massasoit Drive, Warwick, Rhode Island 02888.

*The Genealogist*, published by The Association for Promotion of Scholarship in Genealogy, P.O. Box 1058 Rockefeller Center Station, New York, NY 10185.

*Journal of Genealogy*, Box 31097, Omaha, NE 68131.

Books: *Genealogy as Pastime and Profession*, by D.L. Jacobus, Genealogy Publishing Co., 111 Water St., Baltimore, MD 21202; $7.50.

*Genealogical Research Methods and Sources*, Published by American Society of Genealogists, P.O. Box 4970, Washington, D.C. 20008.

Associations: American Society of Genealogists, P.O. Box 1970, Washington, D.C. 20008.

Association Of Professional Genealogists, Box 11601, Salt Lake City, UT 84147. Annual membership: $35.

National Genealogical Society, 4527 17th Street N., Arlington, VA 22207. Annual membership: $30.

*— Ellen Paul*

# GIFT BASKETS

**Start-up Costs:** $500 for supplies. **Potential Earnings:** $15,000 to $20,000. **Advertising:** Yellow Pages, brochures, business cards. **Special Qualifications:** None. **Equipment Needed:** Good inventory of baskets, ribbons, and small gifts. **Best Advice for Success:** "Know your market and provide good service."

Nancy Kaplan, owner of San Francisco Giftworks, created her first gift basket of champagne and chocolates many years ago for a friend's wedding anniversary. Kaplan always wanted her own business and thought it would be interesting to put goodies in baskets that she would deliver to customers. With that in mind, Kaplan began a business in her house while she held down a full-time computer systems-coordinator position for a major oil company. Putting her coordinating skills to work, she lined up baskets in her hallway, living room, and bedroom.

For the first six months, Kaplan worked at the business part time. She handed out leaflets in the downtown financial district to get the word out about her new business. While she was at work, her answering machine at home recorded orders; in the evening she filled them. During her lunch break the next day she delivered baskets by car or by bus.

Although Kaplan advises those starting out to set up at home, she has invested in a workshop space for her part-time business. With a friend who has a potpourri business, she rents an 850-square-foot converted warehouse space. "I found working at home distracting: I'd stop for coffee or do the dishes," confesses Kaplan.

## The art of giving

In describing what kind of person might want to have a gift basket business, Kaplan says there are several sides to this business. She believes that you should like to sell, shouldn't be afraid to pick up the phone "to tell people about your business," and should keep your business organized. Designing and making the baskets is just a small part of the business. In addition to promoting the business, there is a lot of paperwork and bookkeeping.

Kaplan went to school to be an artist and always had a creative interest; she had long wanted to run a creative business of her own. Some of her most famous customers have been Johnny Carson and Joe Montana, and major accounts include large corporations, hotels, and a travel agency.

Her giftworks baskets are visually appealing and come in a festive variety of shapes and sizes. Here are some examples:

- *Because You're Special*—a flowering plant, gourmet cookies and candy, deluxe nuts, and chocolate truffles delivered in a shapely wicker basket.
- *A Taste of San Francisco*—a picnic basket with bright cotton napkins and matching utensils that carries California wine and cheese, sourdough bread, Italian salami, and Ghiradelli chocolates.
- *Symphony in Taste and Sound*—a bottle of champagne presented in a top hat ice bucket (wine glasses and roses also available) with chocolate truffles, and a gourmet cookbook set.
- *Baby's Bear Necessities*—a cuddly musical Teddy bear, storybook, and a baby bottle filled with jelly beans.

## Do some research

"Don't bite off more than you can chew," is Kaplan's first piece of advice for the beginner. She suggests first reading the business section of your paper to find out which organizations might be worth calling to see what they like to give as gifts. Church groups or civic organizations are also good bets.

In deciding on whether to make yours a part- or full-time business, consider how much you want to work and how much money you want to make. Then write down your costs for materials, utilities, phone expenses, and a minimum advertising budget for a Yellow Pages listing and brochure. Now double that figure. On the plus side, figure a 100 percent mark-up on the baskets.

It is possible to just do the baskets full-time—at Christmas time, for example. You'll probably need help. Start in August and end in January.

Whether yours is a seasonal or year-round business, you'll need a county or city business license and a resale permit from the State Board of Equalization (or your state's equivalent) for charging and paying sales tax and to buy wholesale supplies. If you decide to sell alcohol, you'll need an off-sale beer and wine license from the Bureau of Alcoholic Beverage Control, and you must pay the federal government $250 per year. If prepared food is in your plan, you'll need a food handler's license.

In addition to doing preliminary market research, Kaplan warns against stocking up on too many holiday gift items, such as chocolate bunnies or Valentine's hearts. She suggests having a basic inventory for birthday baskets, baby gifts, wedding anniversaries, and a few holidays. And as for delivery, Kaplan finds that UPS is very reasonable and that hiring a delivery service is more cost effective than doing it yourself.

## Marketing the product

To market her baskets, Kaplan put together a full-color photo brochure with price list and phone number for ordering. She delivers her baskets locally and ships them nationwide. Her prices vary from $20 to $350. If a color photo brochure is too expensive for you when first starting, a simple two-color brochure with your price list can describe your personalized baskets.

Giftworks also creates baskets that appeal to businesses and corporations: baskets for promoting the business, saying "thank you" to employees, and welcoming visitors. Kaplan custom designs multiple orders designed to fit a company's needs and budget.

If you need help at Christmas, ask friends or college and high school students. Or inquire about hiring people from on-the-job training programs for tax breaks. Don't get overwhelmed. Nancy says, "Business *is* problems. If you don't have problems you don't have a business. But don't get frustrated by what goes wrong. Take [the problems] one step at a time."

In Kaplan's experience, the most effective way to advertise is to buy a listing in the Yellow Pages. She suggests installing a separate business phone at home and buying a listing under "Gift Baskets and Parcels." You can pay a column advertising rate if you want a longer ad. The simplest and least expensive way to advertise, according to Nancy, is the basic business card with your logo.

Once you decide on the type of baskets you'd like to offer, you must find wholesale suppliers. Nancy recommends buying high-quality items. "Don't skimp on quality," she says. "And charge a fair price; don't underestimate what people are willing to pay for a good product and service."

Attend regional gift and trade shows for stuffed animals, baskets, and ribbon. Find a good broker (by looking in the Yellow Pages under "Wholesale Foods") and order from their catalogs. Find out how quickly inventory can be shipped. You can buy packing materials, excelsior, types of cellophane, and shrink wrap from manufacturers. For orders numbering over 1,000 you can pay a sheltered workshop to do the packaging.

In addition to running Giftworks since 1984, Kaplan has added teaching to her schedule. She offers a course, "Gift Baskets: Making Presents for Profit" through The Learning Annex. She says she enjoys the experience of having a business, but there is a lot of information she wishes she'd had when she was starting out. Eight years later she has this to say: "Know your market. Work your market, and don't give up. The most important thing is to provide really good service—a dying art—and you will have a successful business."

## For further information see

*How to Start Your Own Gift Basket Business* by Bryce Webster and the editors of *Income Opportunities*. A complete step-by-step manual to help you start your own profitable business. Offers complete start-up information, sources of supplies, marketing tips, and more. $45.90 ppd. for subscribers ($55.90 ppd. for non-subscribers). Income Opportunities Manuals, P.O. Box 40, Vernon, NJ 07462.

— *Paula Nichols*

# GIFT-BUYING SERVICE

**Start-up Costs:** $100 to $300. **Potential Earnings:** $25,000 and up. **Advertising:** Direct mail, telemarketing. **Special Qualifications:** Good taste. **Equipment Needed:** Phone. **Best Advice for Success:** Stress the convenience your service provides; offer a wide variety of gift suggestions.

What can a busy executive do when he or she has no time to shop but must buy a gift for a spouse, a special someone, or an important client? Susan Arpin of Fort Lauderdale has the perfect solution. Her shopping service, The Gamut, handles gift-buying for several hundred business executives, attorneys, physicians, dentists, and accountants.

Arpin's typical work week begins on Monday when she calls clients who have a special occasion coming up to remind them of it and sound them out about their gift ideas. Often the client asks Arpin to make suggestions. Because she keeps a personal data file on each customer, including sizes, favorite colors, gift and jewelry preferences, and previous purchases, she is well prepared. Arpin provides fresh flowers, fine art, gold jewelry, collectibles, and customer gift baskets.

Once a client decides, Arpin shops for the gifts she doesn't have in stock, wraps them, and delivers them to the clients. They pay her the retail price for each gift, plus a service fee for her time and expertise. She charges a 10-percent fee for an article under $200, 7 percent for an item priced at $200 to $500, and 5 percent for any over $500.

The rest of Arpin's week is taken up by shopping, bookkeeping, and finding clients. As most clients come from referrals, she doesn't need to advertise. "People recommend their friends and business acquaintances to me because it's a unique service," she says.

When Arpin started the business from her home, she called potential clients on the telephone and said, "Hello, I have a wonderful service." She gets additional names of potential clients from the Chamber of Commerce (to which she belongs) and by keeping up with the business news of the community.

Arpin still works from her home. "I have a studio with a lot of shelves for my inventory," she says. "A back family room serves as an office. I use my home phone, and I have an answering service. Besides the $50 a month for that, there are no real operating expenses." While Arpin does carry a good deal of inventory herself, she says a person starting out in this business could make good profit without investing in inventory. "You might work out agreements with the stores, explaining that you have an executive shopping service and need a source for clothing or whatever, and ask them what kind of discount they could offer. I have such agreements with certain stores," she says.

One reason Arpin prefers to carry her own inventory is that she likes to put together many gift suggestions herself. "I always look for something special, elegant, and different. On one shopping foray I found a line of Art Deco vases, which I filled with baby's breath flowers, roses, and greens and tied with a big red bow. That sold for $45," she says.

Not only are executives and professional people too busy to shop for gifts for these occasions, Arpin says, but most of them simply don't know what to choose. "They like the idea that you're going to suggest the gift and do all the work for them." Once a client has used her service and discovered its convenience, he or she usually returns for the next occasion. "That's why my choices have to be right," Arpin explains. "If an executive's wife doesn't like a gift, the choice reflects on me and the client won't use me again. So it's my business to find out what the recipient likes. I start out with a list of questions, and I file the answers for future reference. These questions include the recipient's tastes in jewelry and clothing, hobbies, interests, favorite colors, sizes, and so on."

One of the biggest gift-buying occasions is Christmas, and Arpin prepares for it by attending the Christmas Gift Show at the World Trade Center in Texas in July, where she selects most of her Christmas inventory. Then she prepares her annual Christmas Gift Show, which she holds in September. An array of gifts for the entire family is attractively displayed in a "borrowed" vacant townhouse, so clients can make their selections for the coming holiday season. Some gifts may be purchased and carried home, others are delivered by Arpin in early December. Other important holidays for this kind of service are Valentine's Day, Secretary's Week; then a little later comes Mother's Day shopping—well in advance of the month of May. And, of course, July means Christmas shopping.

Being able to shop for those busy executives and knowing what people like has proven rewarding to Susan Arpin. No longer do her clients have to spend business hours trudging through crowded shopping malls—she earns a good income doing it for them.

— *Dana Cassell*

# GREETING CARDS, CREATING

**Start-up Costs:** Vary, but as low as $500. **Potential Earnings:** $20,000 per year once established. **Advertising:** Contacting bookstores etc. consider using a rep. **Special**

**Qualifications:** Talent for art or writing. **Equipment Needed:** Extra room; purchase specialty paper and bulk envelops as needed for print run. **Best Advice for Success:** "Believe in yourself and your work. Feeling passionate about your work is very important."

Robin Spaan is very creative. She does calligraphy, graphic design, and makes greeting cards. She has consistently made money in the card business. Early on she earned only $78.50 for the sale of some hand-silk-screened Christmas cards, but it was money earned doing what she enjoys.

Another holiday season Spaan made twenty-five copies of a two-color card, a drawing of angel with an inspirational quotation on the cover. They sold in just a few days. When she photocopied more the following year, she sold 55 *dozen* to a book store. The next year she sold 111 dozen of that same card, making it that store's best-selling item ever.

Spaan officially started her card business three years ago with no money and netted $2,000 "without even trying." And she did it with no marketing. However, the pressures of trying to operate a business with no capital were great. After taking a business course on managing a small business, she says her goals are to concentrate on her calligraphy items (which have quadrupled in popularity since 1988), to earn enough to reinvest in the card business, and to learn about effective marketing.

Spaan knows that to make big money she needs a sales rep, but there are tradeoffs to consider. She has four card designs and says that reps usually like to have a line of twelve. That has not deterred her. In fact, she says she has been able to work more creatively and keep costs down *without* having a full line. "I look at the cards I have so far as a test market," says Spaan. If people like a certain card and it sells well, she'll then invest in quantity printing to bring the cost down.

**Starting**

Spaan suggests starting part-time and gradually evolving into full time, especially while working. "If you are a small-time card maker, you have to be able to do everything," she says. "You have to be the designer—which is only one percent of your time—the producer, the shipping and receiving clerk—in your living room—and the bookkeeper and the accountant as well." Part of the business equation is keeping track of cost increases and any marketing expenditures.

Spaan notes that her profits have gone up incrementally when she has put in the time for the business. In addition to her calligraphy, Spaan works one week a month as a graphic artist for a local newspaper, "as a safety net."

## Find your market

Spaan illustrates her cards in addition to finding memorable quotes for the covers. But, she says, you must be aware that other buyers may be interested in purchasing the artwork outright—and don't necessarily want verse. If you sell the designs you lose the chance to reprint them as cards.

"There is a full range [of opportunity] between here and Hallmark," says Spaan. The trick is to use your common sense and determine where you'd like to market your work. Bookstores, in general, are among the best places. You may want to market directly to dentists, doctors, and lawyers, who send cards to clients and among themselves to thank for referrals. Postal service outlets, florists, and grocery stores all carry cards for sale. (If you rep yourself, you can keep the profits, advises Spaan.)

Consider attending gift trade shows where retail buyers order cards. Another designer she met at one such show said that she had built a profitable business selling to beauty salons, where customers are a captive audience.

It all depends on how big you want your business to be. Spaan has branched out into doing illustrations for logos and book cover designs and would like to illustrate children's books in the next few years. But her goal is to be able to accomplish all these activities with a card business that supports her. Spaan says it is possible to earn more than $20,000 per year, depending on how labor-intensive the cards are.

## Pricing

To determine how to price your cards, go to stores and see what other cards are selling for. You want to charge comparably. For example, single-color cards might retail for $1.25 and two-color for $1.50. Spaan has sold her original, hand-silk screened cards for $2 each in the bookstore and received $1 profit. But you must then figure backwards to cover your previous costs.

With $2,000 to $5,000 start-up funds, Robin says it may be possible to set up a "friendly business," one in which you pay for supplies, printing and perhaps even a sales rep. But remember, if the card sells for $1, you get 30 cents and the rep gets 20 cents.

You also should learn a bit about printing so that you can put twelve designs on a sheet of paper and set it up so that the printer can just shoot a negative. That way you'll be able to print more cards if you need to, and you'll save money in the process. "The more you know about printing," says Spaan, "the more money you can save." Spaan notes that she also likes to hand-select the rag stock specialty papers for her cards.

Since most stores pay thirty days after invoicing, you must also be prepared to pay mailing and envelope costs. (Never buy envelopes or paper from a printer! The most cost-effective way to buy envelopes is in lots of 250 from a paper salesperson.)

One source of information to write to for learning about the card business is *Greetings* magazine or the *Artist's Market* annual, found at bookstores.

### Finding a Rep

You may decide to shop for a rep at the same trade shows where you are selling your wares. Pick a rep as carefully as you would any business partner, being certain that the person's temperament is in accordance with how you would like your cards represented.

If you write your own card verse, check into copyright protection if you don't sell your work outright. If you plan to quote from books and other written material, check with the publisher or author to get permission to reprint. Be prepared to pay royalties. Spaan says she has been lucky in finding sentiments that have inspired her to accompany her artwork. She has gotten verbal permission in at least one case to print for free, and discovered that some other sayings are not copyrighted.

Spaan strongly suggests that, before you try to allot your initial investment and figure out sales and payouts, you print up about $200 worth of cards so that you can make a small profit and still not have the responsibility of a full-blown business. "It's like growing a bush before you have a farm to plant it," says Spaan. Then find a manufacturer—a quality printer with whom you can have a working relationship. The printer stores all your negatives and keeps your card plates on file for more printings, which can save you money over time.

Since Robin is now using two-color printings, she has simplified the process for printing her cards and made them more cost effective. But gone are the days of selling silkscreened cards for $2. Now she can sell her creations for $7.50 to $25, depending on size and elaborateness. One effective way Robin has found to keep costs down and profits up is to ask clients who are ordering illustrations and lettering for covers of announcements or wedding invitations if they will pay to have extra blank cards printed up (for *her* to sell) in exchange for a reduced design fee.

Robin started teaching "Greeting Cards as a Home-Based Business" with another designer, a woman she describes as someone who "knows marketing." It is a lot of work, she says, but the best way to keep up your interest up is when your cards are your passion. Underlying that passion is "the importance of believing in yourself and your work."

*— Paula Nichols*

# GREETING CARD VERSE

**Start-up Costs:** $25. **Potential Earnings:** From $10 to
$150 per verse. **Advertising:** Direct solicitation. **Special
Qualifications:** Writing skills. **Equipment Needed:** None.
**Best Advice for Success:** Never give up in the face of rejec-
tion slips. Keep trying.

Would you like to be a writer, but haven't got the patience to sit down and
write an article, short story, or novel? Do you enjoy telling jokes or writing
short poems? Have you often become frustrated when buying greeting
cards for friends and relatives because you thought you could create better
verses? Maybe you can.

Many greeting cards are written by people just like you. And the
greeting card business is booming; about seven billion cards are purchased
each year, according to the Greeting Card Association in Washington, D.C.
Between 300 and 500 greeting card publishers now operate in the United
States, generating about $3.2 billion in retail card sales each year.

There are now greeting cards for virtually every conceivable occasion. Somebody has to write them.

What does all this mean to you, the budding verse writer? Since so
much is available in the greeting card field, you have a wide variety of
markets to choose from. If you have artistic ability, you may locate a company that will purchase your verses and designs. Card manufacturers are as
varied as the cards they produce; some are major corporations while others
are small and family-run.

So get out your pen and start scribbling down those verses and/or
pictures that fill your mind. Before you start trying to sell them, however,
remember that there's a right and wrong way of working.

### First things first

Begin your marketing efforts by doing some research. The Greeting
Card Association offers a publication called *Artists and Writers Market
List*. You may obtain a copy by sending $1 to the Association at 1350 New
York Ave. NW, Suite 615, Washington, DC 20005. You might also check
your bookstore or library for writer's reference books and magazines containing listings of greeting card companies that will consider freelance idea
submissions.

Another effective resource in locating potential markets for your
work is a trip to the local card store. Study what's available there. Choose
card designs and verses that catch your eye and make you laugh, cry, or
feel happy. Examine those cards and try to decide what makes them effec-

tive. Talk to store personnel and ask what cards sell most frequently. Ask if there are any kinds of cards that customers request but that are not available. Maybe one of your ideas could fill a market gap. Finally, when you find cards that you like and believe you could have written, note the card company's address. This could be a paying market for your work.

Once you've assembled a potential market list, write to the companies and ask for a copy of their writer's guidelines. Include a stamped, self-addressed business-size envelope with your request. Such guidelines can be extremely helpful to your card writing or design trade, since they contain essential information for submissions. Study the guidelines carefully before preparing ideas. If a publisher wants to buy humor verses and *only* humor verses, he or she will not accept your heartsy, flowery poems. Furthermore, such guidelines will probably indicate how a publisher would like to receive your submissions: one verse at a time or a "batch" of roughly five to fifteen ideas at once. Form is also important; many companies prefer to see ideas typed on 3" x 5" note cards, but again, preferences vary.

Editor George E. Stanley, Jr., of Vagabond Creations, Inc., in Dayton, Ohio, explains that he looks for the following in a verse:

1) Something general instead of a specific situation; it should cover the largest segment of the population possible.

2) It should have a snappy "punch line."

3) It should be as short and concise as possible.

Investigate each editor's general needs before submitting copy. "Most of the idea submissions," Stanley says, "include material that in no way fits the needs of our line. New writers apparently do not study the requirements of each company."

Editorial director Jimmie Fitzgerald of Drawing Board Greeting Cards of Dallas, Texas, looks for "sendability, freshness, and originality" in a greeting card verse. He also recommends that you not submit extremely large batches of verse; twenty is the maximum number favored by Fitzgerald.

Once you've sent out your first batches of submissions, you might expect to receive a series of long, thin envelopes containing checks in response. If rejection slips come bouncing back to you instead, you may feel discouraged enough to hang up your pen and call an end to this fledgling trade. Don't. Persevere and continue sending out your verses again and again, until they are accepted for publication. What was wrong for one company might be just right for another. Look at your rejection slips as business transactions; consider them evidence of your status as an aspiring writer.

## How far can you go?

This is not a field where salaries are easily predictable. Fees for accepted verse range from $10 to $150, depending on the company. When your verses begin selling on a fairly regular basis, you'll probably be able to form a better idea of what your earning potential is.

Meanwhile, if you wish to maximize sales as much as possible, write the kinds of cards that sell best. Of this year's greeting card sales as anticipated by the Greeting Card Association, about half are seasonal while the other half are so-called "everyday" cards. Everyday card sales, particularly those for non-occasion cards, are increasing. As for holiday cards, the most popular are Christmas, Valentine's Day, Easter, Mother's Day, Father's Day, and Graduation.

It's an ever-changing business that may be difficult to break into, but creating greeting card verses can be worth it. Just think: the next time you walk into a store to purchase a card for a friend or relative, the card you select could be created by you.

*— Jeri Watlington*

# HAIR CARE, MOBILE

**Start-up Costs:** $300 to $500 for hair-care supplies (vehicle required). **Potential Earnings:** $16,000 to $32,000 a year. **Advertising:** Word of mouth, senior citizen newsletters, Yellow Pages. **Special Qualifications:** You must be a licensed cosmetologist (check local requirements). **Equipment Needed:** Portable hair dryers, inflatable shampoo bowls, combs, brushes, rollers, perm rods and curlers; professional quality shampoos, conditioners, and permanent solutions. **Best Advice for Success:** Make your business known to everyone. Hand out business cards everywhere. Your business will grow quickly by word of mouth.

Yvonne Conway's idea for a traveling beauty salon got its start thirty years ago with a visit to a nursing home, but it wasn't until recently that the enterprising grandmother took to the road.

In the past nine years, she has racked up thousands of miles taking her supplies and services from her home in Olympia, Washington, to clients in offices, hospitals, nursing homes, and even jails around western Washington. During that time, she has pared her work schedule down to three days a week while building her income up to $16,000 a year.

"Putting wheels under your existing beauty skills and talents is an untapped opportunity," says Conway, age sixty. "Age is not a barrier and set-up costs are minimal. You pick your schedule. You choose your clientele. You decide what services you will offer."

The idea has been so successful her son Craig Conway launched his own mobile salon, Haircuts on Wheels. Unlike his mother, who specializes in serving senior citizens, Craig works full-time providing haircuts and permanents to busy families and executives. He grosses about $32,000 a year.

## The beginning

Conway first came up with the idea of mobile hair services while working for a department store salon in 1984. She earned her cosmetologist's license right out of high school, but abandoned the trade when she got married. However, she never gave up her license. Once her four children were grown she decided to go back to work—but she quickly decided that a hip, bright department-store salon was the wrong place for her.

"I was considerably older. The music was loud kid stuff, the air conditioning killed my arthritis, the clientele was not my type," she says. "I was not in my environment."

She remembered going with her mother years earlier to visit a friend in a nursing home. At the time, her mother commented that it would be wonderful if the women at the nursing home could get their hair done and have manicures and pedicures.

"I said that that would be really nice, but you can't carry a beauty shop with you. Well, I started to think—why *can't* you carry a beauty shop with you?" Conway says.

Before launching her business, she tested the waters by talking to a friend who volunteered at the local senior citizens' center. The woman threw the idea out at a convention of senior specialists in eastern Washington.

"They told her that once I got going I would have more business than I could handle," Conway says.

Her friend proved right. Conway currently maintains a list of about sixty-five regular clients, most of them senior citizens. She also gets calls from local attorneys who wanted to make sure their clients looked well-groomed in court despite being housed in the local jail.

## Putting it together

Before she sat behind the wheel, Conway checked the legal requirements. In Washington, independent licensed cosmetologists can operate mobile businesses without a problem, but other states have more stringent regulations. Some require that you be sponsored by a salon or even own one. Others restrict in-home services to the infirm.

Conway started out with an eight-year-old station wagon and just $311 in supplies. Her son Craig's start-up costs a year later ran approximately $700 more because he purchased a custom sign for the side of his 1947 Dodge pickup truck. However, the expense has been more than justified, Conway says. The classic truck has appeared in local parades, car rallies, and even caught the eye of a local disc jockey who interviewed Craig on the radio as Craig gave him a hair cut.

Conway offers her clients haircuts, coloring, and permanents, as well as manicures and pedicures. Her son sticks strictly to haircuts and perms. To keep the business profitable, Conway never ventures more than twenty miles from home. She also groups together appointments with clients in outlying towns to reduce the amount of time she spends traveling from one place to the next. "Your time element between the appointments is what you want to watch," she says. "You cannot make any money sitting in your car driving." Conway estimates she can be in and out of a client's house in under an hour if the client's hair is short.

When it comes to pricing, the rule of thumb is to charge the same or a little more than the local salons, but never less. For example, Conway called all the salons in her area before recently raising her price for a wash and set from $10 to $12. Tips, as in any salon, vary with the clientele.

When working in someone's home, you must always remember that you are in their territory. Never unplug an appliance without asking first, and always put things back the way you found them. If you work in the kitchen, protect any food left out or see that it's put away.

### Innovate, innovate, innovate

Carrying her beauty shop with her forced Conway to be creative in her equipment and her techniques. One of her first modifications was to take a standard professional sit-down hair dryer, remove the chair, and strap it to a standard aluminum luggage cart. "It didn't stay on very good so I had to revamp it a little bit," she says. The final version includes a pull-out shelf on the bottom. Conway uses the dryer like a mover's dolly, stacking it with small plastic baskets in which she carries her rollers, perm rods, shampoos, towels, and other equipment. The idea is never to make more than one trip to and from the car during her stops. Since she rarely goes back to her house during the day, she always keeps an emergency kit stocked with extra shampoo, hairspray, and other essentials on hand.

Over the past nine years, Conway has worked out a routine. She generally gets to her first client's house or nursing home about 9 A.M., eats a brown-bag lunch between appointments and rolls home about 6 P.M.

During the day, an answering machine catches her messages. When she gets home in the evening, she throws her towels in the washer, gets dinner for her husband, then makes her telephone calls.

Conway believes the key to effective advertising lies in knowing her clientele. She relies primarily on word of mouth and a monthly ad in the local newsletter for senior citizens. In the beginning, she also distributed her business cards to senior centers, nursing homes, hospitals, and jails.

"You want to home in on things that don't cost you very much money," she says. "Go to hotels and motels and give them your card. Most of us know 250 people they say, so give every one of them three cards and tell them to get rid of at least two of them."

Neither Conway nor her son have ever had a problem with being harassed or threatened going into a strange home—or even into the Pierce County jail. One of her male clients once asked her if she wasn't afraid being out on the road alone. "I told him no, I leave a note every day by the telephone of where I am and the phone numbers," Conway says.

A more common problem can be friends and relatives who expect to get free or discounted services at home. Conway advises other mobile operators to be firm, polite, and just to say no. "I do not give home permanents—I give professional service in the home," she says.

### Branching out

Over the past few years, Conway's business has branched out into a variety of enterprises. In 1990, she published her own book, *Mobile Hair and Beauty Services: Your Guide to Profit$ on Wheel$.* The guide includes start-up information, bookkeeping tips, and marketing ideas, as well as step-by-step instructions for coping with special challenges like shampooing clients in beds or wheelchairs and modifying equipment to meet the needs of disabled clients.

"As soon as I started, I knew I was going to write a book, because the service was needed and I love doing it," Conway says. "I started writing notes and then I started reading books on how to write a book."

Conway kept a notepad and pencil in the seat next to her for years. She would go in to a client's home, do the person's hair then write down any problems or solutions that jumped to mind, solutions like how to shampoo someone in bed without getting them wet. It took her three years to actually put the book together and find a local publisher.

Not long ago she mailed a plastic sink manufacturer one of his models which she had modified by bending the round bowl into a crescent shape and adding more drains. The company's engineering department is currently evaluating the innovations and the new sink could be on the market within a year. If that happens, Conway will receive a two to four percent royalty on future sales, an average of about ten to twelve cents per sink.

"The thing is, at my age I've decided to have fun," Conway says. "The kids are grown, the mortgage is paid, so I'm not worried about getting rich."

### For further information, see

Conway's book, *Mobile Hair and Beauty Services*. It is available by mail for $19.95, including postage and handling. Send checks payable to Yvonne Conway, 7424 Holmes Island Rd. S.E., Olympia, WA, 98503. The price of the book also includes a free telephone consultation with Conway.

*— Irene Svete*

# HANDWRITING ANALYSIS

**Start-up Costs:** $500 or less. **Potential Earnings:** Up to $100,000. **Advertising:** Yellow Pages ad; community presentations. **Special Qualifications:** A degree in graphoanalysis adds credibility. **Equipment Needed:** Telephone, typewriter/word processor. **Best Advice for Success:** Understand the process and focus on the best people. To introduce your services in your community, you have to give as many group presentations as you can.

Handwriting experts are hired by business firms to aid in personnel selection, credit risk evaluation, and in connection with employee-motivation programs. Attorneys hire handwriting consultants to help identify certain traits in potential jurors. More than ever, owners of small businesses are hiring handwriting analysts for help in determining the compatibility of business partners as well as employees. With the banning of the use of polygraph testing, handwriting analysis is also becoming a more popular personality testing procedure in the United States. Companies hire handwriting experts to review the positive, negative, and neutral traits of applicants. Employment agencies in ever-increasing numbers are making use of the procedure to place applicants in jobs for which their personalities are most suited.

Elaine Ness, owner of home-based Character In Ink, says, "Handwriting analysis gives better results than the personality and aptitude tests currently used in the screening process."

How did she get started? "I became interested when my husband and I had our handwriting analyzed during a very painful divorce," says Ness. "The understanding I received from that analysis gave me the courage to go on with my life." She received her training from the International

Graphoanalysis Society (IGAS) based in Chicago, Illinois, which offers a correspondence course. "They mail you books and then follow it with examinations. Students have eighteen months to complete the course." The course is tightly controlled by teachers working for the society.

When she completed her certification course, Ness enrolled in the advanced course. Successful completion of this additional eighteen-month course gave her the right to use the title of Master Certified Graphoanalyst. Whereas graphology is the generic term for the study of handwriting, Graphoanalyst and Graphoanalysis are registered trade names of the International Graphoanalysis Society, and only those who have completed the Society's course and testing are permitted to use these titles.

## What is handwriting analysis?

The IGAS method of teaching handwriting analysis was founded by shorthand teacher M.N. Bunker. In 1915 Mr. Bunker discovered that it was the strokes of the writing and the letter formations that provided the key to the analysis. According to IGAS, the principles that the graphoanalyst follows are based on scientific research involving many thousands of case histories. A high degree of accuracy is assured because the techniques are based on a well-defined, standardized method of identifying strokes, relating these strokes to specific personality traits and evaluating the relative strength of the interrelating traits.

Ness, who also received her training from IGAS, refers to handwriting as "brain writing." The theory is that the brain, where one's personality lies, tells the hand how to construct the letters. Handwriting becomes a form of body language that can be preserved.

IGAS, which has trained more than 35,000 graphoanalysts, expects its members to adhere to a very strict code of ethics. IGAS literature puts strong emphasis on the fact that it cannot be used, in itself, to diagnose medical or psychological problems.

"It takes so much of the guesswork out of relationships between people and their aptitudes for a given position," says Ness. "I can't think of a single human relationship that handwriting analysis wouldn't help: lovers, business relationships, vocational aptitude, job compatibility, or simply wanting to have a better understanding of that teenager who is driving a parent crazy."

## Marketing your service

There are at least four main ways to market your graphology service.

- *Mail Order.* You can insert a classified ad, such as the following, in a national magazine:

HANDWRITING ANALYSIS,
$10 AND SAMPLE TO:
NAME, ADDRESS.

Clients mail in a handwriting sample; you analyze it and send the client an analysis. The best magazines in which to advertise are the women's publications. The rates you charge for an analysis should vary according to the magazine. If the magazine is slanted toward the lower- and middle-income brackets, the charge should be from $10 to $15 dollars. For a magazine slanted toward the higher-income bracket, $20 is an acceptable rate.

■ *Personal consultation.* Here the client brings a handwriting sample, usually with a particular question in mind, and you analyze the sample and answer the client's question. Such business is mostly generated by word of mouth or an ad in the Yellow Pages. The charge will depend primarily on how much work you do. If the client only wants a few basic questions answered, $10 is appropriate. If he wants an in-depth personality analysis, the fees should be at least $15 to $20. Some analysts charge lower rates at first and then increase rates as their reputation grows. A word of caution: limit yourself to relating the traits shown in the handwriting. Don't, for example, give the client advice on whether or not he should get married; you might lead yourself into trouble. It may take a while before you start getting the number of clients you desire. Be patient. Your reputation will grow and so will your business.

■ *Roving Analyst.* As a "roving analyst" you go anywhere that attracts a lot of people—malls, art festivals, and shopping centers. Before you can set up an "analyst's booth," you must usually pay a fee for the space occupied. For example, an art festival will charge you a base rate for a booth space. A mall or shopping center may charge you a certain amount for the space plus a percentage of what you make. Since you may be analyzing from fifteen to twenty samples an hour, you rates can be low as, say, $1 to $3 dollars per sample. The analysis need not be detailed. Entertainment value is more important than accuracy. Your service will be a novelty, and it is this novelty effect that will attract customers.

■ *Corporate Analyst.* This is probably the most lucrative area. You'll examine a potential employee's job application and then answer such questions as "Can this person be trusted? Is this a responsible individual? Does he possess a good imagination?" This kind of special work usually requires certification.

## For further information

Educational Programs: American Handwriting Analysis Foundation Education Programs. American Handwriting Analysis Foundation, P.O. Box 6201, San Jose, CA 95150. Offers workshops and other educational opportunities.

Handwriting Analysis Research Library Workshops. Handwriting Research Library, 91 Washington St., Greenfield, MA 01301.

Books: *Handwriting Analysis Made Easy* ($7); *What Your Handwriting Reveals* ($5); *Handwriting Tells* ($7). Available from E.A. Morgan Publishing Co., P.O. Box 1375, Huntington, NY 11743-1375. All three books for $17 ppd.

*Handwriting Analysis: The Complete Basic Book* by Karen Amend. Borgo Press, P.O. Box 2845, San Bernadino, CA 92406.

*— Clarice E. Cady and Mark Cave*

# HERB FARMING

**Start-up Costs:** $500 for plants and seeds. **Potential Earnings:** $12,000 net first year. **Advertising:** Herb and health food magazines, local newspapers, word of mouth. **Special Qualifications:** Knowledge of gardening; uses of herbs. **Best Advice for Success:** Learn by being an apprentice to an herbalist. Diversify your services and products.

Herbalist Shatoiya Jones not only talks to her plants, she listens to them as well. "They tell me what they're good for," she says. While listening to her plants for the past twelve years, Jones has gone from marketing fresh-cut culinary herbs to restaurants to a multi-product and service herb business. "I lived in an area where there were many gourmet restaurants," says Jones, "and I was able to tap into that market. But with the increasing popularity of fresh herbs, a big grower came in and the restaurants were able to order their herbs with the rest of their produce. I just couldn't compete."

So Jones turned to the craft herbs—wreaths, potpourri, and bath herbs. She also experimented with developing an herbal skin care line and studied medicinal uses of herbs by reading widely and attending conferences. She completed a four-month apprenticeship at the California School of Herbal Studies in Sonoma, studying both preventive and curative uses of herbs. Now, aside from her herb-products business, she also runs her own school and has a long list of clients. All of her skin care products are carefully made on the premises, in small batches by hand. "And never when we're in a bad mood," she adds.

Jones is not licensed to diagnose illnesses or prescribe medicine, so she must be careful about her wording when consulting clients. "I might suggest an herb during a consultation," she says, "or tell what the historical use of an herb is." Jones recommends herbs as illness-preventives in foods. "I see people all the time who don't have medical insurance, so they use herbs to stay healthy, and for healing if that should be necessary."

## A growing business

Four years ago, Jones settled on a two-and-a-half-acre farm and has gradually diversified her business. "In the future, herbalists may be able to specialize, for instance with fragrance crafting, but now an herbalist needs a variety of products and services for a successful business." She says if you have a small area for growing and not much capital, you could start with an herb garden in your backyard and sell by mail order. "A good business for a homemaker," she notes.

Jones urges others to learn to market their products, and not just wait for people to come knocking on their doors. "You can't do that and have a successful business," she explains.

For help in marketing techniques as well as development of her business, Jones went to the local Small Business Development Center. Sponsored and administered through the U.S. Small Business Administration and her local community college, the Center utilizes a network of organizations, programs and experienced consultants to assist small businesses. The program is threefold: Business Education and Workshops, Business Consulting and Management Assistance, and Business Development Information and Referral Services.

"After one hour of free consultation," says Jones, "I received low-cost technical assistance. They helped me look at my costs, my potential profits, and to decide whether or not this could be a profitable business." She advises those who want this type of assistance to contact their local Chamber of Commerce to determine what is available. "The consultants were very encouraging and worked with me to develop a five-year business plan."

The business plan included diversification with concentration on the areas where Jones could make the most money, namely her all-natural skin-care line and her educational programs.

Jones learned that a number of successful businesses have developed a certain art type. "For instance," she says, "Banana Republic has an adventure-travel theme; I think a Victorian theme best represents our business, so our ambiance typifies that era. And when we give walking tours of the gardens, we dress in period costume."

For a suggested donation of $3 per adult, Jones gives one-hour tours of her many gardens. She explains that each garden has a specific purpose: "This is our culinary garden, for growing cooking herbs; this is our fragrance garden for potpourri and bath herbs; these are our working gardens where we grow the herbs to make our skin-care products."

Among the several gardens of medicinal herbs, Jones points out her Women's Garden: "All of these herbs are healing for women." Jones has many examples of herbs so her students can come and be with the plants. She explains that in Native American cultures, a child chosen to be medicine-man would sit for days or however long it took to have a vision of what that herb is good for.

Jones's newest garden is very specialized. Several people in the area raise their own sheep for wool and wanted herbs for dyeing the wool.

No insecticide sprays are ever used for insect control. Instead, Jones has rimmed her garden in sunflowers. "They attract the birds who eat insects. We also do companion planting with plants that put beneficial ingredients in the soil for each other or help to repel insects or attract beneficial insects." When asked if she weeds, Jones responds, "No, we graze. Many weeds are edible."

The herbal teas that are blended by Jones are so popular that she has difficulty keeping the shelves stocked. She also custom blends teas for customers who want specific herbs.

Although much of her selling is by mail order, Jones opened a gift shop next to her gardens which carries all of her products. An office and warehouse are presently under construction.

Jones also has a public relations person working with her. "She promotes me," Jones says. "She'll call groups to see if they need speakers; she mails press releases to the newspapers. Soon she'll be in direct sales, working on commission."

Jones advises building your business within your community. "That's what I'm doing," she says. "All the work I've hired to be done has been done by local individuals or businesses. In turn, much of our business has come from our community."

## For further information

Home Herbalist Booklets: "Culpeper's Herbal Remedies" and "Healing Power of Herbs"; both for $10. E.A. Morgan Publishing Co., P.O. Box 1375, Huntington, NY 11743-1375.

*— Arlene Evans*

# HOME PARTY SALES

**Start-up Costs:** In some cases, the cost of the start-up kit, refreshments, gas for car. **Potential Earnings:** Varies. **Advertising:** Word of mouth; some companies have their own advertising package. **Special Qualifications:** None. **Equipment Needed:** A space to conduct parties and a car for deliveries (not always necessary). **Best Advice for Success:** Check fit between company and its product, and your lifestyle. Choose a product you'll enjoy selling.

Have little sales experience and little time, but know a lot of people? You can be successful as a home party sales representative. You sell a product with impulse appeal that sells itself.

The home party plan is a method of product marketing in which you ask a hostess or host family to sponsor a party for their friends. At this informal party you demonstrate your products. The party often includes games, refreshments (a meal, perhaps, if you demonstrate cookware), and party gifts; these variations depend on which company you choose to sell for. According to the Direct Selling Association, products sold in this manner include clothing, cookware and flatware, cosmetics and personal care items, decorative craft items, food supplements, household cleaning supplies, jewelry, personal products, and toys. (See list of home-party companies at the end of this section.)

## What is required

Each company specifies the way it prefers you to stage its parties. Most party plans ask the guests to write out their orders before they leave. Some require immediate payment. Your job is to deliver the products to people after the party, if it is not a cash-and-carry party. You'll probably need to have a car at your disposal, but you may be able to get by with public transportation. It's also possible to go into partnership with a friend, in which the one who likes meeting people does the selling and the one who has the car makes the deliveries.

You can move up in the ranks of your company by becoming a district manager, but you must prove an ability to sell and have the skills to motivate other salespeople. You will often work with a manager until you reach manager status, and part of your receipts, besides the average 40-percent commission, include gifts ranging from jewelry to cars, or even trips for top salespeople. There is usually minimal paperwork involved, but many home-party representatives (often called "consultants") are expected to maintain their own inventory.

The home party plan is a good way for the inexperienced person to learn how to sell and how to approach people while still making money. The experienced salesperson will enjoy even more success. There is often no quota, seldom a territory, but training sessions encourage you to get out and sell more.

## The pros and cons

The advantages of the home-party plan are that you demonstrate the products in the home or office of the person who will be buying and show the product to more than one prospective buyer at a time. You are essentially working for yourself, but you have a company's marketing and research behind you, as well as a proven product that often has appeal to the impulse buyer. This plan is also an advantage to those whose work life must be sporadic because of their home lives. If you must follow your spouse's job, as is often the case with a military family, the home-party method of selling will enable you to keep a job and meet new people wherever you go.

A possible disadvantage would be having a manager who wants you to work more than the one day a week, for example, that you originally decided upon. Another might be the timing of most parties: they are often held at night when you may be accustomed to having your family time. Certainly you can be home during the day with your children while handling necessary phone work, but you will need a sitter for the rallies and the parties.

## Best selling methods

About 80 percent of the home party sales force are women. This is primarily because the representatives ask women to invite them into their homes, and because the products appeal to women as both buyers and sellers. Some companies, such as those that sell cookware, appeal as well to men as representatives. Years ago, when women stayed home, they had Tupperware parties and Stanley parties. This was a great form of entertainment, a way to get friends together and make money or buy a product at the same time. Today, with most women working, representatives of these companies have to be more inventive. They go where the people are. Church members have "home" parties to help stock their church nursery with toys or their fellowship kitchen with supplies. They stage bridal showers where the bride picks out gifts and the guests pay for them as their shower gift; they also order items for themselves. Home party representatives also hold parties in office break rooms during lunch hours.

The tried-and-true method is to gather your best friends and their friends in the hostess's home, serve refreshments, and have a party where you demonstrate various products. If you still live in the community where you grew up, or if you know a lot of people in your town, you'll have lots of contacts among friends and relatives who are just waiting for someone to become a dealer for their favorite home party product. Once you get started, your host company may expect you to ask your hostesses and guests to become dealers also. In this way you can move up the manager ranks, make more money, receive more prizes, and get a cut of your dealers' profits.

Many of the companies that rely on home parties do not advertise. They rely upon word of mouth. You may prefer a company that supports you by advertising.

## Research before you join

Before you decide to become a rep for a company, find out more about it by talking to your friends. Here are some questions to which you should find the answers:

- What are your friends' experiences with this company?
- What is their advice?
- Is there anyone else in your community who sells for this company (in other words, is there currently competition?) Your friends may know a local dealer who would take you on as a trainee.
- Are your friends excited about this company—enough to give parties for you?
- Do local managers press you to hold more parties than you really want to? (There is seldom a limit if you want to hold more and more parties.)
- Is the commission enough to suit you (often around 40 percent, but varying by type of product or by sale price)?
- Do you want to do the paperwork if the commission schedule is complicated?
- Could you eventually afford to go full-time with this company (that is, does it sell as well as you hoped)?
- How are you paid?
- How far do you have to go to pick up your products—or are they sent to you?
- Does the profit come from resales or from a large initial cost for the customer?
- Is there a charge for the starter kit (there is almost always a charge ranging from $10 to $500), or are you considered the owner of the starter kit after you have held a certain number of profitable parties?

If your friends are unfamiliar with a company, ask the local manager of the company these questions.

Pick a company whose product you value. Be your own best customer. If you feel this way about a certain product, that is a good sign that you will be successful, as long as you don't spend all your profits. If you can't be a regular customer of this company yourself, your lack of enthusiasm will show with prospective customers.

## Home party companies

The following companies are among several that sell by the home-party plan. They use part-time contract sales people. Although the party plans are similar, there are differences in style, payment, and commission. Thoroughly investigate each company you consider. Contact each manager and ask for the name and phone number of the local manager and some literature on how to get started with their business.

Mary Kay Cosmetics, 8787 Stemmons Freeway, Dallas, TX 75247. The showcase kit is under $100, and you buy your inventory for around $300 at 40 percent off.

Passport Boutique, P.O. Box 23149, Minneapolis, MN 55423. This jewelry company works on a cash-and-carry basis, so you are paid nightly. The starter kit costs $725.

Discovery Toys, 2530 Arnold Drive, Ste. 400, Martinez, CA 94553. Developmental toys, books, games, and tapes—most under $12.

Perfume Originals, 582A Middle Neck Road, Great Neck, NY 11023. This fragrance company offers a party plan or one-on-one sales. You get a 30- to 50-percent discount and up.

The Creative Circle, 15711 South Broadway, Gardena, CA 90248. Crafts and needlework kits.

The Pampered Chef, 205 Fencl Lane, Hillside, IL 60162. Kitchenware. Per customer sales average $24; per show sales average $325.

Watkins, Inc., 150 Liberty St., Winona, MN 55987. This company offers 250 household products, from cleaning to food products to health products.

Other companies: A.R.T. Direct, 5005 LBJ Freeway, Ste. 1220, Dallas, TX 75244. Oil painting reproductions.

Act II Jewelry, 818 Thorndale Ave., Bensenville, IL 60106. Fashion and fine jewelry.

Aloette, 1301 Wright's Lane, East West Chester, PA 19380. Cosmetics.

Angel Cosmetics, 37053 Cherry St., P.O. Box 873, Newark, CA 94560. Cosmetics.

Brite Music Enterprises, Inc., Box 9191, Salt Lake City, UT 84109. Children's song books, cassettes and records.

Cameo Coutures, 9004 Ambassador Row, Dallas, TX 75247. Clothing, lingerie.

Chambre Cosmetic Corporation, 10138 Huebner Road, San Antonio, TX 78240. Cosmetics and food supplements.

Collectors Corner, Inc., and Affiliates, 5327 W. Minnesota St., Indianapolis, IN 46241. Oil paintings and limited edition prints.

Concept Now Cosmetics, 14000 South Anson St., Santa Fe Springs, CA 90670. Cosmetics.

Contempo Fashions, 6100 Broadmoor, Shawnee Mission, KS 66202. Jewelry and accessories.

Country Home Collection, 1719 Hallock-Young Rd., Warren, OH 44481. Decorative home products.

Custom Nails, P.O. Box 2869, Modesto, CA 95351. Pre-painted artificial fingernails.

Dexi Us, Inc., 6329 Peachtree Industrial Blvd., Doraville, GA 30360. Cosmetics.

Doncaster, Box 1159, Rutherfordton, N.C. 28139. Upscale $700-$800 dresses, coats and outer/sportswear.

Elys'ee Scientific Cosmetics, 6804 Seybold Rd., Madison, WI 53719. Cosmetics.

Emma Page Jewelry, 2201 Northland Dr., Austin, TX 78756. Jewelry.

Heart And Home, Inc., 76 Commercial Way, East Providence, RI 02914. Decorative accessories.

Home Interiors and Gifts, 4550 Spring Valley Rd., Dallas, TX 75244. Decorative accessories.

House of Lloyd, 11901 Grandview Rd., Grandview, MO 64030. Toys, gifts, Christmas decorations.

Jafra Cosmetics, P.O. Box 5026, Westlake Village, CA 91359. Cosmetics and skin care.

Jen Dale, P.O. Box 5604, Charlottesville, VA 22905. Personal care and vitamins.

Kitchen Fair, 1090 Redmond Rd., P.O. Box 100, Jacksonville, AR 72076. Cookware and kitchen accessories.

Lady Finelle Cosmetics, 137 Marston St., P.O. Box 5200, Lawrence, MA 01842-2808. Cosmetics and skin care products.

Lady Love Cosmetics, Inc., P.O. Box 867687, Plano, TX 75086-7687. Cosmetics and skin care products.

Little Bear Enterprises, 11330 Little Bear Way, Boca Raton, FL 33482. Decorative accessories.

Longaberger Marketing, Inc., 95 N. Chestnut St., Dresden, OH 43821-9600. Baskets.

Maya Cosmetics And Skin Care Company, Inc., 2900 Eighteenth St., San Pablo, CA 94806. Cosmetics and skin care products.

Miracle Maid, P.O. Box 97052, Redmond, WA 98073-9752. Cookware.

Noevir, Inc., 1095 SE Main St., Irvine, CA 92714. Cosmetics.

Nutri-Metics International, Inc., 19501 East Walnut Dr., City of Industry, CA 91749. Cosmetics, food supplements, bras.

Oriflame, 76 Treble Cove Rd., North Billerica, MA 01862. Cosmetics, European skin care.

Partylite Gifts, P.O. Box 976, Plymouth, MA 02360. Giftware and decorative accessories.

Petra Fashions, 33 Cherry Hill Dr., Danvers, MA 01923. Lingerie and sleepwear.

Pola U.S.A., Inc. 251 E. Victoria Ave., Carson, CA 90746. Cosmetics.

Princess House, 455 Somerset Ave., North Dighton, MA 02764. Crystal.

QW Fashions (formerly Queensway), 2500 Crawford Ave., Evanston, IL 60201. Women's clothing.

Rickshaw Imports, 311 Richert Rd., Wood Dale, IL 60191. Wicker accessories.

Shaklee Corporation, Shaklee Terraces, 444 Market St., San Francisco, CA 94111. Food supplements, foods, and personal care products.

Society Corporation, 1609 Kilgore Ave., Muncie, IN 47304. Cookware, china and crystal.

Tiara Exclusives, 717 E. St., Dunkirk, IN 47336. Glassware.

Tri-Chem, Inc., One Cape May St., Harrison, NJ 07029. Craft products and paints.

Yanbal Laboratories, 1441 SW 33 Place, Ft. Lauderdale, FL 33315. Cosmetics and skin care.

*— Sandra G. Holland*

# HOUSE-SITTING BUSINESS

**Start-up Costs:** Less than $300. **Potential Earnings:** $50 a day or more. **Advertising:** Press releases to newspapers and local TV; direct mail to real estate agencies; Yellow Pages listing. **Special Qualifications:** None. **Equipment Needed:** As a manager, basic office supplies. **Best Advice for Success:** Get the best, most reliable sitters you can find. Obtain firm contracts.

When families stayed put, it was possible for some family member to feed the pets and water the plants on those rare occasions when someone was absent from home. In today's mobile society, however, a homeowner often has no family member living in the same town and doesn't know the neighbors. So the need for house-sitters keeps growing. You can provide that service, either as a sitter yourself or as a manager of a group of house-sitters.

There are good reasons for having a person watch a home while the owner is away for extended periods. There are natural risks, like storms, lightning, and wind damage. There are man-made risks: things going wrong inside the house requiring the immediate service of a plumber or an electrician. A sitter is good insurance in case of emergencies.

There are occasions when a house-sitter is needed for short periods only: funerals, weddings, or any other event when a public announcement is made that advertises the absence of the members of a household.

## How to obtain sitters

If you choose to be a manager, you'll have to recruit house- sitters to work for you. Women over fifty make the best house-sitters simply because they know more about taking care of houses than anybody else. To find sitters, go where older people congregate: churches, retirement groups, bridge clubs, crafts classes, and other groups catering to seniors. Take along business cards so you can post a notice on the bulletin board. If this doesn't work, run an ad in the classified section of the newspaper under "Employment Opportunities."

*Reliable Sitters.* Clients will often ask if your sitters are bonded. Explain that bonding only covers the loss of money and does not apply to house-sitters. Instead, you must spend time and energy visiting the home of each potential sitter and getting to know her on a personal level. When you visit a potential sitter, allow time to talk. You need to know:

- Does she prefer dogs or cats? Any allergies to either?
- Is she free of responsibilities to family or pets of her own?
- Will she care for plants?
- What are her smoking and drinking habits?
- How does she feel about staying alone? Can she keep busy and content during long periods of solitude?

Give the sitter a general picture of how the house-sitting assignments work. Emphasize that house-sitters are not expected to do any major cleaning, but they are expected to leave the house as they found it with no traces left behind. Tell her how and when she will be paid. When you return to your office, write down your comments and general impressions.

Then telephone the references your applicant has supplied.

## Publicity

The next step is to get the word out about your business. Send a letter to the local newspaper, along with background information that describes generally your house-sitting business. This background information must sufficiently interest the newspaper so that they arrange for a story.

Let real estate groups know of your service. There is often a period of time after the seller moves out and the buyer moves in when the house is empty and unprotected. Leave your cards with travel bureaus and ask that they pass them to clients who may be worrying about leaving an empty house behind. Present your business as an extra service which the travel bureau provides for its customers.

## Charges for three services

Essentially, there are three services you can provide: drive-by, the working sitter, and the twenty-four-hour vigil.

1. *The Drive-By.* Charge by the hour and mile. The sitter begins clocking both time and miles when she leaves her home and drives to the home of the client. It doesn't matter how long or how often each day or week, the cost remains fixed. If the client lives far out of town, the drive-by service can be more expensive than a live-in sitter.

2. *The Working Sitter.* This sitter arrives at the client's house each day at the end of work and stays until the next morning. Charge for this service may be two-thirds of twenty-four-hour service described below. For example, if the twenty-four-hour service is $20 per day, charge $18 per day to remain-overnight. Here is a sample fee scale:

| | |
|---|---|
| 24-hour service | $50 |
| daytime only | $35 |
| remain-overnight | $30 |

3. *The Twenty-Four-Hour Vigil.* This service is the safest concerning the home's security, it is the most supportive for the pets, and it provides the sitter with a sense of identification with the home as her own place rather than as a motel where she sleeps at night or goes to work in the daytime.

   The twenty-four-hour vigil does not mean that the sitter never leaves the house. It means that the sitter will be there most of the time but may go out for an hour's errand to buy groceries, go home to water her own plants and pick up the mail, visit the doctor or dentist, or go for a walk. These errands will be irregular and unpredictable to anyone who might be watching the house to find out when it is regularly unoccupied. The pattern of activity of the twenty-four-hour sitter will be similar to that of a non-working housewife with a couple of young children who is home most of the day.

## Formula for establishing charges

1. *The Work Factor.* The daily rate increases with the amount of work. Ascertain how many pets are to be cared for and how they are to be cared for. Are any medications to be administered? Any special habits or problems to be considered? How much watering has to be done outside and inside? Is there a pool to be looked after? Be sure the house is not occupied by any humans, such as an adolescent who might decide to stay home instead of going along with the family. If there are to be any of the family left behind, talk it over with the sitter to be sure she agrees to the arrangement and, of course, charge extra for the extra responsibility.

2. *The Time Factor.* The daily rate decreases as the number of days absent increases. This works the opposite way as the work factor above. The longer the client is away, the less the daily charge. It makes sense: you have to write contracts, make introductory calls, and go through the entire procedure whether the client is away for a weekend or two weeks. Therefore, you must charge more for a short period and commensurately less as the number of days' absence increases.

3. *The Geography Factor.* The daily rate increases as the convenience of the client's location decreases. The rationale behind the geography factor is that if the client lives way out in the country, it is more isolated and therefore more of a hazard for the safety of the sitter and the security of the household. She will also have to drive further to do her grocery shopping or other errands. Since this will be under her own initiative, she will not be reimbursed for the gasoline used to drive these extra miles. (On the twenty-four-hour vigil she is only entitled to reimbursement for one round trip from her home to the client's house.)

Incidentally, when talking to the client, emphasize that you will try to assign a sitter who lives as close as possible to her house to cut down the cost of transportation. The client will appreciate your concern for her budget.

At the appointed time, arrive promptly at the client's house with the sitter. Show the client the checklist of things to be done and indicate that it might be a good idea to walk around the house so that she can explain how the house runs. Go down the list together. Find out where the sitter is to sleep, the location of the pet food supply, the food dishes, and any medication. Are any of the plants especially delicate? Ask the client to tape directions for watering on their pots. Find out the location of a flashlight or candles in case the power goes off during a storm. How is the telephone to be answered? Ask for a demonstration of the alarm system so that the sitter feels secure with its workings. Assure the client that while the sitter is there, all doors will be kept locked.

After the checklist has been completed and everyone is feeling satisfied that the ground has been covered, produce the contract. The client reads it and signs it in duplicate. She then writes you a check for the stipulated deposit. There are many reasons to collect at least 80 percent of the expected total bill at this point: if anything goes wrong, at least you'll have enough to pay off the sitter.

When the client returns from her trip, telephone her and the sitter to be sure that the service was completely satisfactory. If it was, mail a check to the sitter right away. Show the amount for mileage and the amount for daily sitting. Be sure to thank her for good service and pass along any words of praise from the client.

How much you charge and how much you pay the sitter is your decision. In general, pay the sitter half of the daily charge and all of the mileage. There is no hard-and-fast rule, and you may vary this practice occasionally. If a sitter has been with you a long time and has done good work, give her a larger percentage than a new sitter. If a client's house has been sat for before by the same sitter and there is no need for an introductory visit, you may pass along the savings in time and energy to the sitter in the form of cash reward. If there are many pets and a lot of work, give the sitter three-fourths of the daily charge. If the client is fussy and makes exceptional demands on the sitter, such as never leaving the house unattended, pay the sitter extra. These extras may be put in the form of a bonus so that you can maintain the accustomed daily pay rate.

You may feel that the half-and-half arrangement with the sitter is not to your liking. If you are thinking of cutting down on your portion, don't forget that you are shouldering the expenses of running the business: advertising, telephone, answering service, city license, stamps, and stationary. Also, it falls to you to solve all the problems that arise and, if a client defaults, suffer a possible loss of money. The sitter is always paid but you may lose *your* pay if things go wrong. And last, you are entitled to a reward for having the initiative and energy to start the business in the first place!

Having paid off the sitter, you are ready to send the client her final bill for your services.

Running a house-sitting business develops your skills in judging and dealing with people. Other rewards are many. You will discover one of them at income tax time. If you are running the business from your home, you can deduct that portion of your utilities, mortgage payments, and other relevant expenses that represent your office activities.

### For further information

*How To Run A House-Sitting Business* by Jane Poston. Jane Poston, 1708 E. 9th St., Tucson, AZ 85719. The above was based on Poston's extensive manual. To obtain a copy of the manual, send $38.00 plus $1.00 for handling to Jane Poston at the address above. Her edition includes samples of contracts, letters, advertisements, business cards, and the House-Sitters Code of Ethics.

*— Jane Poston*

# JUNK BUSINESS:
# TURN TRASH INTO CASH

**Start-up Costs:** $500. **Potential Earnings:** $5,000 to $20,000. **Advertising:** Posters and index cards in laundromats, real estate offices, community bulletin boards. **Special Qualifications:** None. **Equipment:** Truck or van, rakes, rubber gloves, trash bags, cardboard boxes. **Best Advice for Success:** Evaluate your merchandise, cart away only what is in good shape and has an excellent resale value.

If you own a pickup truck, you can cash in on the junk business. Second-hand household goods are often sold for less than their true value, given away to anyone willing to cart them off, or simply dumped for the trash man to pick up. If you know how to resell these items, you can make anywhere from $10,000 to $100,000.

If you want to start a business but don't have much capital, this could be the field you've been looking for. In fact, you can begin with your own household junk. By holding a garage sale and selling your unwanted merchandise, you will immediately come up with the capital necessary to go into business for yourself. It's important to distinguish between different types of junk—the kind you can't sell and the kind that has resale value. You'll want to hold on to the valuable discards; they can bring you healthy profits as their value increases.

According to Don Petersen of Westlake Discount Furniture, you will find that just about anything in your home is worth keeping, providing that the item is in decent shape, shows little wear, and has no broken pieces. Petersen started his business out of his home. Today, he has over 6,000 feet of showroom space, owns three buildings and five houses, and is constantly pursuing potential sellers and buyers with good deals on used furniture. But furniture is not all Petersen's store has to offer. You can purchase tools, woodworking equipment, fishing gear, used office furniture, watches, clocks, radios, CBs, TVs, fitness equipment, rugs, beds, and musical instruments. One person's junk is truly another person's treasure.

## How to get started

You could begin your business venture by cleaning attics, cellars, or garages for junk, charging for gas and disposal site fees. You could also start the same kind of business on the premise that the goods worth purchasing are first bought and taken away. Whatever is left will be carted to the dump with the cleaning service included. Buy the valuable merchandise and get it out of the way before offering to clean up the attic, cellar, or garage. The merchandise you carry off is yours to keep whether or not it is worth anything.

Advertising need not cost you much. You can place ads for free in your place of employment, in laundromats, supermarkets, and hardware stores, at homes where garage sales are being conducted, at flea markets, and in hair dressing salons. Ads should be done on 3" x 5" index cards, preferably colorful ones. Make sure you include information on pricing; this will eliminate a barrage of phone calls from people who are "just shopping around."

Homemade posters are also a good way to advertise. Include before and after pictures of a clean-up job. If this doesn't appeal to you, try inserting flyers in mailboxes and at real estate offices. Going directly to the source (someone is moving and needs to have unwanted items carted off) could prove to be your most successful step.

## Evaluating your merchandise

One way of making sure you don't pay too much for merchandise is by doing comparison shopping. Go to used furniture and household goods stores in your area. You should also try giftware shops, antique emporiums, and bookstores. By doing this, you will see what retailers are asking for their merchandise. Remember that this price is based on what the shopkeeper thinks he or she will get for each item, not what the retailer actually paid for the merchandise.

The junk business is one of the easiest small business ventures you can get into. With luck and perseverance, you should be making a profit in no time at all.

*— R.T. Edwards*

# LAWNMOWER RECONDITIONING

**Start-up Costs:** $500 or less. **Potential Earnings:** $75 profit per mower. **Advertising:** Newspaper ads. **Special Qualifications:** Mechanical ability. **Equipment Needed:** Basic tools. **Best Advice for Success:** Buy low and sell high.

In most suburban and rural areas there is a tremendous market for lawnmowers, especially reconditioned ones. Reconditioned lawnmowers are simply used or old, unwanted mowers that have been repaired, cleaned up, and put back into serviceable condition. By selling reconditioned mowers you can take advantage of the demand and line your pockets with extra spending money. Each mower you sell will typically net you five or six times your investment.

The best part of selling reconditioned mowers is that you will probably have little or no competition in your area. Lawnmower dealerships and small engine repair shops will probably have a few used mowers for sale at the beginning of the season, but these sell quickly, and the supply will never meet the demand.

### Getting started

Americans take pride in well-groomed lawns. This means almost every homeowner with a yard is in need of a lawnmower and is therefore a potential customer. The average homeowner will probably go through a half-dozen mowers in a lifetime. Reckon in the number of homeowners in your community, and you can see the potential of this business. As with everything else these days, a new lawnmower can be quite expensive, and many people would rather spend $50 to $60 on a good used mower than go out and buy a new one for $150 or more.

A small workshop can easily be set up in your garage or basement. You really don't need much space; just make sure you have adequate light and ventilation. A small bench with a vise will be helpful. Otherwise, a good set of sockets, screwdrivers, and wrenches are all you will need to get started.

Obviously, you will need a lot of used and junk lawnmowers to fix up. The best way to get them is with an ad in the local newspaper. You can word it something like this:

CASH PAID FOR USED LAWNMOWERS.
ANY CONDITION.
RUNNING OR NOT.
CALL: 555-8605

Once people start reading your ad, your phone will be ringing off the hook, so be prepared. You won't be able to get to every caller in one day, so give yourself enough time and let people know the approximate time you will be over. When you do get there, never ask how much they want for the mower. To save time, explain right away that you generally pay only $5 or $10 for mowers. Most people will be glad to get rid of the mower. If they insist on more money, pay it only if you are sure you can still make a good profit. At first you should buy most of the mowers you look at just to get a good stock of used parts. Eventually you can afford to be a bit more selective, buying only the mowers you can repair with a minimum of time and money.

## Learning to repair lawnmowers

When it comes to fixing mowers, mechanical ability will help, but it is quite possible to teach yourself by tinkering with old mowers. The beauty of buying so-called junk lawnmowers is that one out of every four of them will not be junk at all and can easily be restored to running condition with only a minor repair.

Few people take good care of a lawnmower. You've heard people say that they are getting their car tuned, but when is the last time you heard someone say, "I'm getting my lawnmower tuned"? People expect a lawnmower to run from year to year without any maintenance. As a result, spark plugs foul, air filters clog up with dirt, and ignition points wear out. These are all simple things to repair, but the average person never brings the mower to the repair shop. Instead he will go out and buy a brand new machine, leaving the old one down in the basement to collect dust. You can pick up these mowers for $5 or $10, make a few simple repairs and sell them for $50 or $60 and sometimes $75!

Before you start selling your mowers, clean them up so they will look as good as possible. Buy some degreaser or kerosene and brush it on the engine and body, letting it soak in for a few minutes. Then spray the whole mower down with a garden hose. After the mower has dried, sand and repaint all the rust spots on the handle and body.

## Marketing

Here again the local newspaper can prove invaluable. A simple ad like this should do the trick:

FOR SALE:
RECONDITIONED LAWNMOWERS
Large selection to choose from.
Fully guaranteed.
Call: 613-8605.

Your objective should be to mass-produce reconditioned lawnmowers. Do this and you will soon find out the tremendous potential of your new-found business. Good used lawnmowers are like gold and will sell quickly. Give this unique business opportunity a whirl, and you too could soon be raking in the profits.

*— Scott W. Kendall*

# LITERARY AGENT: INCOME FROM AUTHORS

**Start-up Costs:** $200 or less. **Potential Earnings:** $40,000 plus after the first year. **Advertising:** Small ads, flyers, Yellow Page ad. **Special Qualifications:** Editing skills. **Equipment Needed:** Typewriter or word processor. **Best Advice for Success:** Have the patience to build a strong client base. Be enthusiastic and positive with people.

If you enjoy reading, can recognize quality writing, and have editing skills, all you need is a typewriter or word processor to become a literary agent. Literary agents market the work of writers to publishers. For their services they receive a commission of 10 to 20 percent of the authors' fees. In addition to commissions on sales they can sometimes charge additional fees for reading, critiquing, preparing, and editing manuscripts.

Most editors prefer working with agents to working directly with freelance writers. Many of them do not have the time to consider unsolicited material. Once an author builds a successful reputation, editors don't mind the absence of the intermediary, but new or unknown authors are in a Catch-22 situation: no one will consider their work until they have a good track record, and they can't build a record unless someone gives them an opportunity. That is where a literary agent comes in.

Pamela English, an agent in Mesa, Arizona, says that one of the more important aspects of her job is to match a writer's work with a suitable publication. "You wouldn't expect *The New Yorker* to publish an article on make-up tips for teenagers, but believe it or not, editors see such outlandish submissions. It wastes their time," Pamela says. It's so much trouble that many publications rely on people like Pamela to find suitable articles and stories for them.

Pamela has operated a typing service for several years. She found that becoming a literary agent was a natural adjunct to it. Many agents do not offer manuscript editing and preparation services. Pamela has carved a niche for herself that provides substantial income, income other agents overlook. The skills she uses in preparing reports for business people are the same skills she uses to improve her clients' work. "Editors want clean, easily readable copy, free of grammar, spelling, and typographical errors. Too many mistakes ruin a piece even if its message is excellent," she says. Pamela uses a personal computer with a spell-checker built into the word processing application and a letter-quality printer. It's much quicker than using a typewriter and dictionary.

## Finding clients

Like most service organizations, a good part of a literary agent's effort is devoted to finding and cultivating clients. Some agencies run ads in national magazines. *Writer's Digest*, for example, is a magazine aimed primarily at an audience of freelance writers. But national ads are expensive, and sophisticated competitors may be advertising there as well. Initially, local advertising and contacts seem to produce more results than do national campaigns.

Your local newspaper very likely runs notices of writing club meetings. Join the available clubs, then convince members how much each could benefit from your service. If no club exists, set one up. There are people everywhere who want to be published but who may need encouragement and gentle prodding to overcome their procrastination.

Colleges and universities usually have writing clubs and creative writing classes filled with people anxious to have their work published. Call English departments for the name of writing professors. The professor may well be cooperative, for a teacher's success depends on the success of their students. If a number of students get published, the professor is likely to be perceived as someone who inspires these students and encourages them to try for publication of their works.

While contacting teachers, don't neglect high school composition teachers, especially those who sponsor school newspapers and collections of students' writings. These teachers may be able to furnish the names of people who have the talent and interest to become authors. Many good writers have never seen the inside of a college classroom.

Staff writers for local newspapers may be another source. These are skilled writers, but they often need help discovering topics that interest publishers. Their names appear as by-lines on articles. Call them. Develop story ideas, query different publications until you find one that is interesting, then hand the story over to a staff writer and collect your commission.

One indispensable reference to a literary agent is *Writer's Market;* it's published by Writer's Digest Books and can be found in most bookstores. Updated annually, the book lists hundred of markets, outlining exactly what kinds of material each publisher wants, what their payment schedules are, how long articles should be, and whether they will accept work from freelancers. It also has sections on how to package submissions and the vocabulary of the publishing industry.

This literary opportunity is open to you no matter what part of the country you live in. Contacts between agents and editors are made by mail, fax machine, or over the phone. No licensing or credentials are required—just enthusiasm and basic skills. You can run the business from home, a tiny rented space, or from an existing business. To get started, you'll need letterhead stationery, business cards, a copy of *Writer's Market,* and the ability to promote yourself. This is a business you can easily start for under $200.

Publications: *Writer's Market.* Writer's Digest Books, 1507 Dana Ave., Cincinnati, OH 45207-9988.

Literary Agent. Vocational Biographies, Sauk Centre, MN 56378. Has pamphlet from the Careers in Sales series.

*— Lenn Combs*

## LONGABERGER BASKETS

**Start-up Costs:** $500 or less. **Potential Earnings:** $250 to $300 per party. **Advertising:** Word of mouth; periodic mailings. **Special Qualifications:** None. **Equipment Needed:** Baskets and catalogs. **Best Advice for Success:** Show enthusiasm for the quality of the product—that will translate into greater sales.

Cindy Grace, a young mother of two, liked her career as a registered nurse, but her work hours were often on weekends or holidays. This schedule interfered with the things Grace wanted to do with her husband and children. Then a friend of Grace's asked her to host a party sponsored by Longaberger Baskets. Grace was impressed by the quality of the baskets and the interesting family history behind the company. Longaberger Baskets is an Ohio-based, family-owned business that makes high-quality, antique reproduction baskets sold exclusively at in-home demonstrations. The retail sales of Longaberger Baskets amounted to more than $30 million in 1990.

"The Longaberger Company sells their baskets only through home presentations," says Grace. "They believe this is the best way to explain the history of the company to the potential buyer." Longaberger Baskets began at the turn of the century when J.W. Longaberger began weaving baskets for his neighbors in Dresden, Ohio (where the present company is still based). The company, headed by president David Longaberger, makes baskets that vary in styles from small berry baskets to large market and pantry baskets to cradles that rock. Customers use them for pocketbooks, to hold garden produce or firewood, or for decorative uses such as displaying dried flowers or hanging from rafters in the home. "The baskets are not wicker but are actually 'splint' or 'split-wood' baskets made from three types of wood," says Grace. "All the baskets are handmade, with the weavers initialing and dating each basket they make."

## Becoming a consultant

Grace decided to become a "consultant" and sell the baskets at home "Basket Presentations," as the company likes to call them. With the baskets ranging in price from $14.95 to $57.95, the average party grosses $250 to $350 in sales, from which the consultant can expect to make a 25 percent commission. Since Grace first became a consultant she has held close to 160 parties. She was also seventeenth nationwide in sales, generating nearly $20,000 in revenues for the six-month period.

To become a consultant, Grace bought a start-up kit of eighteen Longaberger baskets at a discounted rate. She uses these baskets in her displays at the presentations. "In less than six presentations I had made up the cost of my investment and began to show a profit," says Grace. As a consultant she also had to sign a contract to have at least six presentations. "Then," says Grace, "I have to sell a minimum of $500 worth of baskets a month, about the average amount of sales two presentations will make." With Grace's success, though, she has been averaging two or three presentations a week.

## The home presentations

At a home presentation, Grace will suggest ways people can use the baskets in their homes. She will also give a brief family history of the baskets. "People are impressed with the quality of the baskets," says Grace, "and they are charmed with the history behind the company and the unique way the baskets are made."

As the baskets are not made until the company receives the orders, it takes about seven weeks for them to be delivered. After a presentation,

Grace keeps former customers informed of latest styles of baskets with periodic mailings. "Many of the baskets become collector items, and some have increased in value just a few months after they were purchased," says Grace.

As a consultant, Grace puts in about four hours of work for each day that she hosts a presentation. That time includes the paperwork and the actual presentation itself. "Some times of the year, such as the weeks before Easter and Christmas, may be more hectic in terms of the number of presentations I book, but I find that with the Longaberger Baskets I have a steady income year 'round," says Grace.

Grace's office is in her living room, and she conducts her business from an antique desk. Longaberger Baskets hang from rafters in the ceiling in a decorative array. She has purchased a mini-van to haul her baskets and display racks, and a cordless phone, which is handy. The van and phone are considered business expenses and therefore deductible, as is the mileage she records.

### Company support

Grace calls her adviser weekly, giving an eight-week projection of upcoming presentations, the amount of total sales her presentations have made in the past week, and the names of any new consultants she has found. "Consultants become advisers when they recruit six new consultants," says Grace. "Then the advisers will receive 5 percent from the sales of those recruits."

The company publishes a newsletter called *The Opportunity* which profiles some of the consultants, the latest kinds of baskets produced, dates and locations of up-coming seminars, and selling hints for the consultants to use. Longaberger also holds a yearly "Basket Bee" for top sales people and other consultants in Columbus, Ohio. Here they are invited to actually make a Longaberger Basket. Special awards are presented, along with an invitation to a VIP luncheon at the home of company president David Longaberger.

"This is an excellent job for a woman," says Grace. "She can set her hours around her family and yet get out among grown-up people." The job allows for creativity in decorating with the baskets and allows men or women at any age to make some extra income."

For more information, write to: Longaberger Baskets, 95 North Chestnut St., Dresden, OH 43821-9600.

— *Priscilla Y. Huff*

# LOT CLEAN-UP

**Start-up Costs:** Less than $100. **Potential Earnings:** $250 per job. **Advertising:** Personally distributed flyers. **Special Qualifications:** None. **Equipment Needed:** Rake, shovel, plastic bags; pick-up truck optional. **Best Advice for Success:** Work to get the jobs that pay the most amount of money.

Randall was home from college. His parents were happy to see him. He was happy to be home and have some time off. But now what? He couldn't just sit around for the next three months, so he decided to find a way to make some extra money—quick. He checked the classifieds and looked at the supermarket bulletin boards, but everything was minimum wage. He didn't want to spend the summer in a fast food restaurant. Then he got the idea to create his own job an at his own price. He would do lot clean-up.

Randall's hometown is situated in an area where there are plenty of vacant lots, most belonging to people who live out of town. These owners can be cited by the fire department if the lots become a fire hazard by collecting debris and tumble weeds. They are subject to a fine if the lot is not cleared within ten days.

The city posts a notice on the lot, and the owner is sent a registered letter notifying him or her of the fire hazard. If the owner doesn't reply within the allotted time, the job of cleaning the lot is made available, and whoever wants to can bid on the job at the city hall. The cost is paid by the city and comes out of the property owner's taxes. Randall got many of these jobs by being the low bidder. Yet the income was still excellent.

Another way he got jobs was by copying off a stack of one-sheet flyers to distribute house-to-house. He offered to clear weeds away from the fence so that residents could pass the fire inspection and to remove unsightly garbage and trash, increasing the beauty of the neighborhood and city, (which also increases property value, of course.) So he was in business.

## Tools of the trade

Randall's initial investment in equipment was minimal. "I went out and got a rake, shovel, and plastic bags. I already had a pick-up truck," he explained. His start up was less than $100.

One thing that he did was to make a homemade drag out of a heavy piece of frame metal—you could also use old springs from a boxspring mattress. He attached his drag to the back of his pickup to rake the lot and help clear the debris, a technique he learned from seeing baseball fields dragged.

Although it sounds like a relatively harmless job, Randall advises that safety is very important. He often had to pull weeds. "I had to keep a hose handy, and always checked with the fire department."

### A lucrative venture

Randall's initial plan was just to make a few extra dollars doing lot clean-up for a couple of weeks, but when he saw how many property owners of underdeveloped property had been cited, he realized there was good money to be made.

Randall tried to get the jobs that would bring in the largest sums of money, and these came from the large, undeveloped lots. Depending on the size of the lot and how much work had to be done, he could get anywhere from $250 up. With homeowners he would offer a flat rate or ask whether they preferred to pay by the hour. "It was whatever they felt more comfortable doing, but I always made out pretty good," says Randall.

The venture turned out to be so lucrative that Randall has decided to continue with the business each year and expand. "Next year I'll be better prepared and maybe go into removing stumps and tree trimming," says Randall.

Even if you don't live in the wide-open spaces, there are lots to be cleared. Someone has got to do it, and they are getting paid for it, so why shouldn't it be you?

*— Jo Ann M. Unger*

# MAIL RECEIVING/FORWARDING

**Start-up Costs:** $500 or less. **Potential Earnings:** $30,000 or more, yearly. **Advertising:** Direct mail; classifieds. **Special Qualifications:** Respect for confidentiality. **Equipment Needed:** Postage meter, scale, labels. **Best Advice for Success:** Be professional, offer a variety of services.

Mail receiving and mail forwarding is a business that can be operated from your home and requires little overhead. Several well-established mail receiving/forwarding businesses operate in the United States and Canada, and demand for their services continues.

These days many people travel a great deal and need their mail reliably remailed at intervals to changing addresses. Some potential clients live in motorhomes or trailers for several months of the year, traveling from place to place. Other clients include overseas employment and military personnel, traveling salespeople, foreign individuals and business firms, separated spouses, and inmates of correctional institutions.

## How it works

When offering this service, you agree to receive mail on behalf of a client at your address and to forward that mail to your client. You act as an agent for handling client mail, and as such you must comply with all postal laws. In the United States your clients have to fill out Postal Service Form #1583: "Application for Delivery of Mail Through an Agent." This form authorizes the Postal Service to deliver a client's mail to your address. The client must fill out the form in duplicate, have it notarized, then return it for your signature. You keep one copy on file, and the other is delivered to the client's postmaster.

In Canada, no forms are required to receive mail as an agent. However, a letter of authority should be obtained clearly indicating an agent's entitlement to receive mail on behalf of a client. It should also be noted that, unlike the United States Postal Service, Canada Post will charge clients a fee for temporarily redirecting their mail to an agent's address. This can be avoided by having clients notify their correspondents to send mail directly to the agent rather than having it forwarded by the post office. In both countries this method helps eliminate a link in the forwarding chain and speeds up the process.

Dependable service, confidentiality, and security are paramount in the mail receiving/forwarding business. Your clients must be assured that their mail will be accorded every reasonable protection. Never open clients' mail without their permission unless legally required to do so, and never divulge client's whereabouts. Any time mail is in someone else's hands, the security of that mail has to be considered. Treat client mail as if it were your very own and handle it with utmost security.

Protect yourself by including a disclaimer on the client's contract, releasing you from any liability for loss or destruction of mail unless it was caused by gross negligence.

## What to charge

What you charge as an agent depends on the going rate in the market. Find out what similar businesses are charging for their services. Some businesses charge a set rate for each piece of mail forwarded. Most charge a monthly rate of $8 to $15 for their services, or an annual $80 to $150 fee. Decide whether you are going to include postage costs in your base price or charge extra for them. Both the United States Postal Service and Canada Post require that forwarded mail from an agent be repackaged and affixed with new postage. Many mail receiving/forwarding businesses have their clients open an account with them to cover the costs of postage for forwarding their mail. They request an initial $4 to $10 deposit to start this account (more if the client is expecting a large volume of mail). When it is depleted, the mail receiving/forwarding agent notifies the client to send additional money to replenish this account.

Your business should include such services as mail sorting according to client instructions, holding mail until your client requests you to forward it, forwarding client mail at specified intervals (daily, weekly, bi-weekly, monthly), holding some mail and forwarding only specified pieces (checks), and forwarding mail according to an itinerary supplied by a client so that mail is waiting for the client at predetermined destinations.

## Supplies

Buy a few office supplies, some stamps, and plenty of envelopes, and you're ready for business. The sophistication of your business will depend on your volume and the kind of mail involved. But even a person working out of the home can benefit from basic equipment that is cheap and available.

By using a typewriter or word-processor, your mail pieces will look more professional than if you address them by hand. The fundamental mailing tool is a postage meter, which can be rented, usually for less than $10 a month. A postage meter works best in conjunction with an electronic scale specifically designed for mailing; this usually costs less than 50 cents a day, a small amount when compared to potential losses from overpayment of postage or delayed delivery resulting from insufficient postage. (Look in your Yellow Pages under "Postage Meters and Scales.")

Another item you should consider is a return address stamp or label to use when forwarding your client's mail. This should include your business name and the address your business is working from. You can use your home address for your business or rent a post office box.

## Advertising

If your mail service business is designed for your client's convenience, with services offered at reasonable rates, people will use it. The success of your advertising will depend to a large extent on your ability to identify your targeted group.

Select a company name that reflects the nature of your business and expose your advertising to your target market. Direct mail is one approach. Send a direct-mail package to a membership list from a local R.V. club, for example. The package should include a cover letter that introduces your service and describes its uses and features, a brochure with your price structure, and a response reply form.

Classified advertising is another approach. Try the two-step method of using an ad to solicit inquiries about your service, which then can be answered by a direct mailing. Place your ads in publications that will be read by your target group. If you can successfully target your market, you can provide a needed service and earn an income from your own business.

— *Patricia McEachern*

# MEETING PLANNER

**Start-up Costs:** $500. **Potential Earnings:** $30,000 and up. **Advertising:** Word of mouth referrals; Yellow Pages. **Special Qualifications:** Organizational skills. **Equipment Needed:** Basic home office equipment. **Best Advice for Success:** Thoroughly research the hotels, restaurants, and travel arrangements you will make for your clients.

Christine Smith had never heard of a meeting planning service. She realized, however, that during her nearly twenty years in broadcasting and public relations, she had built up a special kind of knowledge about putting together events, a knowledge that was not available elsewhere. People kept coming to her to ask, "Chris, how do I do that?" or "Where can I find that?" or "How much should it cost?" Could Smith support herself with a company that put together functions, meetings, and conventions for clients? For two years she planned and worried. Then, leaving her public relations job, she took the plunge and set up Meetings, Inc. in her suburban home.

The concept of meeting planning as a specialized professional service is a recent one, and independent firms that do nothing but arrange events are even more recent. But as the success of Meetings, Inc. shows, meeting planning as a business is coming into its own. Today, Meetings, Inc. has grown so much that Smith needs to move it out of her home in order to expand.

In her first year, Smith contracted with twenty-eight clients to put on about forty events, and showed a profit. In the next months she arranged more than a hundred different events for forty clients. These events included a ground-breaking ceremony for a Marriott Hotel; a week-long Oktoberfest celebration for a German-American Heritage Society; a party to kick off a fundraising campaign for the Arts and Science Council; a regional convention for Women in Communications, Inc., a day of coordinated activities for executives' wives for IBM; and a two-day meeting for local and national company officials and their major clients for a paper mill.

Smith's company makes money from hotel commissions and clients' fees. She says about half her events are held in town, the other half out of town. Smith usually sells and develops the program for the client while her son pulls together all the various aspects of the event. He goes to the office every day, and he and his mother coordinate their activities.

## Every detail

When Smith and her company plan an event for a client, they arrange every aspect down to the last detail—from negotiating with the hotels to choosing the menu, flowers, and linen; from handling media relations to providing music and entertainment; and from arranging transportation and tours to taking care of registration. Chris or her son attend every function the company plans in order to do on-site supervision. This often includes arriving twenty-four hours beforehand to see that the limousine arrives on time at the airport, to make sure the client's VIPs get their luggage first, and to examine the VIPs's rooms to ensure that everything is perfect.

"The client only has to concentrate on the content of the meeting, not whether name cards are being passed out or the food will be on time," Smith explains. "We make the client's conference chair look good. We save money for them with our negotiating expertise. We assure the client the best value for the lowest expenditure. We find what is the most expeditious, the most financially feasible. People know it's cheaper to go outside to us then do it in-house."

Meetings, Inc. also helps its clients save money by making cost-cutting suggestions. For example, Smith's firm now owns silk flowers that clients can rent. Each item is budgeted, and Smith guarantees the fee beforehand, no matter what her costs actually are. The firm also offers consolidated billing—the client pays just one bill and Smith pays each individual subcontractor. Since she wants to keep her staff small, she hires all her help on a contract basis. She keeps files on available workers for such duties as tending bar, taking photographs, handling guest registration, and welcoming.

Meetings, Inc. offers post-event evaluation to each client. Evaluation questionnaires are provided at the event, so the responses of attendees are considered.

Before starting her company, Smith began another kind of research that she continues today: staying in hotels to see what they are like and to learn from their managers what they have to offer. She began by staying at two hotels every weekend. During these visits, Smith takes copious notes and asks for a list of previous events held at the facility so that she can contact the groups for more information. "We don't recommend a hotel we haven't slept in, food we haven't eaten, or a bus service we haven't used ourselves," Smith says.

## Fees

The price for each service depends on the time of the event, the amount of time required for arrangements, the number of people Smith must hire, and the expertise required. She estimates fees on an hourly basis, using a range of $25 to $50 an hour. For a special event she charges a minimum of $500, while for a convention the rate is $3 a person per day.

A consistent cash flow has been a problem for Smith's company. Conventions are usually planned four to six years in advance, and the months of December, January, and May through July are off-periods for meetings and conventions. But this difficulty has been smoothed over now, as Smith finds herself doing many more special events than she anticipated.

A special event is any one-shot event, such as a ground-breaking, plant opening or party, that requires special planning and coordination. "They're good money-makers," Smith says. "You're usually in and out of it within ninety days, they're on a fee basis and they're usually backed by corporations, who understand contracts. Special events have given us the good cash flow we needed." Smith says most business currently comes through word of mouth and from hotel referrals. She also works with groups trying to win bids for national convention sites.

Smith expects to continue to center her activities in the Southeast, because she knows it so well and because it will allow her to keep the company personal. "I never want to dilute the corporation; I want to offer quality service, and you can do that better in a concentrated area," Smith says.

*— Beatrice Taylor Quirk*

## MUSHROOM MAGIC

**Start-up Costs:** $16.95 to $300. **Potential Earnings:** $2,500 a year on a $300 investment; more if you grow a larger crop. **Advertising:** Restaurant and health-related magazines; word of mouth. **Special Qualifications:** None. **Equipment Needed:** Spore, logs, wax, wax pan, tarp blanket (optional), drill. **Best Advice for Success:** Carefully follow the step-by-step procedure for maximum mushroom fruition—and maximum profits.

Wherever the expression "made in the shade" came from, it definitely applies to growing shiitake mushrooms for profit. If you have a shady place in your backyard or can construct a shade cover, you can make substantial money by growing the Japanese forest mushroom on logs.

Ray Sohn has his own spawn and says it isn't hard; it merely requires patience and an attention to detail. The basic procedure is simple: freshly-cut logs are places in a shady place, inoculated with the spore and kept damp until the mushrooms begin to sprout. One of the pleasant things about the shiitake (pronounced "shee-TA-kay") is that the crop will continue to come up until the entire log has been consumed by the fungus, which means about five years of crops from one inoculation.

According to a United States Department of Agriculture report, the market for shiitake in this country is expanding and offers an outstanding opportunity with these delectable gourmet mushrooms presently wholesaling at $6 to $8 a pound and retailing at $12.

## How to grow shiitake mushrooms

The most crucial part of fungal growth is proper moisture. Overly dry or overly wet conditions will retard growth. The best way to ensure the correct degree of moisture is to cut the logs during the winter and store them whole (ideally coating the ends with wax) and under cover to preserve moisture, then cut to length at inoculation time. Small scrub oak makes the best logs, but other woods can be used, too.

Many growers soak their logs before or immediately after inoculating if the logs show signs of dryness. This can be done by placing them in a lake, river, or pond; or they can be hosed or sprinkled. What works best is placing the logs in a large stock tank, a method that allows the grower greatest control.

Light and temperature are the next-most-important factors in getting a maximum crop. If you are growing the mushrooms outside, begin the inoculations when daytime temperatures are 45 to 50 degrees. You'll get even better results if you wait until the temperature is 70 to 80 degrees; this promotes the fastest growth. After inoculation, mushrooms grow best in complete darkness or filtered sunlight, but when they are ready to fruit, they do need light. Protect the spawn from direct sunlight.

Mushrooms are spread by spores. Often the growth starts in damaged spots on a tree where the spores can most easily lodge. The shiitake industry prepares spores under sterile laboratory conditions, initiating growth in wood plugs. The grower simply drills a diamond pattern of holes in the logs and inserts the plugs. Sohn advises inoculating a small amount of logs with a heavy dose of spores rather than a lot of logs with a light amount.

A good rule is to place the plugs six to ten inches apart with about two inches between rows. Inoculating near the wood ends also aids rapid colonization. Once the plugs, or dowels, of spawn are placed in the holes, seal them with cheese wax. This will protect the inoculation sites from dehydration without any toxic effects to mushrooms or people. For best results, heat the wax to over 250 degrees and paint it on with a brush or turkey baster. (For log ends, dipping is most efficient. Remember to use extreme care, since hot wax is dangerous.

One final step remains. Mark each log with an embossable aluminum tag to record the date it was inoculated, the strain used, and the supplier. Leave room to record the fruiting results. In this way you can keep track of the procedures and products that deliver optimum harvest in your area.

Advertised spawn strains usually promise fruiting in six to twelve months, but it can take longer if the spawn-run conditions are less than ideal. The signal that the spawn run is complete and the logs ready to fruit is a soft, spongy bark. It's an exciting moment for most growers when they wake up one morning to see the first white buttons forming on the logs.

## Equipment

Sohn sells a spawn kit that will inoculate 1,200 pounds of logs for $16.95 (see his address below). To set up an operation that would promise commercial profits, Sohn estimates that $300 would inoculate a cord of wood (about 4,800 pounds), from which one could expect to harvest 1,500 pounds of mushrooms over a five-year period, if the logs were kept properly. This means a profit of about $2,500 a year on a $300 investment.

Much larger operations are possible, of course. The shiitake grown out-of-doors are harvested both in the spring and in the fall, but some growers are putting up sheds to enable them to harvest all year round. Costs are higher with an indoor operation because of the need for heating and cooling systems, but they are offset somewhat by the greater control the grower can exert over the environment. It's wise to start small and expand as you gain experience.

## Marketing

Shiitake is used mostly by Oriental food markets and restaurants. Smaller growers can easily find a market for their product by simply approaching restaurants. You can also establish clientele by advertising in restaurant and health magazines. Larger growers will probably find it more desirable to approach wholesale food distributors.

Other growers may be willing to share their marketing ideas with you if you affiliate with a group. The Shiitake Growers Association of

Wisconsin accepts members from all states (see address below). It's an open market for someone who has the time and interest.

## For further information

"Cultivation of Shiitake," by Gary Leatham, USDA booklet. USDA, 14th and Independence Ave. S.W., Washington, DC 20250-2200.

"Shiitake Inoculation and Spawn Run Techniques and Indoors Wrap Method," by Ray Sohn, 610 S. Main St., Westfield, WI 53964; (608) 296-2456.

*Shiitake News*, Rte 2, Box 156A, Lanesboro, MN 55949. Published by Forest Resource Center. An information clearinghouse for shiitake growers, three issues a year. $25 initial subscription; renewals $15.

*— Barbara Vroman*

# MUSIC

**Start-up Costs:** $100. **Potential Earnings:** Varies. **Advertising:** Business cards, brochures. **Special Qualifications:** Good musical ability. **Equipment Needed:** Your instrument. **Best Advice for Success:** Make a good-quality demonstration tape.

Susan Bramlett is a housewife and mother who has a great part-time job that's easy, fun, and profitable. Most weeks she makes two to three hundred dollars for just a few hours work. Her job? She sings with a freelance dance band!

George Allen is a computer programmer for a major company. Many weeks he makes as much money in a few nights, playing bass with a pop-rock band, as he does in a week at his regular job. And he usually works only three or four hours a night.

These people are profiting form the freelance music marketplace. Like hundreds of thousands of other musicians, they work an interesting variety of jobs and make a substantial income from their part-time efforts. On an hourly basis they often make incomes that rival attorneys, accountants, and other professionals.

Could you make money with music? Did you play an instrument in high school or college? Do you play in an amateur band or sing with a barbershop quartet? Do you enjoy playing the piano or guitar to entertain your friends? Maybe you too could be freelancing. Many freelance jobs are private events, but they pay well and don't tie you down to a regular schedule. Here are a few examples of typical freelance jobs. There are hundreds of others, but these will give you an idea.

- A country club hires a bluegrass band to play for its Fourth of July outdoor picnic.
- A politician hires a rock band to create excitement and attract crowds at campaign appearances.
- A major corporation hires a Dixieland band to set an upbeat mood at a new-product introduction press conference.
- A rich citizen hires a pianist to provide background music at a private cocktail reception.
- A singing telegram service hires enthusiastic singers to deliver humorous messages.

It isn't necessary to be a virtuoso to play commercial music engagements. If you are fairly competent at your instrument and can play acceptably well, you'll do fine. And if you are outgoing and personable and can work well with different kinds of people, you'll be that much more ahead of the game. What may be more important than your musical skills is the ability to understand how music fits into the overall situation. If, for example, your country band is entertaining during dinner at a convention, keep your level down so that the conventioneers can talk business. Yes, your music is important, but it's not the reason they're together. They are there to talk business. The freelance musician who can "think like a client," will be far ahead of his competitors.

Whatever kind of music you do best can make you money, if your style is in demand. All you have to do is find the clients and book the jobs.

### Getting started

You'll find it helpful to look at music in a new, perhaps unusual, way. Don't think of playing music as an artistic endeavor. Think of it as a service to your clients, a chance to help them in some specific way.

In social situations, the right music can help guarantee the success of parties and festive events, weddings, reunions, birthday parties, retirement or promotion parties, bar mitzvahs, and so on. Music can be used to create many effects: excitement in sales meetings, a social atmosphere for doing business at cocktail parties, dances or hospitality suites, and an upbeat atmosphere at ground-breaking or topping-out ceremonies or at new-product introductions.

### Selling your music

You've got to make sales calls. How else will people know you're available? Prepare yourself before the sales call by knowing what you can offer the client, why he or she should buy from you, and what your music will cost. Think ahead about what your music can do for the client, not vice versa, and show why your music will add just the right atmosphere to the event. Remember, people who buy freelance music aren't supporting struggling artists; they are planning parties or events, and they only want music if it can help their affairs to be successful. Take a few sales aids with you when you visit. Depending on what kind of music you do and how experienced you are, you may find these public relations tools to be helpful.

- Business cards. Leave one with everyone you meet, clip one to all your correspondence, and always have them handy when you are playing a job.
- Brochures may be elaborate but need not be more than a single sheet, neatly typed and duplicated at a local quick-copy center. Your brochure should tell who you are, what your musical experience is, what others have said about you, where you have worked, and what you can do.
- Photographs can be helpful, and a good "head shot" is a staple for all musicians. Be sure the photo you use is of excellent quality, and that it portrays you or your group as professional and cheerful.
- Demonstration audio or video tapes may be helpful. Be sure that they are of professional quality. Nothing makes you look as inexperienced as a poor-quality demo.

### Setting your fees

Resist the temptation to quote a low price. Underpricing your competition can actually work against you; your clients know that they get what they pay for. Check around to see what other groups or individuals get for similar work. The variety is so great around the country that it's impossible to quote an average price here, and you'll probably even quote different prices at different times yourself. In a busy month like December or June you'll probably charge more than in a slow month like August, and you'll charge more for Saturday nights than for Tuesday afternoons.

You may want to join your local musician's union (usually the American Federation of Musicians), which can help you determine what to charge. "Union scale" is an established minimum for an area, and most musicians will observe it.

*— Jim Gibson*

# ODD JOBS

**Start-up Costs:** $500 or less. **Potential Earnings:** Up to $2,500 per week. **Advertising:** Flyers, shopper paper ads, Yellow Pages. **Special Qualifications:** Common skills. **Equipment Needed:** Lawn mower, ladder, miscellaneous tools. **Best Advice for Success:** Start in spring; provide quality work at economical prices.

Maintaining and beautifying a home can be an endless and expensive struggle. Walls and window trim are forever in need of paint; shrubs and bushes require yearly trimming; and light carpentry and yard work are seasonal chores that face every homeowner. Weekends, which were once reserved for home improvements, are now a time to shop for necessities or leisure activities. Many people who work forty-hour weeks are not inclined to pick up a paint brush or seal their driveway. Usually people hire an expensive professional to do the job. The double-income family is less burdened by professional prices—but still sensitive about giving its hard-earned money away.

Senior citizens often own homes that are in need of repair. The high prices of a professional can restrict a cost-conscious elderly person from having work done, especially when certain necessary home improvements are small and do not require a professional.

An inexpensive odd-job service is an alternative to all these problems. There is a definite need for such a service, and an odd-jobs venture, if executed with vigor and integrity, can be the start of a very profitable business. Opportunities for household odd jobs exist wherever there are homes and homeowners, rich or poor, who must contend with the upkeep of their property. You need not take on jobs that require sophisticated equipment. As you develop capital, however, you might invest in a used lawn mower or electric hedge clipper, enabling you to expand your services to weekly yard work.

## Getting started

To begin, you must be close to people who own homes. Most jobs come from middle-class homeowners who need home improvements. The best time to start is in the spring after the last of the snow has melted. With the advent of spring, the homeowner becomes much more conscious of his home's appearance, especially considering the state of the home after a long winter. Snow and freezing weather often tear off branches and leaves, and many yards need thorough clean-ups. Yard clean-ups which are done in fall and early spring, can yield, depending on the size of the yard and amount of debris, $25 to $200 per yard.

## Selecting services

Selecting which services you want to offer your community is a simple task. Any specific skills you have should be emphasized in your advertisements. Don't worry if you do not possess any special skills. Most household repairs are simple enough to be done by almost anyone. Moving furniture, raking leaves, and painting are basically unskilled tasks that you can find yourself hired to do time and again.

Certain jobs, however, should be left for professionals. Plumbing and involved electrical work can be extremely dangerous unless you are qualified and licensed. Test and see what your community needs. Look through the Yellow Pages to see which services have the largest number of businesses listed. You may find an inordinate number of professional painters, indicating that many people had homes in need of painting. This method of determining what your community needs is by no means foolproof, but it can give you a semi-accurate "feel" for your market. As you work in your community, you will begin to become more aware of your customer's needs.

## Pricing

Pricing is perhaps the hardest part of running an odd jobs business. It is impossible to put a specific price on services that vary from job to job. For example, you might be hired to move a refrigerator. Every refrigerator is a different size, and no two refrigerators have to be moved the same distance. Certain moving procedures require more workers or involve more obstacles.

Here are two ways to charge your customers:

- Determine the price of the job by estimating time, labor costs, traveling time, and so forth. Then give the customer a flat rate. An example of a flat rate would be $200 for a yard clean-up. Charging a flat rate means that no matter how slowly or quickly you finished a job, you would get the agreed upon price.
- Offer a wage rate. A wage rate is an agreed upon dollar-per-hour-per-worker rate. An example of a wage rate would be charging a customer $10 an hour per worker. If you are at a job with two assistants, the customer would be charged $30 per hour. You will usually use a wage rate when a customer needs a considerable amount of work done and it is difficult to determine individual prices for all the necessary tasks.

Pricing jobs is a variable issue, and you may wish to accommodate your prices to the income levels and specific needs of a customer. If an elderly couple needs two guys to help around the house for a week, perhaps you can charge them $7 to $8 an hour instead of your standard $10 to $11 per hour. Determine the pricing formulas that will work best in your community.

## Supplies

Do not supply any materials for customers unless you are explicitly asked to do so. In most cases you can make due with the customer's resources. For example, if you are painting outdoor lawn furniture, you can use old newspapers from the customer's garage instead of a drop cloth, saving the customer an unnecessary expense.

Certain materials, however, need to be bought—paint, for example. In such instances, buy the item and give the customer the receipt, or add a surcharge to the price of the item for having to buy it yourself. Giving the customer the freedom of being able to buy materials himself works out well, because the ultimate cost of the job can be defrayed.

## Advertising

Advertise by printing flyers, placing ads in newspapers, or both. If you advertise with flyers, design or draw a flyer that can be run off by a copy machine. The flyer should be a conservative, to-the-point, one-page advertisement. Using catchy phrases is not bad, but the flyer should definitely include some of the services you wish to offer and a phone number where you can be reached. A one-page flyer, if copied at a reproduction store or a local library, can cost as little as 5 cents a copy.

For many households in which both spouses work, food shopping is done on the weekends. Find out when the local shopping centers experience the greatest volume of shoppers. Hand out flyers at this time to get the greatest exposure. You'll often find, while handing out flyers, that you receive on-the-spot phone numbers or invitations to come over and estimate a job.

Flyer campaigns can be successful, but you will probably gain most of your customers through newspaper ads. Most communities have a weekly local paper that is basically a gossip column and a medium for local business to advertise. Advertise in such a paper with a 1" x 1" advertisement.

## Quality Service

We cannot over-emphasize the importance of giving high-quality service. The only aspect of your business that should differentiate you from a professional is your price. Take pride in your work and always be polite, attentive, and professional. Project an image that says that you are reliable and caring.

*— Eric Davis*

# OUTDOOR COLLECTIBLES

**Start-up Costs:** About $200. **Potential Earnings:** $25,000 to $100,000 or more. **Advertising:** Antique and outdoor shows, word of mouth, newspaper ads. **Special Qualifications:** None. **Equipment Needed:** None. **Best Advice for Success:** Let everyone you come in contact with know about your business. Pass out business cards to anyone you meet.

The middle-aged fellow browsed through my show display, picking up an occasional wooden fishing plug to get a closer look. I was wondering (as I often do when a potential customer stops to look) whether he was a collector or just another curious "looker." You never know. Holding an old Shakespeare fly reel in his hand, he looked at me and said, "I see your sign that says you buy old tackle. Do you need more?"

I replied that I did, and after a bit of chatting, I found out he had several boxes of goodies he no longer cared to keep. He gave me directions to his home and we agreed to meet as soon as the show closed. The fellow had a decent assortment of old fishing plugs, rods, reels, and odds and ends. Some of the items were very nice (plugs worth $30 to $40 each) and some of it was flea market junk. I bought the entire lot for $200 and resold it over a period of two weeks for a total of $620.

The above incident illustrates the profits you can make dealing in outdoor collectibles. On some deals I may make less profit, but rarely less than double my initial investment. As with any business involving buying and selling, you have to know your products, what to pay for them, and most important of all, where to market them. My experience may help answer those questions for you.

The collecting of older outdoor-related items has become a serious hobby for a growing number of people in the past two to three decades. In recent years, many folks not only buy to add to their collection, but also buy as an investment. The appeal of a classic split bamboo fly rod, wicker fish creel, or hand-carved duck decoy is not limited to men only. Many women are buying up the old goodies and incorporating them into their home decor. Restaurant and pub owners buy many of the items I sell for use in decorating (especially seafood restaurants and taverns that are frequented by outdoor enthusiasts). In this business you will meet a wide cross-section of buyers. Some collectors will want $1 fishing bobbers (floats), while others will plop down thousands of dollars for a rare fishing plug or duck decoy.

## Start-up costs

You can begin dealing in outdoor collectibles with $10 or $10,000— whatever your budget, time, and expertise will allow. I recommend that the beginner start small, invest and buy carefully, and spend more time learning the business in the beginning than buying. The business of speculating in antiques and collectibles of any kind is not without risks. Remember always that your purpose is to make a profit, not to go broke with a garage full of items that you cannot sell.

To start, I suggest you have on hand $200 to $1,000 in funds with which to buy. This money should be available at all times in order to make quick deals when they present themselves. The vehicle that carries you around today (car, van, or pickup) will suffice for transportation to and from sales, auctions, shows, and "hunting" trips. A typewriter can be useful if you want to send out lists of items you have for sale to collectors and other dealers.

It is well worth the cost ($100 to $200) to invest in memberships to collector's clubs and in reference books and publications (see end of article). It is worthwhile to have business cards made (careful—nothing fancy) and run a few ads in small newspapers and magazines in the "Wanted to Buy" section. You should also figure on spending money on travel, show fees, and telephone calls.

My advice to the novice is to spend no more than $2,000 in start-up costs (I started with less than $200). Once you gain experience and know what to buy, how much to pay for it, and how to market the item, then it's time for expansion. Rapid expansion (too big, too fast) has been the downfall of many small businesses.

## Learning the collectibles market

After a year of dealing in outdoor collectibles (and making substantial profits), I began to think of myself as pretty much an authority. At a tackle collector's meet, I came upon a frog-shaped fly rod bug that I had seen listed in price guides as being worth $30 to $40, so I didn't hesitate to give the seller the $15 he was asking for it. Nearly a year later I finally sold the darn thing for $5! The lesson here is obvious—you'll never know it all about anything! Rest assured that because of this experience, I became a bit more humble, learned not to go strictly by book values, and decided that I had to become more familiar with certain items and what to pay for them.

Books and magazines that feature outdoor collectibles and antiques are very helpful. Photos and descriptions of items will help the beginner as well as the pro identify what's collectible—and put them on the lookout for such treasures. Antique and collector's trade publications often devote space to outdoor or sporting collectibles. Popular magazines such as *Country Living* often show what's "in" for use as decorative items. As with any venture, the successful person will be constantly learning and keeping up with what's desirable or popular at the moment.

Try to team up with someone who's already in the business. You can learn much from observing an old pro as he or she operates. Pay close attention to what he buys, how much he pays for an item, and how he later markets it.

Another means of educating yourself in outdoor collectibles is to attend collectors' swap meets, auctions, and antique shows. Here you can actually see how items are priced and, more important, what they actually sell for. Oliver's, a firm that specializes in outdoor collectibles auctions, sends an illustrated catalog to prospective buyers before a sale. They will later follow up with a list of the items sold and the prices they brought. The address is listed at the end of this article.

## Where to find collectibles

I drove past the old man who had set up a few tables of yard sale items on a lonely stretch of road that runs from Phoenix to Yuma, Arizona. Probably all junk, I thought—the typical assortment of Tupperware, *Playboy* magazines, and worn out tools. But I couldn't resist. I pulled a U-turn and went back.

Most of it *was* junk, and I was about to leave when I spotted a small box of books and went through them quickly. I paid 50¢ for a first edition copy of Robert Ruark's *Use Enough Gun*. (I later sold it for a substantial sum to an outdoor book collector.) After talking to the old desert rat and letting him know what I was looking for, he produced a beautiful set of deer antlers that I paid $2 for and later sold in Virginia for $40!

Yard sales, flea markets, auctions, and outdoor and antique shows are good, steady sources of outdoor collectibles. Junk and antique shops often produce valuable items. There will be days when you will be wasting time going on buying trips, but there will be times when you hit it big.

A common mistake buyers make is not telling the people who are selling what they are looking for. Just because you don't see anything you want doesn't mean the buyers don't have it. At one yard sale full of costume jewelry and baby clothes, I asked the lady if she had any old outdoor items. She called her husband out of the house who produced a fine bamboo fly rod, a box of old tackle, and several ancient shotgun shell boxes from the garage. I bought this stuff for next to nothing and within two weeks had realized a handsome profit.

Antique shops are generally my least productive source for collectibles to resell. If they do have anything, it's generally priced too high for me to make a profit. But these shops are worth investigating. I stopped at a roadside antique shop one day, snooped around, and then told the owner what I dealt in. He replied that he didn't have anything for me at the time, but another browser overheard us talking and followed me to my car. He said he lived several miles down the road and had some items ("junk," he called it) that I might be interested in. I followed him and eventually bought two old shotguns, an assortment of fishing tackle, and several boxes of outdoor magazines dating back to the 1800s.

One of my better "finds" came by the way of a trip to the local landfill! While I was unloading my trash, the landfill operator came over; we struck up a conversation. After finding out that he was an avid hunter and fisherman, I mentioned that I collected old outdoor articles. Two weeks later he drove into my yard with a pickup truck loaded with goodies. I them bought at a most reasonable price.

Consider advertising in the "Wanted-to-Buy" section of magazines and newspapers, but don't expect miracles. If I average one good buy out of ten responses, I'm satisfied. When someone responds to an ad, set up a meeting to look at what they have. Unless I'm dealing with someone I've known and dealt with before, I never buy anything sight unseen. Remember, you must see the condition of the merchandise before you buy; prices paid are always determined by the condition of the item.

## Determining condition and price

The value of any antique or collectible is generally determined by condition, rarity, and consumer trends. Very rare items in excellent or mint condition will nearly always increase in value at a rate of at least 5 to 10 percent per year, sometimes more. Also keep in mind that the country's economy can greatly affect the value of collectibles—and your ability to resell them at a profit. If money is tight, fewer goods are bought, and thus more of these same goods are available. They may therefore bring less than they previously did.

Determining the condition of any outdoor collectible is quite simple, Here's the guideline I use:

*Mint*—New, never used, in original box, wrap, or container.

*Excellent*—Near mint, all parts and pieces intact, paint or finish good, no damaged parts.

*Very Good*—Same as above, but showing some signs of age and wear.

*Good*—Shows age, wear, slight damage, but still all there.
*Poor*—Parts missing, chipped finish or paint, dented, broken.

Below are several examples of determining grade or condition of an item:

Item #1: Paper shotgun shell box, good color, no damage, two-thirds full of original paper shells; grade/condition—excellent.

Item #2: Paper shotgun shell box, faded, part of top flap missing, no shells; grade/condition—poor.

Item #3: Wooden fishing plug, glass eyes unchipped, all hooks and hardware in good condition, a few minor chips, in original box that shows little wear; grade/condition—very good.

Item #4: Bamboo fly rod, used but intact, original wraps, guides, and in original cloth and metal container; grade/condition—excellent.

A final tip with regard to determining the condition or grade of any collectible is this: don't let the excitement of any "find" cloud your vision. Look closely for flaws and grade as if you were a picky buyer on a very low budget.

Pricing outdoor collectibles is tough. I will not attempt to list specific items and prices in this article, but here's the rule I use when determining what to pay for any collectible: *pay no more than half of what you can reasonably expect to sell the item for.* It's best to pay one-third or less of the item's current selling price.

Always remember, you have other expenses to think of: travel, show fees, auction fees, advertising, and telephone bills to name only a few. Also, keep in mind that any item can suddenly decrease in value due to trends and availability. It can be difficult to make a mortgage payment or have a decent meal with a room full of old fishing plugs that haven't sold. (I've tried it).

Price books are okay when used as a rough guideline, but you can't always bet on them. Actually, the worth of any outdoor collectible is what someone will pay for it *now*. The prices I place on items are determined by what I see similar items actually selling for on collector's lists, auctions, and at shows.

## What's hot now

Items to look for as of this writing: snowshoes, wicker fish creels, minnow and bait buckets, tins, old fishing plugs (especially wooden), bamboo rods, old reels, older paper and wooden shot shell boxes, duck and goose decoys, fish spearing decoys, hand-forged fish spears, animal traps, outdoor books and magazines (pre-'60s), outdoor advertising posters, old tackle catalogs (pre-'60s), tanned furs, hides, antlers, old compasses, metal match boxes, knives and hatchets, fishing bobbers/floats (wood), hunting and fishing licenses and badges (pre-'50s).

Just a few of the manufacturers and brand names to become familiar with and look for: Winchester, Remington, Marble's, Peter's, Shakespeare, South Bend, Meeks, Creek Chub, Heddon, Moonlight, Granger, Pflueger, Blue Grass, Vom Hofe, Hendryx, Abbey & Imbrie, Meisselbach, and Martin.

Note: The word "old" is used quite a bit, and I'm sure many will wonder just what is considered to be "old." Any sporting collectibles that were manufactured prior to 1950 are generally very much sought after by collectors. Some items that were still available in the 1960s are now being gathered up by collectors.

### Marketing outdoor collectibles

Once you've been in this business for six months or more, you'll probably have no problem selling your merchandise if it's priced fairly. I can sell faster than I can find or buy simply because there are more eager collectors who are acquainted with my business than there are items to buy.

For someone starting in the business, I recommend joining the National Fishing Lure Collector's Club and subscribing to *Sporting Collector's Monthly* (see end of article). These two contacts will put you in touch with hundreds of buyers and collectors.

Antique and outdoor shows are good outlets for outdoor collectibles, as are wildlife art shows and gun shows. In many instances you will be the only vendor selling collectibles, and business will boom because your products are very desirable and different from everyone else's. Ads placed in newspapers under "antiques and collectibles" are good for sales.

I'm a bit shy on consigning items of high value in just any auction. I recommend placing items that are very valuable in specialized auctions such as those held by Oliver's.

Dealing in outdoor collectibles has been both profitable and pleasurable for me. If you take the necessary time to learn the business, I'm positive it can prove to be a money-making venture for you, too. Remember, be cautious when you buy. There's room for more dealers in this fast-growing business. Good hunting!

### Helpful publications and sources for the collector and dealer

*Sporting Collector's Monthly*, P.O. Box 305, Camden, DE 19934. Subscription: $12 per year. This is an excellent monthly publication that covers all sporting collectibles: decoys, fishing tackle, outdoor books, wildlife art, duck stamps, guns, and hunting gear. A valuable reference to put you in contact with both buyers and sellers. Often lists upcoming shows and auctions of interest to collectors and dealers.

*Gunlist*, Circulation Dept., 700 East State St., Iola, WI 54990. Subscription: $17.95 per year. Another good reference, especially for those who deal in gun and hunting-related collectibles. Lists upcoming events and shows in all states.

*National Fishing Lure Collector's Club*, 2295 Woody Knoll Drive, Portage, MI 49002. Dues: $17 annually. I recommend this organization for those interested in buying and selling any fishing-related collectibles. Members are scattered around the world and are anxious to buy, sell, or trade. Many send out lists of items for sale or items they are searching for. National and regional events are held for members only, and the novice can really learn and benefit from this organization. The club sends its members a complete list of other members.

Highwood Bookshop, P.O. Box 1246, Traverse City, MI 49685. Specializes in books on outdoor collectibles of all kinds. Write for their catalogs.

*Fish Tackle Antiques—Reference & Evaluation* by Karl T. White. Karl T. White, P.O. Box 169, Arcadia, OK 73007. Price: $39.95 + 3.00 shipping. This is an excellent reference book on tackle, a real help for those who need help identifying and determining prices on various items.

Oliver's (auctioneers), Route One, Plaza One, Kennebunk, Maine 04043. Write for info on upcoming auctions. This firm has the reputation as the nation's leading outdoor collectibles auctioneers.

— *Don Shumaker*

# OUTDOOR GUIDE

**Start-up Costs:** $500 or less for equipment and advertising. **Potential Earnings:** $10,000 part-time, substantially more full-time. **Advertising:** Direct-mail brochures. **Special Qualifications:** Knowledge of outdoors, camping. **Equipment Needed:** Tent, backpack, utensils, trail food. **Best Advice for Success:** Provide an enjoyable time that customers can look back on in pleasure, despite any temporary discomforts.

If you have a love for the outdoors and a concern for the environment, you might parlay these passions into an exciting business. Cari Taylor-Carlson of Milwaukee did. Her company, Tripping Lightly, provides guides, destinations, food, and equipment for backpacking, biking, canoeing, and other outdoor adventure trips.

Taylor-Carlson has always enjoyed backpacking with friends and is quite knowledgeable about the environment. This knowledge earned her a staff position for The Girl Scouts National Center West camp. Later, when she served on the staff of a woman's camp, a number of the participants urged her to guide a trip for them. She says, "I started the first trip with myself as guide, using my own tent and utensils, so I didn't have to invest in any equipment in the beginning," Her main start-up cost was the advertising flyer she mailed out.

## The first steps

Taylor-Carlson started slowly. "The first year I guided only two trips," she says. Today, Tripping Lightly employs thirteen additional guides and offers twenty-eight different trips, plus a day hike every Saturday. The trips include such adventures as snorkeling in the Virgin Islands, exploring the Florida Everglades, and rafting the Salmon River, and local safari-like biking in Wisconsin's beautiful Door County and canoeing the lower Wisconsin River. Taylor-Carlson selects her sites and excursions either because she has enjoyed having the experience herself or because she has a reliable guide who is an expert on that terrain. "I never take a group on a trip if I haven't already done it myself or if I can't provide a guide who has done extensive tripping in that area," Taylor-Carlson says.

## Selecting other guides

Many of the guides who work for Tripping Lightly were originally clients, so Taylor-Carlson got a chance to see how they responded to crises, pressure, and other people before she put them on the payroll. She's been fortunate to find people with special expertise and credentials: an ornithologist who specializes in bird-watching trips; a canoe manufacturer who guides canoe trips; and a naturalist with the Department of Natural Resources at the Horicon Marsh. With a little effort you should be able to find similar people in your community who enjoy sharing their knowledge and skill.

The "mind-set" of the guide is important, Taylor-Carlson says. You and your guides must be upbeat, positive, and encouraging. Not all the experiences of an outdoor trip are going to be pleasant. There will be times when people are too hot, too cold, tired hungry, dirty, or stung by insects. It requires patience and compassion on the part of the guide, because people can get "real crabby when they're cold and hungry," says Taylor-Carlson.

The challenge has always been to deliver what Taylor-Carlson feels is the bottom line for Tripping Lightly: an enjoyable time for the clients to look back on in pleasure despite whatever temporary discomforts they may have encountered.

## Basic Equipment

Taylor-Carlson chose Urika two-person tents, which she finds lightweight and durable. She also keeps camp stoves and cooking utensils as lightweight as possible. For the most part she does not use freeze-dried food on the trail, though she does resort to mixes. Main courses are built around sturdy foods like pasta, rice, bulgar, and lentils. She might make a noodle casserole, fettucini, or spaghetti. She likes to provide a satisfying dessert like mousse or cheese cake, which are easily produced from mixes. There are vegetables and no meat, which takes care of the refrigeration problems as well as vegetarian clients. Muffins and pancakes help to make filling, satisfying meals and are also easily prepared from prepackaged portions that only need water added. Taylor-Carlson supplements this menu with dried fruits.

Taylor-Carlson also carries a well-stocked, extensive first-aid kit and a rope. Clients are expected to furnish their personal gear including flashlights, sleeping bags, skis, snorkeling gear, and backpacks.

Groups range from eight to twenty people, depending on the activity. Taylor-Carlson offers her clients a pre-trip schedule of meetings to help answer questions and give additional information concerning gear, the routes and terrain that will be covered, and what difficulties to expect. The pre-trip meetings are also an opportunity for the people involved to meet their tripmates.

## Liability and costs

Liability insurance is crucial. "You wouldn't dare operate without it," she says. It's the single most costly item in running her business, but there is no alternative. Taylor-Carlson carries a half-million dollars worth of insurance.

Her other major expense is for printing and mailings to advertise the business. Taylor-Carlson says that 10 percent of the people who receive her brochures actually take a trip. She credits a carefully targeted mailing list for this success rate. "We only mail to groups we know have a leaning toward outdoor activities," she says.

Taylor-Carlson and her employees get lots of free publicity for Tripping Lightly by giving talks, speeches, and presentations to all sorts of groups. Even though the presentation might be on a topic like preserving the environment, Tripping Lightly is bound to get mentioned, and Taylor-Carlson always has brochures to hand out.

## What to charge

The fees charged for each trip are determined by the fixed expenses plus whatever special costs the trip might require, with the necessary profit then added. She requires clients to pay half the fee upon registration, of which $50 is non-refundable. The balance is required three weeks prior to the trip. She also sets registration deadlines for some of the trips and charges an additional $25 processing fee for late registrations, since they demand extra effort on the part of her and her staff.

Taylor-Carlson's final bit of advice: "Don't repeat the same trips all the time. They'll get stale." You have to keep your own romance and joy with the trips or you won't be able to share the sparkle and enthusiasm that make a good trip. Ultimately, it is that sharing that makes a trip a special and unforgettable experience for your clients.

*— Barbara Vroman*

# PAPER RECYCLING

**Start-up Costs:** $300 or less, assuming you have a vehicle for paper pick-up. **Potential Earnings:** $46 per short ton. **Advertising:** Flyers distributed door-to-door; store bulletin boards. **Special Qualifications:** None. **Equipment Needed:** Vehicle for pick up. **Best Advice for Success:** Establish well-organized routes.

The pile of newspapers you hauled to the basement last week for temporary storage can, in relatively little time, fill an entire corner of the room. The larger the pile grows, the more difficult it seems to get rid of. Still, a pile of yellowing newspapers can be a money-making opportunity for someone with a little hustle.

Increased environmental awareness has led many people to embrace newspaper recycling. It isn't always convenient, however, to bundle these papers together, load them into the car, and drive to the nearest recycling center. That inconvenience presents the chance to turn yesterday's papers into a profitable part-time or full-time livelihood for the person with the initiative to provide a pick-up service.

John Gilbert discovered just how much money there is to be made in the newspaper scavenger business. Gilbert has been collecting newspapers for over fourteen years, after learning the business from a neighbor. When the neighbor retired, Gilbert took over. "I never really planned on being in this business, " he says, "I just sort of happened into it."

Gilbert collects about eighteen short tons of newspaper per week, selling the paper to Superior Recycling, a Vancouver-based paper reclamation plant. "Paper is a very volatile product," says Gilbert. "The price varies with the local market and particularly with the international market." He presently receives $46 per short ton, no small piece of change for simply picking up bundles of discarded newspaper.

The one piece of equipment you will need is a vehicle. While it's possible to use a station wagon in this business, a pickup truck is much more practical, if only because it can carry more newspapers. With a small truck, Gilbert can back right into the bin when loading or unloading.

## Finding sources

Having a pickup is only the first step in setting up a newspaper collection business. You need to find sources of newspapers, and lots of them, if you are going to get your business off the ground. John Gilbert has an established route that keeps him busy collecting papers five days a week. He visits between 300 to 400 apartment buildings each week, as well as over 500 individual houses.

Apartment blocks are one of the best sources for old papers. Pay a visit to the manager or caretaker of the apartment, inform him of your collection service, and offer to remove any newspapers the building's residents throw out. Set up a regular day for newspaper pick-up and then make sure the papers are collected on the designated day. If you aren't consistent with your pick-up, you might lose the apartment as a source. Residential houses are also a good bet for obtaining discarded newspapers. So are hotels, businesses, warehouses, and even newsstands.

Make your service known to the largest possible number of people. Print flyers and distribute them door-to-door in neighborhoods. Put business cards on bulletin boards at shopping centers, community halls, and churches. Consider taking a weekly ad in the local paper. If your service is good, word of mouth will add more apartment buildings and houses to your route.

You should have a place to store the papers until they can be taken to the recycling center. Gilbert stores the newspapers he gathers in a bin supplied by the recycling depot that buys his papers.

Some sorting of newspapers is required. Glossy advertising flyers and magazines have to be separated from newsprint. Slick paper is not without some value, however. Gilbert is able to get $5 per ton for it.

Gilbert says the key to running a successful paper salvage operation is being able to organize routes properly, picking up a maximum amount of paper with a minimum amount of driving. "You have to be as efficient as possible," he says. "You can't spend a lot of time going to places with only small amounts of paper. In this business a large amount of paper is 200 pounds."

There is competition for old newspapers, in the form of school- and church-organized paper drives and even more from community- sponsored recycling programs. The government-subsidized recycling operations often include curbside pickup. Such competition does not deter Gilbert. "I go one better by going in people's homes, basements, and porches. I try as much as possible to cooperate with the people because they're not getting paid for it. They want to get rid of their papers and I'm trying to make money at it," he says.

John Gilbert is not alone in recognizing the income potential to be had in newspaper salvage. Albert Guilbault operates a bottle exchange and has recently begun dealing in discarded newspapers. "It's there to be had," says Guilbault about newspaper salvage. "It's just a matter of getting sources line up. I'm surprised there aren't more people trying it."

*— Fred Garcia*

# PET CARE

**Start-up Costs:** About $500. **Potential Earnings:** $30,000 a year. **Advertising:** Word of mouth; notify pet shops and veterinarians of your service; Yellow Pages. **Special Qualifications:** Patience; love of animals. **Equipment Needed:** Grooming table, clippers, shears, cages, driers, shampoo, and muzzles. **Best Advice for Success:** Visit a groomer to see what the business entails. Investigate grooming schools. Learn by being an apprentice.

As Sandra Mason was trimming Precious, a toy poodle, her deft fingers worked quickly and exactly. Precious, a regular customer, gets the works—a check-over for warts and tumors, bathing, drying, clipping, brushing and combing, toenail clipping, cleaning of ears and eyes, eye drops, breath spray, and coat conditioner spray—every six weeks. "Some come in once a month," says Mason.

Before Mason began her home-based pet-care business, she worked full-time while taking a three-month dog-grooming course. Juggling her business and her family like a pro, Mason says, "It can really be a family affair." Her youngest child visits the dogs after school and sweeps. Mason's husband helps with the heavy work, repairs, and cleaning. Mason started out in one room in her basement with four cages and a table. Today she has a kennel in addition to her grooming business.

## How she operates

It takes from an hour and a half to two hours to groom a dog. She and her part-time apprentice clip and groom fifty to sixty dogs a week. With the cage dryer, Mason can take care of two dogs at once.

Mason checks the dogs carefully before she begins to groom them. If she finds any signs of disease, she calls the owner. Fleas and ticks are automatically treated. Fungus and other skin diseases are not uncommon, according to Mason. "If you notice a dog with a skin disease, you take the dog to the vet and find out what it is," she says.

Like any business, dog grooming has its hazards. Chows, according to Mason, are unpredictable, and she won't work with pit bulls. When a dog is vicious, the customer is told to take it to the vet and have it sedated before it can be groomed. Mason strongly recommends that all groomers get tetanus shots on a regular basis.

Mason grooms very few cats. But once in a while, if a long-haired cat won't let the owner brush it, Mason will bathe and shave it regularly.

## Setting up shop

The most important purchase a groomer will make is a grooming table. The beginner also needs cages, shears, clippers, one cage drier, and one fluff drier. A tub on legs with a hose, and a floor drain for big dogs is also helpful. (You can suspend a leash from the ceiling above the floor drain.)

Mason advises that you visit local groomers to see what the business entails. Investigate grooming schools in your area and be sure that they are state certified. A good way to learn is by becoming an apprentice to a good groomer. Mason is now a certified pet groomer; she suggests checking with local authorities to find out whether certification is necessary in your area.

Before you renovate your home to accommodate a dog-grooming business, check the zoning in your area. "I had to send certified letters to neighbors to see if anyone had any objections," says Mason. No one did; in fact, two neighbors now work for Mason.

In the beginning Mason didn't need to advertise, because she clipped for friends and co-workers. From there her business took off by word of mouth. Mason advises building a working relationship with the local vets. Clip a dog and then take it to each vet so that he or she can see your work. Mason's advice: "You've got to have a lot of patience and really love animals."

Training: International Professional Groomers, Inc., 4020 McEwen, Suite 105, Dallas, TX 75244-5019.

Wholesale Supplies: Oster Division, Sunbeam Corp., 5055T N. Lydell Ave., Milwaukee, WI 53217.

*— Nancy Miller*

# PHOTO BUTTONS

**Start-up Costs:** $200. **Potential Earnings:** Up to $300 a day. **Advertising:** Appearances at festivals and community celebrations; flea markets. **Special Qualifications:** None. **Equipment Needed:** Button assembly machine, button parts, instant camera and color film, circle cutter, backgrounds. **Best Advice for Success:** The more experience you have in taking pictures, the more confident you will be. Anyone can do a good job with an automatic instant camera.

Candy Anderson's photo button business earns as much as $300 profit for eight hours' work. She works two or three days a week in actual set-up time and another day or two designing and making unique handcrafted items that showcase her photographs, which are sealed and crimped inside metal badges. The profits are great.

"I set up my booth at a May festival," Anderson says, "I couldn't believe how many people stood in line waiting. In eight hours I cleared $300!"

She knew that other people were already making and selling photo buttons, so she started searching for something that would make her photo buttons unique. "I was already involved in handicrafts, such as tole painting and sewing. I decided to put that experience to use in designing wood plaques, cloth rosettes, and pillows that would be a natural showcase for photo buttons. I can also personalize photos by hand-lettering captions for them." she says. This variety enables Anderson to increase her sales without adding a lot to her investment costs.

"I invested $600 in equipment and inventory when I started but later realized I could have gotten by with less. In fact, most people could be doing this with less than $200," she says.

## Equipment needs

Anderson lists the following items as basic equipment: button assembly machine, button parts, camera with instant color film, circle cutter for cutting photos, simple background, small, sturdy work table, padded stool, and a display with samples. Other helpful items include a camera tripod, a free-standing shelter for setting up at street fairs and festivals, professional-looking signs that attract people to your booth, and several backgrounds so your customers can have a choice.

"You can purchase an instant camera for about $75. It should have automatic focusing and flash, as well as the ability to take close-up pictures," says Anderson. "I chose the Polaroid 660 and it has worked out well."

For backgrounds Anderson uses colorful beach towels. She simply stretches the towels around sheets of 3-by-5$\frac{1}{2}$-foot $\frac{3}{8}$-inch plywood and fastens them with large thumb tacks. On the back of the plywood she attaches a hinged board that allows the background to stand alone, like a large easel. Her customers sit on a padded stool in front of the background when posing for a photo button.

Instant color film is the most expensive item in Anderson's inventory. Anderson has been buying her film at retail stores at a cost of about 80 cents per shot. She has looked into the possibility of buying film from a wholesale jobber, which could reduce the cost to 50 cents a photo.

Anderson sells her photo buttons at a base price of $3 each, so she tries to set up each picture for a one-time shot. "Working on location in the street and at fairs the way I do, people don't expect studio-quality pictures," she says. "The photo buttons are considered novelty keepsakes and are bought on impulse. I can usually take the photo and have it in the badge and mounted the way the customer wants it in three minutes."

You'll also need a circle cutter for cutting photos to fit the badge face. "You can use scissors, but it's time consuming and will usually leave the edges uneven and discolored," Anderson explains. You can buy a portable circle cutter from most badge manufacturers for $20 to $50.

The largest single investment you'll make is for the button machine. These can cost from $30 to $500, depending on the size, durability, and versatility you want. Several companies sell these machines; a list is included below. Anderson uses a hand-held model because it is easy to pack and easy to use on location. You can buy button parts from the manufacturer of your choice, but be careful to order the correct-size parts for use in the machine you buy. Button parts come in sizes ranging from 1" to 3" in diameter and cost anywhere from 5 to 50 cents each.

### Pricing and location

Consider marketing costs and economic conditions in the area where you live. Anderson charges $3 for a pin-back photo button, $5 for a photo button mounted on a small wooden plaque, and $8 for a ruffled pillow with a photo button pinned to its center.

How does Anderson go about finding locations to work? "I set up where I know there will be a crowd. To find out about event opportunities I read area and statewide newspapers. Most states have an agency which publishes a list of festivals and arts and crafts shows in their state, too. At each event I attend, I ask others working where they plan to go the next week. Usually, a festival or show that has a history of drawing a crowd of people ready to spend money will continue to live up to its name. For the most part, I've found that festivals and community celebrations that attract teenagers and young parents are the most profitable locations for a photo button set-up," she concludes.

## Expanding

The business can be expanded in many directions. Anderson uses her ability to paint on wood as an excellent way to showcase photo buttons and increase her profits. Other crafters could adapt their work to photo buttons as well. Examples include a family photo button tree, a carved stand, photo buttons embedded in plastic, photo button name plates, a key rack with a photo button of each family member positioned above a hook where his other keys hang, hand-painted hats that showcase photo buttons, leather bands or fobs designed for photo buttons, and magnetic frames for displaying photo buttons on refrigerators.

### Manufacturers of button-making machines and button parts

Badge-A-Minit, 348 North 30th Road, Box 800, LaSalle, Illinois 61301-0800.

Badge Parts Incorporated, 2320 West Greenfield Avenue, Milwaukee, Wisconsin 53204.

Mr. Button Products, Inc., P.O. Box 68355, Indianapolis, Indiana 46268-0355.

The Debbeler Company, 3912 W. McKinley Avenue, Milwaukee, Wisconsin 53208.

Button Designs, Box 34333, Indianapolis, IN 46234; (317) 852-7200.

*— Roy Halliday*

# PHOTO POSTCARDS

**Start-up Costs:** $500. **Potential Earnings:** $25,000 to $40,000. **Advertising:** Direct mail; Yellow Pages. **Special Qualifications:** Some photography know-how. **Equipment Needed:** Good 35mm camera, lenses, flash. **Best Advice for Success:** Offer add-ons such as posters and business cards to boost your profits.

Each year the Post Office handles millions of postcards sent by people who believe a picture is worth a thousand words. Some are the kind purchased by travelers; other are used by businesses to advertise their products or services. Who produces these cards? You can!

If you already have a good 35mm camera, or can borrow one, your start-up costs are almost nothing. Once you understand the product and its market, your income is limited only by your ambition. You may choose to sell just a photo to a postcard manufacturer, or you may want to locate a distributor for postcards you've developed. Consult the following from your local library: *The Buyer's Guide, The Gift and Decorating Accessory Buyer's Guide,* and *Photographers Market.*

The best markets for travel postcards are chambers of commerce, government tourism bureaus, and government agencies. Big or small, such organizations are looking for photos that have a broad appeal and accurately represent their area. Good subjects for these photos include skylines, natural features, and human interest (a horse-drawn buggy or a street performer, for example). The object is to present something they don't already have; a new subject or fresh angle on an old subject.

Businesses are probably the best potential market for photo postcards. To sell a business on your product, emphasize the following benefits:

- Postcards are inexpensive to produce and mail. A 3-½" by 5-½" postcard costs only fourteen cents postage.
- A postcard is more likely than other "junk" mail to be inspected by the person who receives it.
- A postcard can incorporate coupons.
- Because a photograph imparts information so vividly, that information is more likely to be remembered.

## Your market

Three common subjects for business postcards are products, personnel, and facilities. You can combine any or all three of these—just don't try to include too much in one picture.

Auto dealerships are a good potential market. Because they maintain extensive customer records, they already have mailing lists. Photo subjects include the sales staff, new car models, and new or expanded facilities. The front of the card can have a coupon for service or parts, or the dealer can announce buyer incentives such as special financing, extra trade-in allowance, and free options packages. The same approach can be used with any dealer of personal property. Don't overlook dealerships that sell boats, sporting goods, office equipment, or recreational vehicles.

Real estate agents and developers could use a photo of a stately home or large office building with the agent's sign in front. Manufacturing firms can use photo postcards to announce new products or facilities. Use your imagination. New buildings or building expansions, new businesses, or buyouts of existing firms are all opportunities waiting for you.

### How to start

Unless you can afford to hire a professional photographer, you'll need a camera. You can buy a good 35mm camera with through-the-lens viewing for $80 to $150. A good flash will cost $50 to $100. Pawn shops, the used-equipment department of camera shops, and the classified ads are all good sources for complete camera/lens/flash packages, sometimes for as little as $150.

### What to photograph

When taking pictures, be creative. An aerial shot may be the best way to express the size of your customer's facility. Sailboats, motorcycles, and other leisure products create attention-getting images when pictured in use. If your client is a manufacturer, it may be best to take his product with you. You can set up a small studio in your home using seamless paper (available from photo shops).

Be prepared to shoot a lot of pictures. This "shotgun" approach assures that you'll wind up with a picture your customer is crazy about, even if he has to sort through three dozen shots to find it. Protect yourself by involving your customer every step of the way. Although you will want to advise him in selecting a photo to be used, the final decision should be his. Show him a proof of the postcard, usually provided by the printer, before ordering production run. And get a non-refundable deposit of half of the order total, with the balance paid on delivery.

### Printing

Go to a professional photo lab for quality results. A lab will be able to help you with any photo problems you may have and will assist you with custom work like push processing, cropping, retouching, and enlarging. Check the Yellow Pages of the nearest large city for printers equipped to product post cards.

Printers require minimum runs, usually two or three thousand postcards. They have several sizes available. A rush order may be done in ten days, but average delivery time is more like three weeks. While most printers can work from prints, slides, or negatives, it's best to check their requirements in this regard. Depending upon the quantity and size ordered, postcards will cost you two to 20 cents each. The printer will expect a deposit of 30 to 50 percent, at least the first time you order. Additional charges can be expected for these common add-ons: matte finish; additional text or two-color printing on the front side; a title on the picture side; and full bleed, where the color of the picture extends all the way to the edge of the card.

There are a number of related products to bear in mind when talking with your customer, including poster-sized enlargements from your photos and bill-stuffers. These can be add-on sales or used as an incentive for him to order.

### What to charge

If you get a 100-percent markup on the price of the postcards plus freight expenses, you can easily cover your other costs, which will include buying and developing film, depreciation on your photographic equipment, and your time. Don't overlook incidental expenses like custom photo or printing work.

There are a few potential legal tangles in creating photo postcards. Get a signed model release from any person you photograph to protect you from having that person come back later and demand compensation for the use of their picture.

Whether their business is tourists or tie tacks, sightseers or sports cars, there are thousands of companies out there waiting for you to help them carve their niche in the marketplace. So sharpen up your sales and photographic skills, and go get 'em.

*— Richard Ries*

# POTPOURRI

**Start-up Costs:** $100 or less. **Potential Earnings:** $5 to $10 per bag; more for a glass bottle. **Advertising:** Shopper papers; sell directly to department stores. **Special Qualifications:** None. **Equipment Needed:** None. **Best Advice for Success:** Try to get the flower ingredients for free from florists and other sources mentioned.

The flowers you enjoy in your garden next summer can be a source of income for the following winter—right in time for the busy holiday buying season. Now is the time to plan. Potpourri (pronounced POE-POOR-*EE*), a fragrant blend of dried flowers, spices, and scented oils, is a big seller today, with the growing emphasis on romance. You can easily make potpourri at home from ordinary garden flowers or by taking advantage of free flowers available in every town.

Potpourri is a simple mixture of five basic ingredients: dried flower petals or other natural materials, herbs, spices, essential oils, and fixatives. The resulting fragrance, whether spicy or delicate, woodsy or tangy, depends upon the dried materials used and the aroma of the oils blended into those natural materials.

The basic potpourri recipe can be varied dozens of ways. You can make it with a heavy floral fragrance for bedrooms and dresser drawers. You can blend a citrus mixture that will add a tangy scent to kitchens. You can even concoct a mixture with the fresh aroma of a pine forest to add a holiday fragrance to the home during the Christmas season.

Rose petals are the primary ingredient in most traditional potpourri recipes. Roses, along with lavender and tuberoses, are the only flowers that retain their natural scent when dried. However, you can use any garden flower to add bulk and color to your potpourri. You can even create a scent with the spices and oils you blend into the flower petals.

## Think color

The best potpourri is enjoyed for its color almost as much as for its scent. Some of the best flowers for color are roses, hollyhocks, larkspur, cornflowers, marigolds, heather, purple violets, lilacs, strawflowers, blue delphiniums, and lavender. Drying almost always softens the natural color of flower petals (strawflowers are an exception), so to get brightly colored potpourri you should choose flowers with the brightest or deepest tones. Most white flowers (except baby's breath) dry to an unattractive beige, so avoid too many of them in your mixtures.

If you don't have a garden from which to choose flowers, now is the time to plan for spring planting. Flower seeds are inexpensive and available from many sources. If you haven't the outdoor space for flower gardening or don't want to get involved with the gardening aspect, don't despair; you can have all the fresh flowers you need for making potpourri—free, just for the asking.

One source is your neighborhood florist. Florists can sell flowers only at the peak of their freshness and beauty. Roses must still be in the bud stage; carnations must be fresh-cut and perky; tulips and jonquils can be no more than one day away from the plant. As hard as they try, even the best florists can't sell every blossom before it begins to wilt. Passe flowers must simply be discarded, and most florists are happy to give them to anyone who asks. (The only exceptions are florists who make their own potpourri to sell as a sideline in their shops.) You will be almost guaranteed of getting all the flowers you need for potpourri if you make a point of visiting florists on Mondays. However, the best times to get literally buckets of free blooms, including dozens of roses, are the days after major holidays or events. Valentines Day, Easter, Mother's Day, and graduation day can be real bonanzas. In any event, be sure to call ahead. Otherwise, the flowers may well hit the trash before you arrive.

Begin preparing the flowers for potpourri shortly after they've reached their peak. If you use garden flowers, pick them in the morning on the day they first begin to lose their freshness. Flowers you've cut to enjoy in a vase indoors are fine too. Just use them before they droop. Commercially grown flowers should be dried immediately.

## Drying and preserving

Spread the loose petals in thin layers on trays. Place the trays in a dry basement, garage, storage room, attic, covered porch, or any area away from direct sunlight and where the air is dry and still. Allow the petals to dry until they are crisp. Depending upon the kinds of flowers and the humidity in your area, this step can take from a few days to two or three weeks.

You might also dry a few small whole flowers separately to add a decorative touch to clear glass canisters filled with potpourri. Naturally flat blooms, such as pansies and purple violets, can be placed between sheets of newspaper and weighted during the drying process. You can preserve the shape of flowers with more dimension, such as tiny rosebuds or miniature marigolds, by burying them in dry sand. Strawflowers make excellent accents for potpourri. Cut the flowers in full bloom and hang them upside down in a dry, airy closet or garage for a few weeks. The dried flowers are quite stiff and hold their brilliant colors well.

Once the loose petals are thoroughly dry, ladle them into a plastic bag or crock with an air-tight lid. Continue adding dried flowers to the container throughout the growing season or as you get them from the florist. Once the growing season is over or you're satisfied you have enough dried petals, you're ready to start the preserving process. In addition to the dried materials you'll use dried herbs, most of which are available at any grocery store. You can grow your own herbs, too. Some of the most popular herbs for potpourri are rosemary, tarragon, dill seed, thyme, bay leaves, sage, and marjoram.

You'll use essential oils to enhance the fragrance of the flowers and herbs. These can be found at large health food stores, craft shops, and drug stores. Shop for the best prices. You might want to buy several aromas: rose, lemon, orange, lavender, sandlewood, and eucalyptus. Each will impart its own distinctive "flavor" to potpourri, and will give you a wider variety of fragrances to offer your customers.

Spices are as necessary to potpourri as the flower petals themselves. Most experienced potpourri makers prefer to crush whole spices (cloves, cinnamon, nutmeg, allspice, vanilla bean) rather than use powdered spices. The powdered type can darken the dried petals, obscuring some of the lovely color. Just place the whole spices on a wooden cutting board and crush them with a rolling pin. You can buy these spices at any grocery store.

You'll add a small amount of fixative to "set" the fragrance of the potpourri and make it last. Orrisroot and coriander are the most common fixatives. Check your library for books containing potpourri recipes. You can buy either at grocery stores and health food stores.

### Packaging and marketing

Potpourri is traditionally packaged in two ways for selling. You can pour it loose into large clear glass canisters, adding a few whole blossoms for the sheer beauty of their color and shape. Potpourri so displayed is often sold at the cosmetics counters of fine department stores. The salesperson simply ladles it into a plastic bag for the customer. It can be priced by the ounce or bag. If you decide to market your potpourri to stores in this way, you'll probably want to offer at least two different fragrances so customers have a choice. You might have a floral blend in one canister and a woodsy blend in the other.

The easiest way to sell potpourri at craft and holiday bazaars is in small fabric bags. Select a firmly woven fabric in a color and design appropriate to the season. For a summer bazaar you might choose an old-fashioned floral print. For a holiday bazaar you could package your potpourri in bright red and green fabric. In either case, use pinking shears to cut circles or squares of fabric about nine inches across. Place about two tablespoonsful of potpourri on the fabric, then bring up the edges and tie with a piece of pretty narrow satin ribbon.

Potpourri can be marketed for a variety of purposes. A small bag will perfume a closet or dresser drawer for months. Bags can be tucked into gift boxes of lingerie, handbags, or sweaters, thereby adding a whole new dimension to the gift.

*— Jacquelyn Peake*

# RECYCLED GLASS ART

**Start-up Costs:** $500 or less. **Potential Earnings:** $5, $20, and up per piece. **Marketing:** Art shows, fairs. **Equipment Needed:** Kiln, enamel color, glass. **Best Advice for Success:** Take a class to become skilled in the various techniques. Then put your creativity to work.

The display draws you in. The glass plates and decorative items sparkle in the sunlight, their colors dazzling and brilliant. Here's the face of a lion, there's a sea anemone. The designs range from cute and quaint to avant garde, with something for every taste. Customers and browsers murmur words like "beautiful" and "fantastic."

You'd never guess that these striking objects just missed going to the city dump, but everything in the display is made from recycled glass. Old window panes, fish tanks, and small containers have been transformed into decorative plates, dinnerware, ashtrays, and candlesticks, which explains why Lynn Gable, Susan Hamusek, and Val Hamusek call their business "Trash Glass with Class."

A plate that looks like a mass of amethyst crystals came from a discarded shower door. The shatterproof glass was very difficult to break up. In fact, Gable and a friend had to cover it with newspaper and attack it with a sledge hammer! "It can be fun—like coloring in a coloring book. But it's not as easy as you might think. You have to know the techniques and you have to respect the properties of glass," Lynn says.

Gable studied art in school and has a certificate in ceramics from the Ceramic Art Institute in Sacramento. She also studied glass to qualify as a judge at craft fairs. "Ideas kept popping up," she says. Her first effort with recycled glass was a six-inch plate with a zebra. Later she created a complete safari series, including lion, tiger, leopard, cheetah, elephant, and rhino designs. Her plate decorated with the face of a tiger is on the cover of *Ceramics* magazine, and she has written several articles for publication.

When her kitchen was remodeled, she took the old windows and made them into a set of dishes. She quips, "You may not be able to eat off my floors, but you can eat off my windows!"

Soon Val and Susan Hamusek became interested, took classes, and began creating their own designs, letting Lynn do the firing. Then one day late in 1990 when the three ladies were together, Gable said to the others, "Let's make this a business!"

So they did. The other two had no ceramics experience, but they uncovered artistic talent they didn't know they had. Val, retired from her job at city hall, creates designs that include flowers and other things from nature. Susan's designs include sea horses and anemones, reflecting her fascination with creatures of the deep and undersea colors.

## Taking the show on the road

The three women take their work to craft shows and fairs. They appear at large convention centers as well. Not every show is right for decorative glass. First, the customers must be able to spend a fair amount of money, and second, good lighting is required to show their wares to best advantage. Some of the better shows, however, have long waiting lists.

The first show where they took their work was a charity event. As Gable explains, "People paid $25 to get in. We were the 'guest artists.' We took in $1,100 in two days and gave $200 to the charity."

Many people who sell items at craft fairs consider $1,000 as a rea-sonable amount of gross sales for a two- or three-day event. Some consider $1,000 to be the bare minimum. "I hear people say that if they don't make $1,000, it's not a good show," says Gable. "There are all different types of shows and they're worth attending for different reasons." She observes that the feedback you get from people can be valuable even if you don't make many sales.

Their most expensive items are priced at $50 and $60, with many at $35 and under. As Val Hamusek explains, "Sometimes you work on some-thing for days and you know it ought to sell for several hundred dollars, but people don't have that much money." She notes, though that she spends a lot of time to satisfy her own quality standards.

## See if you like it

Gable recommends that anyone considering recycling glass first take a class. The class will probably focus on working with new rather than throwaway glass, but many of the principles are the same. What's vi-tal is becoming skilled at cutting glass and learning how different types of glass react at high temperatures during the firing process.

"See if you like it first," advises Gable, who has taught classes her-self. Many adult schools also offer such classes. So do product manufac-turers, often through hobby shops. In a class you'll learn how to use a kiln before investing in one of your own. Anyone ill at ease around a hot oven could be more than a little nervous "baking" things at 1,500 degrees Fahr-enheit. Working with a good teacher, however, a person who is motivated can overcome the fears which may surface at first.

## Getting started

The equipment you need to start could cost as little as $500 or less. The kiln is the largest investment for anyone taking up glass as a hobby or a business; a kiln made for hobbyists can do the job if you decide to start a business. Gable, who already had two ceramic kilns, notes that they work fine for this purpose, too. Her smaller kiln has interior dimensions of 7 x 7 inches and sells for $130. Her larger one is 8-sided, 14 inches in diameter and 27 inches high with shelves. It sells for about $800. She doesn't have a special studio. She keeps the smaller kiln in her bathroom and the larger one in the garage.

Overhead can be kept relatively low. There are energy costs, how-ever, which vary considerably in different parts of the country. Most kilns are electric, but gas-powered ones are also available. It makes sense to have a number of projects ready before firing up the kiln.

The colors or enamels used to make designs can seem costly. Reds, purples and blues are higher priced than yellows, greens and whites. "You can easily spend $20 on a tiny bag of enamel, but it may last through a number of projects," Lynn explains.

You also need ceramic molds or learn to make them yourself. These are the forms on which glass is shaped using gravity as it heats up and softens. The greater the variety of things you make, the more molds you'll need.

### A perpetual scavenger hunt

The glass itself is free, and there's usually no scarcity of it—once you've put out the word and people know you want it. "Finding the glass is part of the challenge," says Susan Hamusek, and these three, who seem to be on a perpetual scavenger hunt, are ready to haul their finds. Val drives a truck, Lynn a van, and Susan, a sports-utility vehicle.

You also need a place to store pieces of glass until you use them, such as a shop or a portion of the garage. What's left over when you've extracted the glass you can use must then be taken to the dump. Small pieces of glass, however, can become earrings and other jewelry.

### For further information

*Warm Glass* by Shar Moorman; 127 pages, fully illustrated. Covers such topics as behavior of glass in a kiln, compatibility of different glasses, molds, and step-by-step instructions for two projects (including the firing process). Available for $20 (price includes shipping and all other charges). Check or money order to CKE Publications, 2840 Black Lake Blvd., Suite E, Olympia, WA 98502. Phone: (206) 352-4427.

*— Ruth Halcomb*

# RESEARCHING BIRTH DATES

**Start-up Costs:** $200. **Potential Earnings:** $25 to $50 per report. **Advertising:** Classified ad; booth at fairs, church auctions, etc. **Special Qualifications:** Patience for research. **Equipment Needed:** None. **Best Advice for Success:** Use your imagination for entertaining reports.

What took place in the news the day you were born? There were world events happening that day—perhaps a war ended, the sound barrier was broken, or a president was inaugurated. Even if history was unspectacular that day, there were still hit records, fashions, and other interesting things going on. If you like to write, why not offer services as your area's "Special Day" researcher-writer? You can write fact-based stories based on these events for birthday or anniversary gifts. The story can be lighthearted and amusing while offering a composite view of the birth date's news and cultural events. This part-time pastime will be interesting and enjoyable and could even help tide you over financially until your Great American Novel gets published. Prospective clients are as varied as the people in your community—anniversary celebrants, children who want to mark an elderly parent's birthday, or a group of friends who'd like to put together a gag gift. Don't underestimate the potential market.

If you already have a reputation as the "local writer," getting your business known will be somewhat easier. Have you written for local papers, newsletters, or businesses? Just let people know you are also channeling your talents toward birth date reports.

## Looking into the past

Begin by finding the newspapers and magazines you'll need. The library's reference section will be your most helpful tool during this research. Some libraries have special computers that can make your task much easier. Familiarize yourself with your library's services.

Collect as much information on your client's birthdate as possible. Record every fact you think is interesting, even if you're not sure you'll actually need it; these miscellaneous tidbits may come in handy later while you're writing the report. Be sure to double-check everything for accuracy. Keep a list of each source used so you'll remember where all this information came from. Newspapers will provide one of your quickest hands-on records of what happened on a particular date, but don't rely just on headlines. Interesting and colorful items, those which add the most texture to your report, will come from the newspaper's interior sections, where fillers and features and other miscellaneous items hide. Look at comic strips, recipes, advice columns, and horoscopes.

Pulling information from magazines will be somewhat different from newspaper research. Try poring through several varied categories—women's, men's, sports, etc. Use this information for background material, which will provide the "backbone" of your report.

As you conduct research through magazines and newspapers, you might become frustrated if no truly earth-shattering events took place on your client's birth date. This doesn't have to be an insurmountable challenge; sometimes it can actually be more creative and fun to write a birth date report without the anchor of a major historical event. What other famous people were born on that date? This is easy to research through world almanacs. For instance, if you're researching April 3rd, you'll discover that Doris Day, Marlon Brando, Wayne Newton, and Eddie Murphy were all born on that date.

If you still feel you need some kind of anchor, try collecting your research around a central item, such as a popular song, movie, or anything else that captures your imagination. You'll use this element as the "lead" or "hook"; it could help everything else fall into place.

When writing a report on a birthdate that coincided with a major historical event, you'll need to use your imagination. The birthday celebrant most likely knows he or she was born on the same day as the political assassination, royal wedding, outbreak of war, etc. Devote coverage to that major event, but your report's main value will be the coverage it gives to other events that took place. Such events have probably been overlooked by media and history; your birthday celebrant should enjoy learning what else happened on that special day.

### Putting it together

Don't be overwhelmed by all the information you've gathered. Sit down and decide how it will be presented. Knowing what form the report will take should help you decide how to organize information. Here are some possible options.

*Newspaper Article.* If you have a reporting background, or just feel most comfortable writing from a nonfiction vantage point, try composing a mock newspaper article covering all the points you need. Although you're presenting facts, remember that you're also writing entertainment, so the overall tone of your report should be lighthearted and fun.

*Fiction Story.* If writing fiction is your love, create an interesting tale. Is your client a science fiction or mystery buff? Turn your birthday celebrant into a space traveler arriving on earth, or have a detective uncover the birthdate mystery. A special tour guide can lead them through the events of the day or week, creating their own "excellent adventure."

*Just the Facts.* You can play your report straight, address your client in the second person, and simply present the birthday facts. "On the day you were born, astronaut John Glenn was orbiting the earth." This approach can be just as creative as the others because you'll need writing skill to carry it off.

While only a few forms of stories have been mentioned, you can devise entirely new forms on your own. When advertising for business or dealing with clients, you'll have the best chance for success if you offer a choice of possible report options. Then you can please the client who wants a serious report, a fanciful one, or something in-between.

## Back to business

How much should you charge for your services? You might be tempted to set a high hourly rate and pay yourself well for your research time. Doing this may leave you open to competition from local writers and entrepreneurs who may pick up on your idea. Set your fee based on several factors: the number of potential competitors in your area, the range and difficulty of research, and your professional background as a writer; $25 to $50 for each birthdate report is a reasonable fee.

Keep copies of your best birthdate reports (after obtaining permission from the appropriate clients, of course) and put together a portfolio. This should help increase business and reputation.

This kind of writing may never pay as a full-time career. As part-time work, however, it can bring a tidy amount of cash and provide writing practice, if you're hoping to publish that Great American Novel. You also may find that researching and writing for special dates is a lot of fun.

*— Jeri Watlington*

# RÉSUMÉ SERVICE

**Start-up Costs:** $200. **Potential Earnings:** $30 to $60 per résumé. **Advertising:** College bulletin boards, Yellow Pages, local papers, flyers. **Special Qualifications:** Typing, writing skills. **Equipment Needed:** Good-quality typewriter or word processor. **Best Advice for Success:** Once your business begins to thrive, add new services.

Before anyone embarks on a job search—whether he is a veteran in the work force or a recent college graduate—he'll need a résumé. Since résumés play such an important role in a job hunt, they demand special attention. Writing, designing (choosing paper, typeface, and format), and producing them may be a job you have a knack for doing. You may have heard about résumé-writing services, but never knew how they alone could sustain a business. This service is something that is always in demand, can easily branch out into other forms of typing services, and requires little overhead or start-up capital.

There are several kinds of résumés, chronological and functional being the most popular. The chronological résumé is the traditional detailed format most often used by beginners and those who have not had many job changes. For someone with a diverse or broken job history, the functional résumé may prove best; it concentrates the most pertinent information in a useful length.

You will discover that your customers prefer one or two basic formats. Most people will allow you to format it for them. Others may show you exactly how they want the formatting done. In the end, use something that looks good on one page. Always proofread a résumé, checking for typos, grammar, and meaning.

To write a résumé, you must know what one looks like. Check out books on résumé writing at the library, or buy your own at the local bookstore. Keep samples of anonymous résumés to refer to (don't show one customer another's résumé).

A résumé requires the job seeker's name, address, and phone number at the top of the page. List work experience and education in sections under the subheadings "Experience" and "Education." List achievements in reverse chronological order. Your client must also decide whether she/he wants to include a career objective, and whether to have her/his experience come before her/his education or vice versa.

Allow résumé clients to call you at night, because some can't call during the day with an employer hovering nearby. Treat all résumés like rush jobs. People who are out of work hate the waiting game. Since you are at home, you can receive the information "after work hours," finish the résumé after supper, and have it ready the next morning for the job seeker to take to an interview. Request that they stop by a little early in case there is anything you need to change before their job interview.

With a typewriter or word processor (with letter-quality printer), a few office supplies, and a set price for each service—both typing and writing—you're ready for business.

## Profits

What you charge depends on the going rate in your market and what part of the country you live in. Find out what résumé services in neighboring areas charge before setting your price. Some charge a set rate, some charge by the page (from one-page to three-page résumés), and others charge by the hour. You might charge $5 for typing, for example, except in large cities where typing alone runs $25 an hour. Some city services charge from $30 to $60 or more for writing a résumé. Where no one else has this service, charge $5 to $10 to attract job seekers of all economic means. If you must charge more later, you can, but it's easier to go up in price than to go down after you have gained the reputation of being expensive.

## Branching out

You don't have to be a great writer to run this business, but you may be asked to write a cover letter or customized letter to a specific company to accompany the résumé. Sometimes the client knows what he or she wants to say in the cover letter and can provide specific information, but doesn't want to do the writing. Some job-seekers will ask you not only to write a résumé and cover letter but to help them fill out their application, especially if it is a detailed, difficult Civil Service application. This, of course, represents extra income.

Once your business begins to thrive, you can add other typing services. Areas to consider are brochures, flyers, newsletters, and college student's reports and thesis papers. If you just want to stick to résumés, that's okay, too. No matter what you decide to do, by starting a résumé service you are providing a needed service to your community and earning a living from a business that is yours.

### For more information

*The Resume Catalog: 200 Damn Good Examples* by Yana Parker. Ten Speed Press, P.O. Box 7123, Berkeley, CA 94707; $10.95.

*Resumes That Work* by Tom Cowan. New American Library, 1633 Broadway, NY, NY 10019.

*Resume Writing Made Easy* by Lola M. Coxford. A Careers Book, Gorsuch Scarisbrick Publ., 8233 Via Pasea Del Norte, Ste. E400, Scottsdale, AZ 85258.

*Resumes That Get Jobs*, 4th Edition, Jean Reed, Ed. Prentice Hall, 200 Old Tappan Rd., Old Tappan, NJ 07675; $4.95.

*Resumes That Knock 'em Dead* by Martin Yate, Bob Adams, Inc., 260 Center Street, Holbrook, MA 02343; $7.95.

*Better Resumes For Executives And Professionals* by Robert F. Wilson and Adele Lewis. Barron's Educational Series, 250 Wireless Blvd., Hauppauge, NY 11788.

*— Sandra G. Holland*

## SELF-PUBLISHED BOOKLETS

**Start-up Costs:** $200 to $500. **Potential Earnings:** $5,000 and up. **Advertising:** Classified ads. **Special Qualifications:** Some writing/editing ability. **Equipment Needed:** Electronic typewriter or desktop computer publishing system. **Best Advice for Success:** Choose a unique topic on which you can write authoritatively.

Most freelance writers struggle to earn a living, churning out ream after ream on trusty typewriters for little more than ten cents a word, virtually guaranteed to remain poor forever. Most freelance writers haven't learned about booklet writing—the best-kept secret in publishing today. If you'd like to write for a living, are willing and able to do the research required, and have the persistence and drive to see a task through to completion, you can succeed in a booklet-making business and earn up to $100 a word or $1,000 per hour!

Booklets, reports, manuals, and portfolios, are potentially more lucrative than most other forms of writing, can be produced more easily, and virtually sell themselves. The cost of manufacturing booklets can be quite low, and the process is seldom difficult. In fact, once you are into the swing of producing a product that makes money for you, it becomes rather fun.

The three elements of this process are writing, manufacturing, and marketing. We describe these three categories in detail below so that there will be no doubts in your mind when you set out to begin your booklet-making business.

## Selection of a topic

This is the most important element in insuring the financial success of your booklet. Apply a great deal of attention to the subject you intend to write about. The more unusual your subject, the better your chances for success. Creating a booklet on a topic that has already been widely written about spells disaster. For example, many books and booklets have been written about making a fortune in real estate, recipes, wine making, and a host of other subjects you'll find in the classifieds. The most successful booklets are those that meet people's basic needs, like love, acceptance, and safety. Earning money is the most popular topic today. Self-help and self-improvement booklets follow a close second. The topical substance of these two categories is unlimited: anything from how to impress the opposite sex to an acne cure; how to lose weight to legal advice (but avoid writing about medical or legal advice unless you happen to be a professional in these areas). The best subjects are those for which you possess first-hand knowledge: a hobby, work, sports, recreation, crafts, collections, investments, homemaking, special skills, gambling, or love. Almost any adult has the raw material for at least one booklet.

As topics vary, so do approaches. The "how to" format is the most successful. More than 7,000 books now in print include "how to" as a part of their title. Successfully coupling needs with the "how to" format virtually guarantees success. Any booklet in which you can combine plans, formulas, drawings, or sketches with easy-to-read instructions will make the booklet more appealing to the consumer.

## Writing

Any booklet, whether for the glamorous national market or for the smallest of special-interest groups, should begin with a good idea supported by a statement of purpose. State the purpose as one of assistance, how-to, self-improvement, or information for the reader.

Next, choose a writing style. Decide on the character of your book's language, whether it is scholarly or adventurous, technical or general, personal or formal, humorous or serious. Then turn to your outline, which will serve as the skeleton of the booklet; it will gradually develop until you finally fill the frame with details, explanations, and anecdotes.

## Manufacturing

You can reproduce a booklet in a variety of ways, but the two most common methods are photo offset and photocopying (Xeroxing). Photo-offset—sometimes called offset lithography—refers to the printing method by which the ink is transferred to a rubber blanket and then onto the paper. Photocopying uses copy machines like those manufactured by Xerox, Canon, and several other companies. The technical aspects of these two forms of printing your booklet are unimportant. Your local print shop or copy shop can accommodate you. You should know, however, that photo-offset produces high-quality copies and is therefore the more expensive of the two methods. The quality of photocopying, on the other hand, has improved so much in the last few years that its results may be satisfactory for most booklet publishing. It is also less expensive.

If your booklet requires the use of color or the reproduction of photographs, photo offset should be your choice. If you don't need color and merely have line drawings as illustration, photocopying will suffice.

Another decision you will have to make is whether to have the booklet professionally typeset or simply produced on a typewriter (or word processor). Naturally, a typeset book will have a more professional look; yet many booklets that are successfully sold have been produced on writers' typewriters. Just be certain that your typewriter or computer printer produces neat, legible characters (no dot matrix). By either method, you'll want an attractive, easy-to-read appearance. If you're willing to shell out big bucks, another manufacturing alternative is one of the remarkable desktop publishing systems now available for home computers. With the right software and a laser printer, even a novice can produce almost professional-looking results that approach the quality of typeset copy.

## Marketing

This is the final step. There are basically two methods: direct-response mailings and classified advertising. Classified advertising can be an excellent and low-cost means of testing new booklets. for relatively small sums you can test several offers simultaneously to determine which work and which don't before investing in large scale advertising. Many self-publishers rely solely (and successfully) on classified advertising.

You can use direct mail and media for advertising, but always within a budget. Keep careful records of the returns from ads and mailings. This will indicate which ads pull and whether any season or time of year produces better results than others. Use letters, circulars, brochures, or other direct mail procedures as tests to determine the best copy appeal, most effective art work, right price, and other features.

Despite the increasing costs of postage, printing, and paper, direct mail continues to be an effective and profitable means of selling. Mailing lists covering virtually every conceivable kind of market and customer base are available from a great variety of sources.

Writing is a business. The sooner you approach it as such, the more successful you will become. It is important to remember that good, accurate writing is the main purpose of booklet writing. However, it is also true that a poorly produced booklet will attract few buyers.

— *Joseph L. Overman*

# SHARPENING SAWS AND TOOLS

**Start-up Costs:** $500 minimum. **Potential Earnings:** A full-service shop will have unlimited potential. **Advertising:** Business cards, flyers and handbills, direct mail, word of mouth. **Special Qualifications:** None. **Equipment Needed:** Saw and tool sharpening machine. **Best Advice for Success:** Hard work and professionalism will bring business to your door.

By sharpening saws, shop and garden tools for the home, and haircutting instruments for barber, beauty, and pet shops, as well as honing cutting bits for industry, you can be on the cutting edge of a great business. A few suppliers of sharpening equipment, like Foley Belsaw, offer many opportunities based on an all-purpose machine called "Sharp-All." The company also supplies technical training. (See address below.)

## Setting up shop

If you start out small, you can easily get by with a ten-foot by ten-foot area in your home. If you plan to have a full-service business with all of the specialized machines, you will need roughly the space of a two-car garage. Set up your sharpening machines so that you can move around easily. Create work stations so that everything you need to complete a job is at your fingertips. By streamlining your business in this way, you will save time and energy. However, don't streamline to the point that the quality of your work suffers. If you turn out shoddy work, customers won't come back.

Another point to consider is your electrical supply. Refer to the sharpening machine's manual to see what the electrical needs are for each machine you will be operating. Then set up your work area with enough electrical outlets so that no one circuit is overloaded. If you aren't sure that your home or office location has enough electrical supply to operate your equipment, contact your local electric company. For little or no charge they will come out and check to see whether your electric service is adequate.

## Advertising

Your advertising should tell people that you are in business and what services you provide. Here are the tools you'll need:

*Business cards.* Whenever you are telling someone about your business, hand him a card that has your name, business name and logo, phone number, and address. Not only does that put your business in front of him, it also says that you are a professional, not some fly-by-night business. If you operate your business professionally, you'll gain the respect of your community and customers will come to you with all of their sharpening needs.

Flyers. Flyers are a good house-to-house form of advertising They should include all of the information that is on your business card, a list of the services your business provides, your business hours, and an incentive to draw new customers (a discount, for example). Hand them out yourself or hire neighborhood teenagers to take one to every door in your area you wish to reach.

*Newspaper classifieds.* These are used periodically to inform the public that you are in business and to announce specials and discounts. You should also use the newspaper to announce any new services your business will be providing. Yellow Pages advertising is used to attract someone who is looking for a saw sharpening shop for the first time. For the fee you pay, you get an ad in almost every home in the community for an entire year.

These are all good forms of advertising, but the best advertising is free or one-time-cost **Advertising:** word of mouth, a business sign in front of your business, and your name and logo on your car or truck.

### Start up costs

The amount of start-up costs will depend on the kinds of services you plan to offer when you open for business. If you plan to start out small, working out of your home and building as you go, you can buy a machine that specializes in household sharpening needs. With approved credit you can buy equipment from Foley-Belsaw with little or no money down. If you get their start-up package, it is possible to start out with as little as $500.

For more information about equipment and business opportunities, you can call the company toll free at (800) 468-4449 or write them at Foley-Belsaw Company, 6301 Equitable Rd., Box 419593, Kansas City, MO 64141.

*— Charles Hayes*

# SILK PLANTS

**Start-up Costs:** $500. **Potential Earnings:** Up to $400,000. **Advertising:** Direct mail; Yellow Pages. **Special Qualifications:** An artistic sense. **Equipment Needed:** None. **Best Advice for Success:** Have a variety of supply sources. Offer extra services for your customers.

Kerry Robins has breathed life into inanimate objects and nurtured a risky business venture into a blooming success. Just over two years ago Robins was an interior designer with no retail experience. Now, with her new business, The Silk Petal, she oversees an operation whose annual net sales are $400,000!

Silk plants, which Robins calls "plants of convenience" or "plants of today's age," are presently enjoying a tremendous popularity because of their good looks, maintenance-free quality, and trendiness. Silk plants are a necessary alternative to real plants in many environments. For instance, health clubs, with drastically abrupt temperature changes, find that real plants cannot survive. The same goes for restaurants and hotel lobbies, which lose plants in their smoke-filled environments. Homeowners, too, realize that the weekend condo or summer home cannot double as a greenhouse since real plants need constant care. "Most people don't have a green thumb, and these plants look good from the start and stay that way," says Robins.

The Silk Petal Inc. works with individual homeowners and corporate customers to "design" plants that will blend in with the office decor. "We match up the plant you want with the design of the room you want them for, and then it's maintenance-free," says Robins. Silk plants don't attract bugs and disease, don't need light (they can be put anywhere), don't need water (so there is no possibility of staining carpets and furniture), and don't wilt or spot, and the leaves don't dry or fall off the branches.

Robins, who always enjoyed gardening and crafts as hobbies, was raised in Texas, Louisiana, and Florida. Gardening in her native South was never a problem. Then she and her husband moved to Denver, where she found the Colorado winters did not provide favorable conditions for her pastime. Finally settling in the Washington, D.C., area, she gave up plants once and for all—at least the real ones. She traded her interest in horticulture for one in silk plants, and in this field her crafts interest was piqued.

With a silent partner to help her financially, Robins concentrated her efforts on her newly founded business. "I've always been a little bit of an entrepreneur, but not on this grand scale," says Robins.

## Her company grows, even if her plants don't

One of the most delicate matters she had to settle initially was the hiring of employees. She made it quite clear that all of her employees had to have some, however minimal, background in art. "There are many facets to the artist," says Robins. "Not just a paint brush is needed. I look for people who work with their hands—that is a must—even if they have only decorated cakes."

Since her business relies so heavily on interpersonal behavior, amiable and articulate employees are also imperative. "I use a weeding-out process over the phone when hiring new help. First, I notice if a candidate has a good phone voice. Then, I always lean towards people who have pleasant, positive things to say. And again, they must have an art foundation—even my sales people," says Robins.

Now two years old, The Silk Petal is booming. Of course, as a new businesswoman Robins is learning on the job and learning from her mistakes. Poor financial advice and inexperience cost her heavily in the beginning. "My mark-up structure was too low—my profits were non-existent," says Robins. She advises all newcomers to take inventory at least two, if not three times a year and be aware of their profit margins.

Another piece of advice she offers dictates that one have more than one supplier of stock. "I had only one supplier, an import/export outlet that purchased flowers from the Orient. They were always poorly stocked in greenery and would run out of colors, parts, and specific size flowers," says Robins. With no desire to import flowers herself, Robins has become an adept shopper and investigator. "You can't just sit in the store. Investigation is important, even if it means going to the library to look up importers from around the country," says Robins.

Robins stresses the importance of keeping customers happy, and for this reason The Silk Petal has a policy of offering free arranging of the flowers on any plant, so customers can feel as if they have acquired a new plant without making an investment. "We want to keep our customers satisfied," says Robins. She also offers classes on design (both flower and greenery) and arranging (contemporary, oriental, and traditional).

Robins is a motivated woman who successfully cashed in her green thumb for greener pastures. The striking quality about The Silk Petal products is how genuine they appear. "Premium quality silk plants are our product, and realism is vital," says Robins. "Our trees are so natural looking, sometimes even we can't tell the difference."

*—Lance W. Gould*

# SIX WAYS TO PICKUP TRUCK PROFITS

**Start-up Costs:** $500 to less, assuming you have a pickup. **Potential Earnings:** Varies according to service. **Advertising:** Word of mouth; local shopper papers. **Special Qualifications:** None. **Equipment Needed:** Varies. **Best Advice for Success:** Use your imagination.

If you own a pickup truck, you're in luck, because it can start delivering cold cash. Here are six ways to make that hauler bring in income for you in just about any part of the country. The following are only suggestions; they've worked for others and they will for you, too. But don't restrict yourself to these. Look around and you may find some that are better.

## 1. Hauling landscape rock and wood

In many housing developments, landscape building materials consist of little more than cement block. Block walls stretch as far as the eye can see, but many homeowners would prefer something more distinctive, if it could be delivered to the site. Here's where you and your truck come into the landscaping picture: wherever there's running water (beaches, rivers, even small creeks) there are smooth stones, often of amazing beauty and diversity, and equally lovely driftwood. All you do is bring your pickup—loaded to the gunwales with selected rocks and wood—into a higher-prices, rapidly sprouting tract, and show your wares to both homebuilders and contractors.

One rock seller gets $150 to $200 per load.

## 2. Motorized hayrides

Kids in the suburbs may have heard of hayrides, but how many of them will ever join in a pastoral, moonlit tour of nearby country roads? Not many, but a lot of them—and their parents—would pay well for the chance. This is an income idea for which you need do no actual hustling: contact church and community youth group officials and tell them what you have in mind. Hay's cheap, the overhead is negligible, and you'll be pleasantly surprised at the reaction. This has become a regular weekend job for several West Coast entrepreneurs. Youth groups are always looking for wholesome ways for kids to spend Saturday evening; they'll supply refreshments and do all the tiresome organization. And getting $50 or more for taking a pleasant drive in the country ain't exactly hay. Check with your insurance agent about adequate coverage before offering this service.

## 3. Appliance repair-shop delivery

Have you ever watched somebody groan, sweat, and curse while trying to wrestle a power mower or television in to the trunk of his car? You can be sure he'd much rather have someone else—you—do the job with a suitable vehicle—your half-ton. But he can't stand that extra $10 for a service call. All you have to do is set up a pickup and delivery service for one-man-shop repairmen, most of whom would rather stay in their little shops and tinker than shuttle from customer to shop all day. Incidentally, it's almost a reflex for customers to dispense healthy tips to eager-beaver deliverers—a "gravy" addition to the fee from the repairman.

## 4. Hay supply

In most suburban areas are neighborhoods zoned light agricultural, which almost always means horses, not vegetable gardens. Junior equestrians have their own horses, usually kept in small backyard paddocks. Those pampered hayburners are your in: as the hayman, you become as indispensable as the milkman or the mailman. Actual ranches, of course, have their hay shipped in by the twenty-ton load. But the ever-present suburbanite horseman must drive miles for his steed's staff of life, then hoist those heavy bales in and out of the trunk of his compact car every week or so. So you get in your truck and canvass these one-horse "ranches" and offer to provide a weekly hay delivery service. If you're planning to become the fodder mogul for, say, twenty customers with twenty-five horses, buy a twelve-ton load (the price of hay fluctuates with the season), jerry-rig a shed to cover it, and distribute a three-quarter-ton per week to the score of horses. You can easily charge $10 per bale, more if hay's scarce, and clear a tidy $80 to $100 for an afternoon's work one day each week.

### 5. Economy towing service

What does Joe Motorist do when he's stuck on a muddy stretch of lonesome road? He beats it to the nearest gas station pay phone, calls the nearest neighborhood towing service—and gets stuck for $50. Actually, though, you, your half-ton pickup, and a standard-length tow chain can do the job for half the price and still make a comfortable profit. In order to catch the motorist's attention before the fast-buck towing serviceman (who has a $16,000 rig to pay for), you simply spend an afternoon pasting notices in out-of-the-way phone booths. With emergency road calls averaging ten million per year in the U.S., and a good number of those being simple soft-shoulder pullouts and empty gas tanks, you can bet that your phone (and your wallet) will get a real workout. Don't worry about your hauler; it can yank a passenger car out of anything short of quicksand with negligible wear and tear to either vehicle. A couple of sandbags in the truck's bed insure traction under wet conditions—and don't forget that gallon of gas. Don't sell yourself short; a stranded driver is a captive customer and will be happy to pay $20 to $30 to have wheels again.

### 6. Shopping center delivery

Anywhere there's a modern shopping complex offering lower prices and centralized location, there's also a group of older, smaller, neighborhood businesses that must offer better service to avoid going under. One way the little grocery, pharmacy, and liquor store can compete is by delivering. This way the little guy can keep his old customers and gain new ones: housewives stuck without a car all week, oldsters too tired to hoof it to the nearest shopper's "mall" and others who prefer personalized service to slightly lower prices. Unfortunately, small butchers, bakers, and grocers can't afford full-time delivery service. So what you do is contact members of a neighborhood shopping area as a group and farm yourself and your hauler out to as many of them as are interested. Work out a schedule that gives each of them one or two "delivery days"—and everybody profits.

— *Will Borgeson*

# SNAIL RANCHING

**Start-up Costs:** $50 or less. **Potential Earnings:** $25,000 plus **Advertising:** Direct contact with restaurants. **Equipment Needed:** A place to breed the snails. **Best Advice for Success:** Start with 200 snails. Pick one or two clients and sell six dozen a week to each at 60 cents apiece. In six months you can add eight more customers.

Ralph Tucker, a seventy-one-year-old retired insurance agent from Fresno, California, had never tasted a snail in his life until he went to Hawaii on vacation and ordered escargot. He found the dish forgettable. The bill, however, was not.

"I paid $12.50 for six shriveled-up snails," he recalls. "Back in Fresno, I had snails by the thousands in my garden. I told my wife right then and there we had a gold mine on our hands."

Today, Tucker reigns as founder and president of the Snail Club of America, 900 strong, with members in every state and in seventy-two foreign countries. Although Tucker says his herd is small, some members boast backyard herds of up to 10,000 head. Their product has displaced canned imports at the tables of such celebrated restaurants as Kansas City's American Restaurant. "Imported snails taste like shoe leather or rubber," says Kenneth Dunn, the American Restaurant's chef. "California snails are plump and extremely tender."

## The art of ranching

A plumper snail takes time, however. En route to the garlic and butter, Tucker's gastropods amble about a vegetable patch, their diet supplemented by orange peels and whatever else the neighbors throw over the fence. On hot summer nights, Tucker may water down the patch. To keep the mollusks in a mellow mood, he often pipes out classical music from his ranch-style home. ("They love Mozart," he claims.)

To keep the herd corralled within the wooden fence, Tucker has ringed it with a band of copper, which gives snails a slight static-electricity charge when their antennae touch it. Roundup is easy. Tucker sprinkles their favorite food, Bran Flakes, around the rim of his garden and they scramble over. (Well, maybe not exactly *scramble*.) After the roundup, Tucker purges the snails of grit.

"Put the ones you've selected in an empty container," Tucker says. "Put in some yellow cornmeal, lettuce, and some water. The end of the second day, remove the lettuce. At the end of the third day, remove the cornmeal. The last two days, give nothing but water." At last the snails are ready. Tucker boils them in water with a squirt of lemon juice, and after three minutes in the hot bath he liberates them from the shell. They're ready to be frozen.

Replenishing the herd after harvest is no problem. Snails are more prolific than rabbits, what's more, most snail ranchers can get lots of replacement stock from the neighbors. One rancher has a night depository on her front porch in which people can dump buckets of snails culled from their gardens. One snail rancher, a retired police officer in California's wine country (where snails are plentiful) patrols the sidewalks at night with a flashlight for extra snails, which she sells to restaurants nearby. "It's just like an Easter-egg hunt," she says. "I don't make a lot of money, but it's a lot cheaper than playing golf."

## Snail sense

In its slow dawdle through the centuries, the snail—or escargot, as the French know it—has been the hors d'oeuvre of kings, play food of the *bon vivant*, and a kind of "soul food" to the French. Ambling along at three inches a minute, growing a half-inch a year, and resting as long as weeks at a time, the snail simply can't keep up with the world's desire to eat it.

Only sex and food might quicken the snail's pace. Snails are hermaphrodites, possessing both male and female organs. Thus courtship, snail-style, means that after a love match, both partners become pregnant. About three weeks later each digs a hole, lays about sixty eggs, and leaves them to fend for themselves. Those that survive indulge in a relentless lifetime pursuit of food, gorging on lettuce, artichokes, fruits, and vine leaves until they consume their own weight each day. Small wonder the Department of Agriculture considers the common brown snail to be the worst plant pest in the country. Last year California farmers spent an estimated $30 million to keep it from munching their crops.

On the other hand, California gourmets spent $16 million to import snails for the table—and the product isn't very good. An estimated 80 percent are the giant African snail, chopped to brown-snail size and canned in Taiwan. Purists are repelled by the taste.

The lure of capturing some of this escargot market has given the despised brown snail (*Helix aspersa*) a new charisma. Perhaps the most impressive evidence of this changed perception has been the establishment in 1984 of the U.S.'s first snail cannery. Located in the northern San Francisco Bay Area, it is called Enfant Riant, French for "laughing child."

## Big business

These days, it's Enfant Riant's Tracy Brash who is laughing—all the way to the bank. Gross sales in 1987 were $250,000 and have continued to grow. The business was launched nearly eight years ago after part-time writer Tracy Brash interviewed a Frenchman who was raising snails and selling them frozen. Inspired by the story, Brash began collecting snails, and one evening served some for dinner to a friend who owned a restaurant.

"Where did you get these?" the restaurateur asked.

"In my back yard," Brash answered.

"I'll take sixty dozen a week."

Brash's backyard couldn't supply 700 snails a week, but the idea intrigued him enough to start taking snails seriously. And while the Frenchman who originally inspired him was unsuccessful with his frozen snails, Brash is now firmly rooted in the world of heliculture. He gathers his crop from 1,600 acres of pesticide-free farmland and brings it to Enfant Riant's "ranch," which consists of two greenhouses and a processing plant. The snails live like royalty, with a special diet for five weeks. Brash bathes them daily, and with the aid of air conditioners, keeps them at an optimum temperature. They sell the snails through specialty stores and wineries at a retail price of $9 per 7.5-ounce tin containing thirty-six snails. They also send out 300,000 to nearly 500 restaurants in forty-two states.

Ralph Tucker believes that supplying restaurants and gourmet cooks is where the snail future lies. "Our members can supply the chef with live snails, or they can take them out of the shells after parboiling for three minutes and send them by air express in airproof plastic bags with blue ice anywhere in the country."

Tucker has sold his snails for as much as $1.25 apiece, but the average runs more like 60¢ to 75¢ each. He says the club has set an absolute minimum of 50¢ per snail. It costs about 8 to raise a snail.

## How to start

No matter how many snails a gardener thinks he has in his back yard, it's not going to be enough for quite a while. "You ought to have 10,000 snails before you start selling seriously," Tucker advises. "It will take about eighteen months to get that many, and then they have to be the exact size of a perfect snail, 1" long. At that size you can depend on three things: it is seven months old, it has laid eggs once, and it's right at the time it's the most tender, succulent, juicy food you can find."

Some ranchers have made the mistake of offering their crop to chefs before they've established a large enough herd. Take Jim Hauck in Memphis. He spoke to the Restaurant Association and they all gave him orders. Now he's overwhelmed. He has orders for 300 snails a week, and he's had to go into his breeding stock. The same thing happened to Ginger Harr in Ojai, California. After a story appeared in the newspaper, people flocked to her place and she couldn't meet demand. Unfortunately, if you use up all your snails, you're back to square one.

Tucker advises starting with 200 snails. In eighteen months there should be enough snails to sell a few. "Pick one or two clients," he suggests, "and sell six dozen a week to each at 60 cents apiece. Use this as a blueprint for future sales, then in six months you'll have a feel for the business, and you can add eight more customers. Aim for twenty customers at the end of three years. That's about as much as the average small business can handle."

Not every state of the Union provides a natural habitat for snails.

When the temperature gets below 50 degrees, snails stick themselves up on a rock or wall and hibernate on food they've stored inside. A lot of the snail is water, so if the weather gets cold they get what appears to be pneumonia. Still, this hasn't stumped determined snail ranchers. In Minnesota, Connecticut, and Iceland, they build greenhouses, sheds, or raise them in basements where they can maintain a 50-degree temperature. Prospective snail ranchers in such climates don't have the advantage of being able to walk into the backyard to get a herd started. They buy breeding stock from other snail ranchers.

Right now, according to the U.S. Department of Agriculture, snails represent a $200 million market nationwide. Most of the snails restaurants use are imported from Taiwan, where snails grow to the size of a man's fist. Cut into curlicue pieces that look like the snails epicures favor, restaurants serve them in reusable ceramic shells. "Snail fraud," Tucker calls it.

Tucker's biggest job now, as president of the Snail Club, is to educate chefs and the public to the taste thrill of snail meat. "We've introduced an exotic food here," he says, "and people are going crazy for it." A recent Fresno food-fest found 2,500 eager takers for Tucker's tasty samples. "It was a milestone," he exclaims. "Ninety percent had never tasted snails before, and they loved them. Now we'll never keep up with the market!" Snails are the cuisine of kings, he says. "Why stop with garlic butter? There's snail soup, snail ravioli, corn and snail chowder, scrambled eggs with snails." Snail Club members will find recipes for all that, and more, in Tucker's monthly newsletter, *The Artichoke Leaf*. The slogan? "If you can't beat 'em, eat 'em.

For a copy of *The Artichoke Leaf* ($3) or information about the Snail Club of America, write to Ralph Tucker, 187 N. Duke Ave., Fresno, CA 93727, enclosing return postage.

Dick Johnson of Frescargot Farms (1610 14th St., Sanger, CA) sells starter snails for $1 each plus shipping costs, sent anywhere in the country via Express mail. (You won't need many; snails lay 250 eggs per year.) He guarantees they're top-notch producers.

*— Phyllis Zauner*

## SWIMMING LESSONS

**Start-up Costs:** $100 minimum, plus insurance. **Potential Earnings:** $180/hour (gross), or $120/hour net. **Marketing:** Brochures; water safety talks at schools; water safety seminars at gyms for adults; board membership with the Red Cross or YMCA. **Special Qualifications:** Teaching format;

Water Safety Instructor credential; Cardiopulmonary Resuscitation credential, and a Standard First Aid card. **Equipment Needed:** Children's kickboards, water toys, swimming pool with commercial filtration system. **Best Advice for Success:** Love water and kids; ability to see yourself as a motivator.

Like most small children, three-year-old Tommy feels insecure about putting his face in water. But swim instructor Sue Royston knows how to allay his fears. "Watch how *I* put my nose and mouth under water," Sue says softly, while gently holding Tommy's hands. Sue blows some bubbles, then smiles at Tommy, continuing to hold him close. "Tommy, I know you can get your face wet just like I did," Sue says encouragingly. "And don't worry, I'll be right here next to you, so you will be perfectly safe."

Every summer Sue Royston charms 400 children like Tommy into taking that first frightening plunge into water. It's a job she adores—and best of all, she only works hard for one month a year. Her gross income for that month's effort: $30,000.

Royston says that you, too, can start a successful private swim instruction business if you answer "yes" to the following two questions. Do you love children? Do you love the water? These two qualities are the keys to Royston's economic success.

Always enchanted by water, Royston gave her first swim lesson when she was only seven. By age nine, she had so many customers that she started charging for her time: 25 cents per hour. Today, customers still clamor for her lessons, which now cost each student $75 for ten half-hour sessions.

Royston's teaching method is based on gentleness and kindness. After she moved to her current home in Nevada City, California, and started teaching swimming classes there, she was inundated by phone calls from hundreds of parents requesting her mellow lessons. "They'd tell me horror stories about abusive things that had happened to their children in other teaching situations," explains Royston. "I felt terrible turning them down for my classes, but there are only so many students one teacher can handle."

Royston was so alarmed to learn that some swim teachers were yelling at children, throwing them in the water, or dunking them, that she felt she had to take action. A few years ago she produced a video called *Swim Lessons for Kids* to share her non-abusive teaching methods with the general public. If you are considering starting your own swim instruction business, you may want to order a copy of Royston's video so that you can see exactly how Royston teaches. In 1988, the American Film Institute named this video one of the four best sports instruction videos of the year, and in 1989, the International Film and TV Festival of New York gave the video a bronze medal for the top how-to video of that year.

## Getting started

Your next step is to find a pool where you can teach your classes. Although it might be tempting to teach in a backyard pool, Royston advises renting time at a pool built for commercial use, because it will have a high-quality filtration system. "Environmental health departments have very strict rules about filtration systems," explains Royston. "It's a good idea to check with your local health department and follow their rules from the start."

Insurance is another basic requirement for private swim instructors. You might be able to use the pool owner's policy, or you may have to purchase your own. Royston's current policy costs her 10 percent of whatever she grosses on her lessons. This is a sizable chunk of money, but one that she gladly pays. "It would be foolhardy for me to teach swimming classes without insurance," she says.

Royston's lessons are now so popular that she doesn't have to advertise. But in the beginning you will need to let the public know that you are available to give swim lessons. You can always run an ad in your local newspapers, but ads tend to cost a lot of money. A less expensive and more effective advertising method is to create a basic brochure explaining your business. Then volunteer to give water safety seminars at grade schools and preschools. After your free talks, leave some brochures. You'll receive plenty of calls, without spending any money.

Another free advertising tactic is to become a board member for your local Red Cross or YMCA. Start networking with the folks interested in swim classes. These contacts will establish your credentials as a swimming expert.

## Building your business

Don't expect to have 400 students the first year. Royston's classes have grown steadily, from thirty students her first year, to eighty, to 120, to 200, and finally to 400 students, which is all she wishes to handle at the present time. She was able to make this gradual growth over a twenty-year period because her satisfied students (actually, their parents) kept coming back for more lessons. Your initial goal, therefore, is to develop a devoted clientele by giving quality lessons to a small number of students.

By growing your business slowly, you will have time to become well-organized. Royston laughs about how disorganized she was when she first started. "Parents would call me repeatedly to find out when lessons began," says Royston. "If I had just set a firm schedule, I could have avoided a lot of those calls."

As more and more students signed up for lessons, Royston became overwhelmed by the communications required for her burgeoning swim business. Finally, she hired a business consultant, Lowell Robinson, who helped her become better organized. "Lowell taught me how to run my business by mail, so that my phone wouldn't ring constantly," says Royston. "He also helped me learn how to be clear with my customers, so that my brochures answered all of their questions before they asked them."

Now that Royston teaches 400 students, she has hired three instructors to help her. Using additional instructors enables her to have twelve children in the pool at a time, which makes the best use of the space she has rented. "I place four students with each instructor," says Royston. "And I move from group to group, overseeing the entire operation."

During the four weeks a year that Sue Royston works, she teaches from 10 A.M. to 6 P.M., Mondays through Fridays. That's sixteen classes a day, which may seem like a grueling schedule—but remember, it only lasts for twenty working days. Plus, you make more money teaching swimming by concentrating your lessons in a short period of time. And that's the bottom line.

Of course, there is always a bit of work to do during the winter months. In December, Royston sends a mailing to her preferred customers, advising them to pre-register their children. Then in March, she sends them a reminder to send back their registration forms with their $30 deposits. As parents register for classes, Royston enters all information about her students into a computer. In analyzing the makeup of her classes, she now notes that two-thirds of her students are ages three to five, an age group which has become her speciality.

## Teaching methods

Working with three-year-olds is tricky, because they tend to be chain reactors. If one starts crying they all do, which can create quite a bit of poolside pandemonium. Royston's talent as an instructor is that she knows how to create a safe space for these youngsters, a space in which she presents herself as the authority who knows everything about swimming. "I let them know they have nothing to fear," Royston explains. "They trust me. They know that I wouldn't ask them to do anything they couldn't do, and that I am right there for them."

As a private swim instructor, you will undoubtedly develop your own techniques to calm and teach your students. Royston uses storytelling, games, and toys to lure the children into learning to swim. Most important, she abhors force, and advises that you never force any student to do anything.

To order the video *Swim Lessons for Kids*, call 1-800-333-0901, extension 41. The price of the video is $29.95, which includes shipping. For more information on starting your own swim business, contact Sue Royston, SwimSAFE FUNdamentals, P.O. Box 312, Nevada City, CA 95959; (916) 273-7319.

*— Geeta Dardick*

# TAG SALES

**Start-up Costs:** Under $500. **Potential Earnings:** 20 to 25 percent of each sale. **Advertising:** Direct mail, business cards, brochures, real estate company referrals. **Special Qualifications:** None. **Equipment Needed:** Telephone, price tags, paper bags, purchased or rented tables and racks. **Best Advice for Success:** You must have an outgoing personality, plenty of energy, and be familiar with all household objects, new and old, and with current prices, even for long-forgotten odds and ends.

Tag sales are never-ending treasure hunts. For anyone who enjoys snooping into boxes, attics, and garages, has a knack for keeping on top of prices, and has plenty of energy, operating this service can be a sound money-maker, assures Beverly Michael, an eight-year tag sale veteran.

Tag sale clients include retired people who are relocating, anyone moving from one home to another, the newly divorced—even homeowners who have decided to get rid of the old and bring in the new. Many people who want their homes cleaned out are turning the job over to a professional who will examine everything from an elaborate dining room set to old shoes, tag the objects, and assume the burden of moving, shoving, and selling.

Michael, who lists her operation in the phone book as "Complete Liquidation Service," depends on referrals from realtors, attorneys, and former clients. Michael prefers to be alerted by would-be clients three months before they move. She also expects them to be sure of exactly what they will keep and what will be earmarked for adult children, who, she has found, can be more sentimentally attached to objects than their parents. She then makes a preliminary visit and conducts an informal inventory. "After I have seen what is at hand," Michael says, "I urge the owners not to throw anything out. Recently, a client, thinking he was doing me a favor, threw out old magazines and bed linens. Both are good-selling items."

## Start-up costs

The start-up expenditure for Michael's tag sale service was several hundred dollars. There were printing costs for business cards, brochures, and signs ("WATCH YOUR STEP," "DO NOT ENTER," "ITEM SOLD"). Office supplies were needed—sales receipts, pricing tags, hand tags, and labels. A box of cleaning supplies was also a necessity. "You can't sell furniture unless it looks like new," Michael comments. She often uses her own washing machine and dryer to give a fresh, clean appearance to linens.

Once Michael gets the go-ahead for a sale, she does a formal inventory, carefully checking the quality of each item. She goes to the house with sandpaper, steel wool, oil, touch-up pencils and crayons, and enamels for chipped furniture. She has also acquired display tables, garment racks, showcases, and matching table covers to help underscore the professional look of a sale. She found them at sales she conducted where she was able to pay minimal prices.

Michael spends $100 or more for pre-sale ads that run for three to five days in two to four newspapers. The telephone bill and replenishing or renting additional tables and racks also total approximately $100.

At this time she asks the client to sign a contract. "The owner must understand that I set the prices and I will handle every aspect of the sale, ranging from advertising and arranging the merchandise to removal of the items from the premises," says Michael. The contract also states that the owner will be responsible for retaining heat and water in the house and will carry liability insurance during the set-up period, the sale days, and when excess merchandise is removed. If any items are removed or sold after the formal inventory or after a pre-sale advertisement has appeared, Michael is entitled to her percentage (25 percent of the total sale).

Michael holds sales two or three weeks before a house closing or the moving date, with a two-week period before and one week after the sale also reserved for Michael's activities. She needs two preliminary weeks for advertising in local newspapers and for cleaning the furnishings. Before a sale, sets of items like china glassware are boxed and shoes are tied together. Michael price-tags each item. The action is fast and frenzied on the sale day. "If someone is going to buy," Michael says, "They will buy on the spot. By the second day, people think objects will go for any offer. But this is seldom so." Two or three-day sales are limited to "enormous homes."

## Getting attention

Michael's duties begin early . She posts signs around town with arrows pointing to the sale. She attends to last-minute tagging and arranges a desk with an adding machine, sales book receipts, a generous supply of pencils, paper bags, and wrapping materials, and ropes and tools to expedite the removal of bulky furnishings. The desk is always close to the door that will be used for both entry and exit. Michael places a large container outside this door filled with numbers for shoppers. By regulating entry by the number, Michael can maintain a reasonable number of people in the house and keep the sale orderly. She has learned that this is an especially important procedure at the opening hour, when it is not unusual for hundreds of eager shoppers to appear.

Michael encourages clients to leave during sale hours. "Their personalities change when they see people tearing apart the home that took them so long to create," She also posts a sign at the entrance stating, "ALL TRANSACTIONS CASH ONLY. OBJECTS IN AS-IS CONDITION ONLY." An interior sign reminds shoppers that merchandise must be removed from the premises by a certain date.

During a sale, Michael must be alert and ready to sell only at what she considers a fair price. Bargaining is expected, she says, "because this is not new merchandise." In fact, on some items, Michael places bid sheets stating: "If you like this, make us an offer." If the object isn't sold, Michael calls the highest bidder after the sale. "That's our bit of insurance that the item will be sold," she explains.

According to Michael's contract, she is responsible for "broom cleaning" the premises. This means that any unsold articles—clothing, pots, pans, furniture—must be cleared away.

Conducting tag sales can be a full-time, profitable venture, maintains Michael, "provided you stage at least two sales every weekend through the year." It is important to know antiques very well and the current market value of household items of every type. To keep on top of the market, Michael is a regular visitor at museums and fine antiques show, where she checks styles, trends, and prices. She is also a frequent visitor at quality resale shops and rummage sales.

It is essential to know "a lot about many different things," Michael stresses. She remembers a sale when she was offered a dollar for a wrench. "But I knew better. It was a commercial pipe cutter. And it was valued at over $100." She also recalls a punch bowl set the client said she had purchased for $25. Michael recognized it as a valuable signed piece. It sold for $450.

Michael says that a tag sale entrepreneur must be outgoing, possess quick thinking to place on-the-spot prices on objects that may not have been tagged, and have the ability to win the confidence of both clients and potential customers.

Once in the business, make it a policy to conduct thorough inventories, Michael advises. If there is a workbench in the house, examine every inch of both the bench top and the drawers. It is not unusual to find coins or a rare handmade tool. Sewing baskets, too, can be treasure troves. "Women always threw their thimbles into the baskets and these can be antiques. Pure silk or cotton threads are prized by doll enthusiasts, who use them to mend old costumes. Ivory sewing notions, old political pins, and even precious lace can be tucked away into a sewing basket."

*— Mildred Jailer*

# TALENT AGENCY FOR TRADESPEOPLE

**Start-up Costs:** Under $500. **Potential Earnings:** $65,000 to $100,000 annually. **Advertising:** Flyers, newspapers, word of mouth. **Special Qualifications:** Familiarity with construction basics, devotion to quality and customer service, and assertive nature. **Equipment Needed:** Second phone line, answering service, computer. **Best Advice for Success:** "If you look out for your clients, the money will follow."

When Teddi Kessie bought a fixer-upper house as an investment, she was shocked by the incompetence of tradespeople. She says, "I kept getting ripped off. The real problem was I didn't know how to screen them."

There were people who charged too much and people who showed up late or not at all. A few times Kessie had to order work torn out and hire someone else to start over. Kessie realized she needed a better way of finding help. Surely there was a referral service that would recommend reliable, congenial tradespeople. Her investigations turned up one service, but it wasn't nearby and it catered to people living in very expensive houses. She also learned that many other people, like herself, experience difficulty in finding qualified painters, plumbers, electricians, and carpenters.

"I knew there were competent, ethical workers out there. The trick was to find them," Kessie says. So the idea for her business, The End Result, was born. Whether it's major remodeling or replacing a screen door or light fixture, people can call on Kessie for the names and numbers of competent workers. She has a total of 185 active names on her list.

## Getting off the ground

Kessie started out with three partners. She and her partners invested a total of just $160. Because your initial costs will be for marketing the business, printing flyers, and getting the word out in various ways, a larger investment can yield results quicker.

She doesn't charge tradespeople up front to list with her service, which means they have nothing to lose and everything to gain. They bill the clients, and she earns her profits—10 percent of the total bill—after the job is finished.

"Keep it simple," Kessie advises. She believes that many business people make things unnecessarily complicated. "You don't need a computer or even a typewriter, if you don't mind addressing envelopes by hand," she says. She recommends having a second phone line and, especially if you're working at another job, an answering service. Starting out, you'll also need stationery, business cards, and flyers.

As for required special skills, Teddi says, "You've got to like people and enjoy helping them." She sees herself as helping people get work done around their homes as well as helping qualified workers keep busy. Sadly enough, in this business, you must sometimes detect who's not sober and who's lying. You must be able to give directions, too.

It also helps to be familiar with the building trades. Kessie relies on her experience with fixer-upper houses, and notes that some parts of the country have classes in construction trades for lay-persons. She urges everyone—with or without previous experience in construction—to consider this opportunity if they have a genuine interest in people.

### Getting tradespeople

You aren't in business until you get tradespeople to sign up. For starters, Kessie suggests having fifteen to thirty names. "We knew some tradespeople who were real gems, so we asked if they'd be interested. We got names of others from friends and neighbors. If we drove past a building site, we'd stop and watch the work and look at the condition of the truck. If we liked everything we saw, we'd stop and talk to workers," she explains. They asked tradespeople for names of others who were skillful, reliable and honest.

Careful screening of workers is vital to keep clients happy and be sure they call again. Before giving out a tradesperson's name, she asks for three or four references and she follows up on each. Kessie interviews each individual carefully. "We have a conversation in which I ask how long they'd been doing this work, what made them get into it, what they liked about it and what they didn't like. I'm looking for people who take pride in their work and who care about the people they work for," she says.

### Profiting from past mistakes

"We made mistakes starting out," Kessie admits. "We spent money on advertising. Handing out flyers was more effective, but our first ones were too homemade looking." She's a great believer in publicity, but cautions, "Be sure you're ready for it." Her business really took off after a local magazine did a story. Kessie made copies of it and sent it to other media. A major local newspaper soon followed with another story. "We had more calls than we could handle," she says.

In about three years The End Result had net profits in the range of $18,000 to $20,000, and it has expanded steadily ever since. "We grew slowly because we had no model to follow." She's certain that it's possible to build a business more quickly. "You can be earning $200 or $300 a week after three or four weeks, and in a year or so, you can be earning a very handsome living."

Kessie acknowledged that money isn't her main motivation. "My main purpose is to see that clients are satisfied. "I've seen people who are motivated by greed who don't stay in business long. If you look out for your clients, the money will follow," she says. Six years ago, Kessie met a woman who wanted to follow in her footsteps. She was able to benefit from Kessie's mistakes and she threw herself into the business seven days a week and distributed 1,000 flyers each weekend. Her earnings now exceed $100,000 a year.

When Kessie started out, she thought only big cities needed a service of this kind. However, people from small towns and rural areas now call her, telling her they see a need for referrals in their communities, too. "If the world were a perfect place where everybody could trust everybody else, we wouldn't need what I do."

### For further information

*The End Result: How To Run A Home Referral Service.* Teddi Kessie, The End Result, 13061 Hartsook Street, Sherman Oaks, CA 91423; or phone (818) 784-1572.

*— Ruth Halcomb*

# TEN WAYS TO EARN VACATION MONEY

**Start-up Costs:** $100 to $500. **Potential Earnings:** Paid vacation, plus profit. **Advertising:** Posters, brochures. **Special Qualifications:** Varies. **Equipment Needed:** Varies. **Best Advice for Success:** Before the season begins, visit the area where you'll spend your working vacation.

Wouldn't you like a free vacation this year? You and your family can enjoy a few weeks, or the whole summer, in a resort area and go home with more money than you brought. How? By starting a summer business that serves your fellow tourists. Surprisingly, many vacation spots offer only the basics for their summer guests. There are motels, of course, and souvenir stands, specialty shops, restaurants, and gas stations. But businesses catering to tourists, apart from these, are not often seen. Where they do exist, they are booming and profitable.

With a little imagination and a general knowledge of the resort area where you'd like to vacation, you can find several services that are needed and choose the one that seems most interesting to you. Here are some ideas to consider:

## 1. Photographs

Frank J., an instant photograph buff, pays for his own vacation by photographing other tourists, working the beach areas during daylight hours and restaurants at night. At a charge of $2 per picture, he averages a very nice weekly profit. His only expenses are for film. There are no darkroom or mailing charges. When customers like the results well enough to want extra copies, he simply shoots more pictures in the same pose right there.

There are numerous locations where such a photo service would be appreciated: fishing piers (to record the "great catch"), amusement parks, scenic areas, county fairs, and playgrounds. Special activities, such as a church picnic or a scout outing, might also be covered. Obtain a weekly calendar of events from the local chamber of commerce or parks and recreation department in order to know in advance about other events where picture-taking can be profitable.

## 2. Lessons

A number of tourist arrive at a vacation area with big plans for water skiing, scuba diving, fishing, and hiking, but actually have limited knowledge of these sports. If you're skillful at any of these, or if you have experience in any other vacation activity, consider your knowledge. A combination of private lessons at $12.50 to $15.00 an hour, and group lessons at $5 an hour per student, can result in $300 to $400 a week. You'll be able to arrange your teaching hours around your own vacation plans and will be getting paid to participate in an activity you enjoy.

Parents on vacation may be eager for their children to have instruction during the holiday. With this in mind, you can also plan an occasional field trip—such as a day spent backpacking or out on a fishing boat—for children only. These special programs should be scheduled and publicized well in advance. Since the majority of your potential customers stay at local motels, posters announcing your service should be placed in each lobby or registration office. You'll also want to let the hotel employees know of your availability, so they can pass this information on to guests.

Contact local sporting goods stores to sponsor one free lesson for every customer of the store who spends a certain amount on merchandise. This will bring new students to you while boosting the store sales.

## 3. Vacation service

In resort areas, some year-round residents travel during the tourist season. This has led to a rash of burglaries in empty houses. Two years ago, Bill and Matthew W. started a service which helps these absent home-owners. They first asked the police for advice on ways to deter a criminal and learned that professional thieves watch for the tell-tale signs of vacancy—piled up newspapers, uncollected mail, no trash cans set out on pick-up days, unmowed grass, and so on. The brothers now provide a form of security protection by handling the tasks police spelled out on a regular basis for clients who are away from home.

They find their customers by going door to door in appropriate neighborhoods and by speaking with local clergymen, who recommended them to parishioners. They charge $35 to $45 a week per house, depending on the size of the yard.

To protect themselves, they never accept a key to the house. Clients are responsible for setting up light timers and other devices designed to make the interior of the house appear occupied. The young men proudly report that no break-ins have been attempted at any of the addresses they care for. They believe that the mere fact of their presence on a regular basis adds to the appearance of occupancy.

Before beginning this service, discuss your plan with local law enforcement officers and a legal advisor. You'll want to protect yourself from liability should a house be burglarized in spite of your best efforts.

## 4. Guided tours

Many vacationers are unfamiliar with the region around a resort area and some are too timid to explore on their own or lack the necessary transportation. A guided tour may be the answer for them and for you. Depending on what attractions are available and how far away they are, you might offer one hour of general sightseeing, a half-day trip to a scenic spot, an evening tour of nightclubs, or some combination of these. You can use your own vehicle if it is large enough, or rent a minibus. One popular beach resort tour features a dune buggy as transportation. Riding in this is a new experience for many people and adds to their general enjoyment. It is also easier to maneuver in sandy places.

As you plan the tour route, begin by listing all places of interest in the area. Consider including a beautiful residential district or some examples of unusual architecture that may not be mentioned in guidebooks. After you decide what to offer on the tour, determine how long it will take to drive past all the points. It may be more logical to create two tours, each focused on a different category of interesting places. You can charge $5 to $6 per hour per person. Publicize your tour with a sign at the departure point and posters in motels and restaurants. Be sure to list starting times and tour lengths. It will probably pay to advertise in a local tourist magazine or newspaper, if one exists. You may be able to develop trade-offs with specific restaurants, in which each of you promotes business for the other. For example, you could agree to distribute a sample menu to each tour passenger in exchange for a specified number of free meals for yourself.

Develop a monologue to make riders aware of what they are seeing. Try the tour out first on family or friends. Ask them to make suggestions on your route and your speech, then make any necessary adjustments. Offer a reduced price for children and a discount for groups or families. This will help to build business quicker.

### 5. Artist on display

If you are a craftsperson or artist, you can offer to work in public view—in a store, in a display window, or in an outdoor restaurant. Your presence will bring interested bystanders to the place of business and will almost certainly increase sales for the owner. At the same time, you'll be receiving a rent-free work area and attracting customers who may wish to buy your handicrafts or art.

If you're not artistic, consider bringing a craftsperson and an appropriate store owner together in exchange for a percentage of sales during the first week. All three of you stand to gain.

### 6. Mobile produce stand

Business at summer roadside stands is steadily increasing each year, but unless you happen to live on a farm near a tourist area, you probably won't be able to sell your own produce in this manner. However, you can earn money by purchasing produce at such a stand, driving to a central spot near where tourists gather, and reselling it from the back of your car at a marked-up price.

Customers like this service for several reasons. They get fruits and vegetables with just-picked flavor; they don't have to stop their activities to find a store; and they needn't change out of their bathing suits or other casual clothes to shop. With a growing number of people devoted to natural foods, this service can be popular and profitable.

Establish a schedule of times when you will be at each stop you make. Photocopy announcements of your service and distribute these weekly to all motel rooms with kitchen facilities. Families who rent these units often avoid restaurants to save money and will be likely customers for you.

## 7. Taxi shuttle service

Parking is almost always at a premium in resort areas. Vacationers often have to fight for a space to leave their cars and then walk several long blocks to their destination. Tony D. realized this situation last summer and started a taxi shuttle service.

First he located a deserted lot about a mile from the center of town and persuaded the owner to make it a parking lot. The two men split the cost of signs directing people to the new lot. Tony also ordered a sign announcing his every-twenty-minutes shuttle service to the downtown area. Drivers leave their cars on the lot and ride with Tony in his station wagon the rest of the distance. He charges $5 a passenger.

At night he converts the shuttle into a taxi to take vacationers to restaurants, nightclubs, and other popular places where parking is scarce. The charge is agreed on in advance, based on the number of passengers and where they are going. During shuttle service hours he tells riders that he is available for night driving if they need transportation, thus creating a form of free advertising.

A shuttle service can work profitably on a variety of routes. Some examples: along a large beach, around a popular shopping district, from a campground to a nature trail, or between a hotel and a fishing spot.

Check in advance with the appropriate authority to learn whether you'll need a license. Also make sure that storekeepers and others along your route know of the service so that they can inform their customers.

## 8. Laundry service

People on vacation would like a holiday from doing the family laundry, but clothes continue to get dirty. This means that someone has to stop having fun and go off in search of a laundromat. You can fill a very real need by offering to collect soiled clothing, wash it, and return it dry and folded. A reasonable charge for this is $10 to $12 per machine load.

Publicize your service with photocopied announcements distributed in smaller motels (large ones usually have laundry facilities on the premises) and through real estate agents who handle summer cottage rentals.

Give each customer of supply of plastic bags such as the one sold to line trash cans. One of these can serve as a makeshift laundry hamper and, when full, will be easy for you to carry. The system also helps you keep each family's laundry together.

## 9. Beach lockers

There is often no good way to keep valuables safe around an outdoor recreation area or beach. People dislike leaving money, credit cards, or watches behind in their rooms, and they sometimes need these during part of the day. You can help by starting a locker rental service. A charge of $2.50 to $3 a day is reasonable. Used lockers can be purchased from a school or at an auction.

Set the lockers up on a direct route between the parking area and beach or near hotels. In some places you may be able to locate them right on the sand. Use combination locks rather than those that require keys. Seal the combinations in transparent plastic and provide a safety pin.

## 10. Restaurant delivery service

Vacationers who want to eat in after a day of sightseeing or physical activity have trouble finding restaurants that deliver. However, many of them do have food to go. You can combine these two facts into a profitable service delivering take-out food to tourist motels, if you have your own transportation.

Marian and Brian H. found a seafood restaurant that packaged dinners to go but was losing business because it was not centrally located. The couple proposed a food delivery route using their camper. The restaurant agreed to test this for one month. At the end of that time, business had picked up almost 20 percent and everyone was happy.

## Finding the right summer business

Before the season begins, visit the area where you'll spend your working vacation. Use a day or two to look over existing services and talk to local business people. They may be able to tell you what services last year's tourists had trouble finding. If possible, locate some people who have spent a holiday in the area; ask the same questions of them.

When you have narrowed the field of possible business down to one that seems best for you, discuss your idea with as many people as you can. The chamber of commerce and the police department may also have helpful information for you. Be sure to ask if a license or permit will be needed.

Prepare your advertising and promotional materials ahead and set up a distribution system. Then take a well-deserved rest and look forward to June. This may be your best summer ever.

*— Margaret Opsata*

# TRAVEL WRITING

**Start-up Costs:** $200 to $5,000 a year. **Potential Earnings:** Up to $50,000 for experienced full-timers. **Advertising:** Direct queries to publishers. **Special Qualifications:** Writing ability. **Equipment Needed:** Typewriter or word processor, camera, pocket tape recorder. **Best Advice for Success:** Be persistent, learn from rejections, and always give your editors and readers top quality, plus a little extra.

Last year, writer Katy Williams explored the streets of Bangkok, visited Moscow and Berlin, and rubbed elbows with most of the best marathon runners in the world. Claire Walter skied some of the finest slopes in Europe, and North and South America. I bungee-jumped out of a hot air balloon, ski toured alpine lodges in the Rocky Mountains, and climbed Sicily's volcanic Mt. Etna.

And someone else paid for these adventures!

Travel writing is a little-known "lifestyle" profession. While you probably won't get rich doing it, with persistence and ingenuity you can travel virtually anywhere in the world for free, and get paid for writing about your wanderings.

Thumb through the magazines at your local newsstand. *Backpacker* magazine urges you to climb mountain paths. *Gourmet* magazine describes the ultimate coffee shop. *Travel and Leisure* touts expensive cruises and Parisian boutiques. In fact, most of the magazines on the rack run travel or travel-related articles.

Travel writers routinely fly around the world to wine, dine and adventure their hearts out, all at someone else's expense. They can do this because countries, sporting events, restaurants, tour operators, and all sorts of other organizations need and want publicity to bring in tourism to finance their cause. Travel writers are often the cheapest, most effective way for these groups to get this exposure.

Travel writing, however, is a highly competitive business. For the amount of effort you as a writer expend, the pay is often terrible. Many travel writers write part-time for the travel perks, and support themselves with another job.

## Getting started

First, educate yourself in the business of travel writing. Read *The Travel Writer's Handbook* by Louise Purwin Zobel (Writer's Digest Books), and *The Traveling Photographer* by Ann and Carl Purcell (Amphoto Books). Their clear, step-wise approach will give you the foundations of how travel research, writing, and selling is done.

*Get a Story Idea.* It doesn't have to be exotic to you, as long as it is interesting to someone. Mating season at the local zoo might seem a recycled, passé idea to you, but each spring also brings in a new generation of students fascinated by baby bear cubs. Scan back issues of magazines and newspaper travel sections to get ideas, and don't be afraid to recycle old ideas with a new slant or focus.

*Research the Idea.* Glean enough facts, tastes, smells, and sounds to interest an editor. Your immediate purpose will be to write a one- or two-page query letter which will sell your magazine editor hook, line, and sinker on your irresistible idea. You are not yet ready, however, to do a lengthy, exhaustive research on an idea which may or may not sell. Libraries, bookstore travel sections, personal contacts, and the traveler's "grapevine" are all useful sources of research information.

*Determine Your Markets.* Thousands of periodicals around the world publish travel articles, many of which are described in the publications listed below in "Markets." Cull through the publications to see which might find your idea interesting, make a list and prioritize it, usually from highest paying to lowest paying.

*Query Markets and Get an Assignment.* To reach out and grab your prospective editor, your one- or two-page query letter must concisely present your idea in an irresistible fashion. You should tailor the idea to fit the length, style, and needs of that particular publication. Though formerly frowned upon, the only practical way to make money travel writing is to query many different publications with your idea at once. Experienced writers may have fifty or more queries on a dozen ideas circulating at any given time. Read *The Travel Writer's Handbook*'s excellent chapter on the art of query-letter writing. The query is your single most effective sales tool.

### Free travel

Get free travel, if the destination, event, or subject is not located near you. Though many writers salivate over the thought of free travel, many don't realize how easy it is. The key is to first have an assignment from a magazine or major newspaper. With this powerful tool in hand, approach tourism boards, race directors, cruise companies, and foreign embassies for free travel and accommodations. For example, Katy Williams got an assignment to cover the Coast-to-Coast Triathlon in New Zealand for *Triathlete* magazine in America. She then called the New Zealand Tourism Board, informing them that she was a writer on assignment, and asked if they could help with travel costs. They responded by paying her air ticket, arranging free lodging, and even went so far as to chauffeur her around the country to glaciers and rain forests for two weeks, while she gathered information for several other travel articles.

Why will tourism boards and other associations give writers and photographers free travel? Because their business is to promote travel, tourism, or specific events on a limited budget. It is simply more cost effective for them to spend $3,000 to import a writer to write an article, than it is to take out advertisements of equal size, which might cost $15,000 or more. More to the point, the traveling public reads articles thoroughly, whereas they most often ignore ads. Your article has a cash value to them: they measure its column inches when printed, then call the magazine's or newspaper's ad department to find out how much an ad of equivalent size would cost. You end up being the most effective and cheapest way to promote their cause.

## Produce the article

When you travel, gather every last scrap of information, including travel costs, the price of a cup of coffee, the taste of yak cheese, the smell of the incense wafting through the temple, the clamor of the marketplace, and expressions of children, peddlers, and of yourself. Your article must do two vital things at once: inform and entertain. Your readers must smell that baboon, hear the rattle of the rickshaws, and taste the acrid smoke of the cremation. Use a pocket dictation tape recorder, a notebook, and a camera to capture all the facts and emotions of the scene. Then, when you write your article, immerse your readers in a sea of sensations.

*Take Photographs.* Photos greatly increase the worth of your article, and are a great sales tool. Become proficient with a good 35mm camera (pocket instamatics don't cut it), and shoot color slides (unless asked to shoot black-and-white or prints by your editor). Take action shots, "survey" shots of the entire scene, "midrange" shots of people or groups of people, and closeups of supporting items (flowers, pottery in shop windows, etc.). Try to capture people doing something in at least 80 percent of your photos. Take 200 photos and send the best ten.

*Polish Your Article.* Rewrite it, and then rewrite it again until it flows and glows. Then put it down for a few days and repeat the process. When you lick the stamp, your manuscript should be as good as you can possibly make it. Make absolutely sure of your facts, spelling, and other details. Always try to give something extra, above and beyond the norm, to grab your readers and hold them. Your manuscript should be a complete package, with photos and slides neatly captioned, with all relevant data included, and with a cover letter to the editor. Editors are often harried, overworked, and underpaid former-writers who would rather see themselves sunning on that beach than nursing a half-hearted, amateur manuscript. Be professional, and make their lives as easy as possible, and pretty soon they may be calling you with assignments. Quality counts.

## Other markets

Newspaper markets are somewhat different from magazine markets. While small papers get most of their travel articles from staff or from the wire services, large papers like the Los Angeles *Times* and Boston *Globe* regularly use freelance work. Instead of querying the travel editors with an idea, you simply write the article "on speculation," package it up, and ship it to them with a self-addressed, stamped return envelope. If they like it they will call you. If, however, you get the manuscript back in the mail a few weeks later with a form rejection, you simply package it up again and ship it off to the next paper on your list. While you can sell your story once to a magazine with national circulation, you can sell the same article many times to non-competing newspapers with different regional or city circulations. These multiple sales make newspaper writing monetarily practical.

International magazine markets can be even more lucrative than domestic American markets. To overcome the long time delays associated with international mail, experienced writers regularly query European, Asian, African, and other magazines by fax. Fax services are readily available in most towns. If you find yourself selling overseas regularly, get a fax machine of your own and subscribe to AT&T's Reach Out World plan to reduce phone costs. Faxes also help you coordinate your travel plans with tourism bureaus and other destination organizations.

## Personal habits

You will need to cultivate a thick skin. Editors will reject your ideas over and over, because the idea does not fit their current needs, because your query failed to interest them sufficiently, or because they already have the same idea in the works with another author. Be persistent!

Read all the magazines and newspapers you can get your hands on, every week. By being well informed politically, socially, and in other ways, you can beat competing writers to the punch on new trends, destinations, and issues. Analyze other writers' travel articles. Why does one article make you sweat with anticipation while another tastes like sawdust? Integrate the good techniques into your own style.

Just do it. As a freelancer, you are your own boss. While this sounds good at first, you will soon realize there is no manager storming down the hall, whip in hand, to get you moving. You must crack your own whip. Procrastinators don't make it as travel writers.

## Add horsepower

Regular sales of your articles means regular trips and cash in your pocket. Since travel writing, like most freelance writing, tends to be 75 percent marketing (which pays nothing) and only 25 percent actual writing (which puts bread on your table), shift the balance away from marketing by obtaining regular work.

To get a reliable stream of assignments, cultivate a personal relationship with your editor so he or she knows you, is comfortable with your ideas, style and quality, and finds you reliable and timely. These personal relationships are extremely important. Editors are far more likely to assign a story to a writer they know and trust than to a stranger who sent them an unsolicited query letter. If an editor accepts one story from you, hit him again and again and again with more ideas. And do it within a few weeks of your first story. Show an interest in them, and they are more likely to show an interest in your ideas.

Attend travel and tourism conferences. "It's a source for trips, it's a source for sources. I got offered a trip through the Swedish canals just by meeting a tour operator," said Katy Williams. Hand out your business card at every opportunity.

Another way to add clout to your image is to join two nationally known writers' societies. Since you must sell a certain number of articles per year to join them, your membership is a prestigious calling card on your letterhead which proves to editors that you can produce quality, saleable work.

The American Society of Journalists and Authors (ASJA) is a network of writers all around the country. In addition to its many writer support and information services, the psychological advantages of regular meetings with other writers include networking, idea pooling, and friendly shoulders on which to cry. Requirements are eight to ten recently published magazine features, two books, or a dozen or more recent newspaper articles. Contact: ASJA, 1501 Broadway, Suite 302, New York NY 10036, (212) 997-0947.

The Society of American Travel Writers (SATW) is composed of the cream-of-the-cream of travel writers. Entrance standards are tough—roughly twenty or more different magazine features (reprints don't count) in high circulation publications within a period of one year. Benefits are equally good, however. Members are routinely called for free travel, editors seek out SATW members for assignments, and your status as a producing writer is high in all arenas. Call (202) 429-6639 in Washington D.C. for more information.

If travel writing sounds hard, it is—full-time. The secret is to start part-time and get something published somewhere. Then build on it. The benefits come after the hard work.

## For more information, see:

*Travel Writer's Markets* by Elaine O'Gara. Harvard Common Press.
*Writer's Market*. Writer's Digest Books (yearly).

*Travelwriter Marketletter*. Robert Scott Milne, Waldorf Astoria,
Suite 1850, New York NY 10022. Keeps you up to date on who is buying
what topics; $60/year.

*Travel Publishing News Newsletter* c/o Elaine O'Gara, Editor. Win-
terbourne Press, 2015 17th Ave., San Francisco, CA 94116; (415) 731-
8239. Covers travel related books.

*Markets Abroad Newsletter*. Strawberry Media Inc., 2460 Lexington
Drive, Owosso, MI 48867. Covers international publications.

*Travel Free: How To Make A Fortune And Travel Absolutely Free.*
207-page book explains how. E.A. Morgan Publishing Co., P.O. Box 1375,
Huntington, NY 11743-1375; $21.95.

— *Erik Hyypia*

# TUTORING

**Start-up Costs:** $500 or less. **Potential Earnings:** $12 to
$15 an hour per student. **Advertising:** Referrals from teach-
ers and parents. **Special Qualifications:** Teaching experience. **Equipment Needed:** Textbooks. **Best Advice for
Success:** A primary goal should be to instill self-confidence
in the student—that's half the battle.

Deborah Schadler and her friend Karen Horoschak were often frustrated in
their years of public school teaching in not being able to give individual
help to those students they knew could benefit from one-to-one tutoring.
They simply didn't have the time. Schadler and Horoschak retired from
teaching to raise their children, but still tutored friends' children as a favor.

When Schadler began to tutor almost every day, she decided to turn
it into a real business. First she established accounts with the major publishers of educational materials. Establishing these accounts was important," Schadler says, "because I would often have to place a phone order so
I could have materials delivered the next day and be billed later. I couldn't
wait weeks to have an order processed through the mail, especially when a
parent wanted his child tutored immediately!"

Schadler conducts her business from her home. Its unclassroom-like
atmosphere helps students feel relaxed and ready to learn. She tutors students in grades K-12 from five surrounding school districts throughout the
year. "We begin with a few students in September," says Schadler, "and by
March we are packed with students who need help to pass a course or

work toward a scholarship." Schadler and Horoschak get very few students through newspaper advertising, even in the special educational issues. Most of their referrals are "by word of mouth." Parents will make the first initial contact, then Schadler and Horoschak will contact the school district and the student's teacher and guidance counselor.

## Working with teachers

Schadler and Horoschak strive to work with the school district and teachers, but they have found the biggest problem in schools is "the lack of communication between the teacher, student, and parent," The two have compiled a simple, quick checklist for the teacher to fill out initially, then weekly, so Schadler and Horoschak can monitor a student's progress in the subject for which he or she is being tutored. This checklist has been valuable in bridging this communication gap.

With such support, students soon realize Schadler and Horoschak really care about their progress. The students, in turn, try harder to improve. Parent involvement after the first initial contact is one of support. "Sometimes," Schadler says, "we have to 'educate' the parent into stressing the positive, not the negative." After assurance from the parents that they will give positive encouragement, Schadler and Horoschak begin tutoring.

With an elementary student, Schadler never tutors the student without a recommendation from the teacher. Promoting a good self-image in a student of this age is one of the most important factors. For this reason, Schadler and Horoschak like to have elementary students referred to them at as early a grade level as possible. Schadler says they find that by fourth grade many students are already "locked-in" to a certain concept of themselves.

With the elementary child, Schadler and Horoschak will also use totally different texts from the classroom texts, so that the material will be new and interesting for the child. This makes it easier to keep up the child's interest in learning.

With the secondary student, after the initial request for tutoring by the parent, Schadler or Horoschak will contact the teacher, then report back to the parent as to what areas the student needs help in. Schadler says the objective for students of this age is usually to pass that particular course. They want the student to "get through" that course on a report card basis.

Schadler and Horoschak do not tutor only students who are having difficulty. They also tutor honors students who are competing for scholarships and preparing for SATs, and some who are attending college. When students who are having difficulty in a subject hear that such "top" students are being tutored by Schadler and Horoschak, they don't feel so "dumb."

## What to charge

Because most of the students are from middle-class families,

Schadler and Horoschak try to make their service affordable. They charge $12 to $15 an hour, which covers the cost of materials, maintenance of the equipment, and their profit. Schadler says, "The biggest cost is having to buy books from the same companies as school districts, which do not, as a rule, shop around for the best prices." These materials are expensive.

There have been some surprising sidelines to Schadler's and Horoschak's business. Schadler teaches at the local high school's adult evening school, and both Schadler and Horoschak teach homebound students who are recuperating from illness, accident, or an operation. A surprise for Schadler was the number of requests from the parents of her students who said they had never quite grasped a subject and would like some extra help. Schadler schedules these adult students to come in the daytime, before the school students begin to come in the afternoon at 3 p.m.

At first Schadler was afraid the material for adults would be too juvenile, but found most publishing houses have good educational material at the adult level. For a fee of $100, Schadler will give the adult student a complete battery of tests to determine the adult's level. Included in the fee are the materials and tutoring by Schadler or Horoschak until the person completes the course.

Another branch of Schadler's business was the establishment of study groups. Students come with others at designated times to do homework and research, and prepare for tests. If they need help, Schadler and Horoschak are there to help them.

## More sidelines

Local businesses have approached Schadler and Horoschak to provide still another business sideline. One business hired Schadler to teach a grammar "refresher" course to fourteen men who were promoted to managerial positions. The company president wanted the men to be able to use the correct business English and grammar to "fit" their new positions. Still another local business asked Schadler to help the large number of Hispanic employees become better acquainted with English.

The most exciting sideline of Schadler's business is the summer program she and Horoschak direct. "This is our program!" Schadler says. "We don't have to follow any other teacher's plans. There are no limits to the creativity we can put into the sessions," which they call the "Summer Reading Maintenance Program." There are incentives and rewards for the students as they work on reading skills so they will not fall behind in the summer months. Schadler and Horoschak hold a party at the end of summer for the students who attended their program.

*— Priscilla Y. Huff*

# TYPING PROFITS

**Start-up Costs:** $500 to $3,500 (depending on equipment purchased and extent of advertising). **Potential Earnings:** $240 to $500 per week. **Advertising:** Writer's magazines, postings on college bulletin boards, brochures and business cards, word of mouth. **Special Qualifications:** Excellent typing skills. **Equipment Needed:** Electronic typewriter or word processor or computer with word processing software. **Best Advice for Success:** Deliver what you promise when you promise it.

Can you type? Do you own a typewriter, word processor, or home computer? If you answered "yes" to both questions, then you've already completed the first two steps of starting your own at-home typing business. A typing business is an ideal home business. The equipment can fit into the corner of a room, and you can set your own hours and work at your own pace.

In today's economy, companies both large and small are down-sizing their personnel. This means that more and more work is being "farmed out" to freelance contractors. One type of work frequently sent outside the office is typing, or, to use today's business vernacular, "word processing."

Word processing refers to typing on a computer or word processor rather than a typewriter. But whether you're using a state-of-the-art computer or an "old fashioned" electronic typewriter, you can profit.

## Learn to type

If you can't type, or if your typing skills are rusty, you can take a course at a local community college for around $50. Most people who are thinking about starting a typing service know how to type. However, you might discover that to compete in the marketplace, you must invest in a word processor or computer. If you've never worked with computers before, it may take a few weeks to learn the word processing software. Take the time to become familiar with the program *before* you start taking in business. Most community colleges offer courses on the more popular word processing software packages, such as WordPerfect.

## Equipment

Consider your equipment options carefully. If you already have a good electronic typewriter, it can get you started in business. The advantages of the word processor or computer, however, make it a worthwhile investment. Electronic typewriters cost between $200 and $700. Word processors start at $500 and can cost over $1,000. Computers (with necessary software and printer) will run between $2,000 and $3,000. With the constant improvement in technology, however, there is a growing "used computer" market. You can opt for a used computer system and save quite a bit of money. The "dated" computer is most likely three to five years old. It will be considerably slower than new models, but will otherwise work fine for your purposes.

Word processors and computers give the added advantage of being able to offer your customers spell checking, multiple type styles, and "on disk" storage. Computers, while initially more expensive that the word processor, give you the added advantage of being able to expand your business beyond word processing. With a computer, you can build onto your typing business in the future (with desktop publishing, data processing, and other services).

When selecting a printer for your computer, you have two choices: a daisy wheel printer or a laser printer. (A dot matrix printer, even the most expensive, can't produce the letter quality needed by your customers.) A daisy wheel printer is similar to a typewriter in that metal or plastic keys strike the ribbon against the paper. Although different typestyles are available (by changing the type wheel), you can't easily alternate type styles within a document. The laser printer provides high print quality and the greatest flexibility with type styles.

When selecting equipment, also consider the supplies you will need. A ribbon for a word processor or daisy wheel printer is considerably less expensive than the toner cartridge used by a laser printer. In addition, consider the cost of paper, and the cost of floppy disks (if using a computer or word processor).

### Finding customers

Who needs a typing service? Customers can be broken down into two main categories: individuals and businesses.

*Individual Customers.* One individual who hires typists is the professional writer. Writers often hire typists to type final versions of plays or manuscripts. You might be typing up copy from a rough typed draft, or from a handwritten draft, or even from an audio cassette. Unless you limit yourself to local writers, you will probably be working with writers through the mail. That is, they mail the rough copy or cassette, and you mail back the typed pages.

College students are other potential customers. Students are often willing to pay to have term papers, thesis, and dissertations professionally typed. College students are seasonal customers. You'll get most of the work from college students near the end of the term when papers are due—and very little the rest of the year. If you are willing to work long hours, you can make extra money doing rush jobs at the end of the term.

Students, as well as others, also pay typists to prepare their résumés. College students can bring the work to you, or you can offer pick-up-and-deliver service on campus.

*Business Customers.* All sizes and types of businesses hire outside typists to handle routine word processing. One way to get your foot in the door with business is to contact a word processing agency (look in Yellow Pages under "Word Processing"). Often, these companies farm out excess work that they get from business. Working for these companies can often be easier than contacting numerous businesses directly. When working with businesses, they will most likely expect you to pick up and deliver the work. However, in some cases, businesses may use a courier to deliver work.

## Advertising and promotion

Promoting your service can cost pennies or hundreds of dollars, depending on the type of customer you are trying to solicit. If you live near a college, you can place flyers on announcement boards free of charge. You might also consider advertising in the college's newspaper.

You can reach writers through listings in the many writing magazines and journals. The cost for this varies tremendously. One of the largest periodicals for writers is *Writer's Digest,* which charges $100 for a six-line listing. Another publication, *Writer's Journal,* charges 80¢ per word (approximately $10 to $30). You can find a lengthy listing of writer's magazines in a copy of *Writers Market* at your local library.

In your ad, along with the basics of name, address, and phone, also list any special services you provide (spell checking, disk storage), as well as special skills (such as knowledge of medical terms).

You can also contact businesses directly. When working with businesses, the professional approach is always the best. Create an attractive brochure about your typing service, and have some business cards printed up. Although you can work in ripped jeans and a sweatshirt, you should be sure to dress professionally whenever you visit the business to pick up or deliver work.

Of course, the best form of advertising for any type of customer is good word of mouth. You can help promote word of mouth advertising by providing each customer with quick, quality service.

## Setting your rates

How much should you charge for typing? Usually, you will charge per page, rather than per hour. This is good news for the fast typist, not so good news for slower typists. However, the amount you charge per page is up to you. When setting your per-page rate, consider it in light of an hourly rate. This is simple to do if you know your average typing speed—that is, how many words per minute (wpm) you type. (You can determine your wpm by using a stop watch or timer. Type for five minutes, count the words typed minus any mistakes, then divide by five. For example, if you typed 253 words in five minutes with three mistakes, your wpm would be fifty.)

The average double-spaced page has 250 words. So, if you divide that by your wpm rate, you will know how long it take to type one page. If you divide sixty by that figure, you know how many pages you can type in an hour.

For example, if you type fifty wpm, it will take about five minutes to type each page. That means you can type twelve pages in an hour. If you charge $1 per page, you are earning $12 an hour. However, if you type twenty-five wpm, it will take ten minutes to type each page, and you would have to charge $2 per page to earn $12 an hour.

Along with using your wpm, also compare what other typists are charging in your area. A quick glance through a recent copy of *Writers Digest* sets the per-page rate anywhere between 95¢ and $1.50. If you advertised at $2 per page, you probably wouldn't get many customers.

The average typist (50 wpm), charging the average per-page rate ($1), can easily earn $180 to $240 a week, working part-time. A full-time typist could earn $500 a week.

### Building a strong customer base

As with many service businesses, a typing business won't make you rich overnight. It will take time to build a customer base through advertising and word-of-mouth. However, with a typing business, you can count on repeat business from many customers—if they are satisfied with your work. Once you have established a customer base, you can count on a steady work load—and a steady income.

*— Denise Osburn*

# VIDEO SERVICES

**Start-up Costs:** $500, if you already own a camcorder. **Potential Earnings:** Up to $50,000 or more. **Advertising:** Word of mouth, flyers, classified ads in local newspaper. **Special Qualifications:** None. **Equipment Needed:** Camcorder(s), light kit, and sundry accessories. **Best Advice for Success:** Experience in videotaping is recommended. Enroll in a night class to learn the basics. Professionalism comes only from practical involvement—something you'll want to acquire once you've learned the basics.

Vince Taylor is a self-made millionaire who started shooting videos as a hobby. His company, Taylorvision, started videotaping at a small profit using simple components. "I videotaped anything I could—weddings, dances, bar mitzvahs, you name it," says Taylor. The fact is, anybody can make money shooting videotapes for interested clients. And you don't need a special license either. Earning money by shooting video footage is uncomplicated, artistically rewarding, and offers not only the promise of a good second or even primary income but also a chance to indulge your creative urges.

When Taylor began, he contacted local businesses and produced videos for realtors, restaurant owners, and any other businessperson who accepted his services. In one of his first years in business, Taylor grossed $50,000 working out of his home. But he didn't stop there. He went on to produce an original idea called the "Welcome Channel" and sold it to local hotels. "I ran cable to their rooms," he recalls, "and on an unused channel showed videos of things in the area such as shops and activities. Of course, that also meant I could go to the local stores and produce low-rent commercials for them, to show on the Welcome Channel."

## Equipment and its cost

You'll need video equipment to start this venture: a camcorder, light kit, and sundry accessories. Some experience in home shooting is also recommended. It might help to enroll in a night class at a local college where they'll teach you the basics. Fundamental knowledge is all you really need, since professionalism comes only from practical involvement—something you'll want to acquire once you've learned the basics.

There are a variety of camcorders available. Price is usually determined by features, and you should shop around before buying. Read up on the matter (many video magazines give helpful hints on selecting camcorders designed to be used for specific purposes). Local libraries have a variety of books and magazines on the topic of video cameras and accessories.

You'll also need at least one microphone (wireless microphones are best because there are no cords that can get in the way), a tripod, and a few other accessories.

As is usually the case, beginners can't always afford to spend all their start-up funds on equipment. And you really don't have to. You can rent everything you need at a fraction of the price it would cost you if you were to buy it. You can rent video lights with stands and reflectors, extra cables, extension cords, headphones for monitoring sound, and a host of other equipment. Renting is by far the cheaper way to start up.

## How much to charge

Working out of your home cuts down on expenses, compared to working out of someone else's studio. Here are some guidelines to consider before you quote a price. Just remember that the price you charge must be based on a realistic assessment of your costs and on competition:

1. How much time will the shooting take? How much money are you worth (or willing to work for) on an hourly basis?
2. Will you be renting extra equipment for the job? Will you need to rent extra transportation to cart equipment and people around?
3. Will you need to hire an assistant? How much will this cost you? (If the hired hand is a professional, most likely his rates will be expensive.)
4. Does your customer need "raw footage" or edited tapes? How much longer will it take you to edit the tapes if this service is required? If you send the tape out to be edited by someone else, what will be the cost?

You may also charge clients on the caliber of your equipment and your personal qualifications. If you're a beginner, of course, your prices should be kept at a minimum and be competitive. After a year's involvement, your experience is worth more money and, since you've presumably upgraded your equipment, your investment should have a higher return value.

## Good ideas are worth a million

Here are some ideas you may be interested in turning into profits:

■ *Instructional how-to videotapes.* Consider a series of how-to videotapes on household repairs and chores. For example, some car owners don't know how to change their oil. You could develop a short, twenty-minute videotape showing step-by-step instructions on how to do this. A short videotape showing how to unplug a clogged sink could be a best seller. Produce a video showing how to remove old roof tiles and how to install new ones. Once you have your series of how-to tapes, the whole world is your market.

■ *Special occasion videos.* How many parents would refuse to experience the thrill of seeing their newborn baby on tape? This kind of engagement could become a long-term contract, in that the baby could be taped not only in its crib at the hospital but for years afterward as it develops. This kind of long-term engagement requires that you call back periodically to see when the parents are ready to tape again. Weddings are another opportunity. Traditionally, the still portrait was favored by most newlyweds. Today, however, the trend is videotape. A video can capture the wedding ceremony in a way still pictures cannot.

- *Business videos.* Offer your services to conference speakers, entertainers, retail business people, professional and amateur sports people, and school teachers. How about coin and stamp collectors? With the close-up power of a macro lens you could capture on tape the fine points and flaws of a treasured collection. In fact, most serious hobbyists would be more than happy to have their distinguished collections on tape. You could advertise in many publications that specialize in any specific hobby (stamps, coins, porcelain, dolls).

- *Educational videos.* Develop educational tapes for the Board of Education of your state or province. This means hiring the services of other professionals, such as math and history teachers, for example, or dance and sports instructors. It involves long-term planning and invariably demands greater investments of both time and money. However, the financial rewards are larger, as well. Moreover, once you've created just one successful project for any school board, this reference will act as a springboard, leading you to other related jobs for which you can charge more.

You can come up with all sorts of ideas on how to earn money shooting pictures if you'll just use your creative imagination and open your eyes to the events that unfold daily in your community.

*— James Amodeo*

# WORM FARMING

**Start-up Costs:** Less than $50. **Potential Earnings:** Up to $75 per hour. **Advertising:** Check out all possible markets. **Special Qualifications:** None. **Equipment Needed:** A good bedding box, red light, and nutritious worm food. **Best Advice for Success:** "A good product establishes a good market." Patience and a love of worms will produce a high-quality product.

George Sroda calls himself the Underworld Czar. He has no connection with organized crime, but his title is appropriate. Sroda is an oligochaetelo-gist—an expert on earthworms. "Earthworm farming is big business and getting bigger each year," Sroda says. "It is not uncommon for earthworm breeders, particularly in the south, to have an income of $40,000 a year."

The earthworm business is one anyone can get into for as little as $10 to begin with, according to Sroda. Kids can easily clear over $500 in a summer. He cites one case where a couple of older women started out in Denver with a $12 investment and in four years were grossing over $150,000 a year.

## Free inventory

There are few businesses you can start where the inventory is free. Worm farming is one of them. Worms are yours for the effort. Night-crawlers, which are probably the fisherman's favorite, can be bred in cap-tivity, but Sroda does not recommend it. Nightcrawlers burrow to a depth of ten to twelve feet to lay their eggs, which makes breeding them imprac-tical. However, you can hold, condition, and grow nightcrawlers indoors once you have "harvested" them. It is possible to keep them all through the winter and have a thriving business with ice-fishermen.

Redworms can be successfully bred because they lay their eggs only six inches below the surface, and because they multiply at an astonishing rate. One thousand redworms will multiply into one million in just one year.

Sroda recommends investing in some simple but effective equip-ment to facilitate harvesting the crawlers and to insure their protection from injury. Since nightcrawlers usually come out only at night (generally around midnight), you will need a light. A flashlight will encumber your hands, so Sroda suggest buying a light on a head-band similar to those used by miners. This kind of light has the added advantage of easy adjust-ment to shine in any direction. Tape red cellophane or plastic over the light; worms are sensitive to white light.

The second and most important piece of equipment is the container into which you gather the worms. Don't use a tin can. A container devel-oped by Sroda has many tiny holes for aeration, is large enough to gently accommodate the worms, has a handle for convenience, and is amply pad-ded with worm bedding.

Unless you choose to go barefoot, the third necessity for successful harvesting is a pair of soft-soled shoes or rubbers, because the worms are extremely sensitive to vibrations. Some harvesters use electrical or chemi-cal means to drive the worms from the ground, but Sroda frowns on these methods. Electrical means force the worms out too quickly, he says, often rupturing their crops (top section or "head") or injuring their segments. Chemical means kill baby worms in the soil and destroy the natural odor of the adult nightcrawlers, which is what attracts fish to them. You can, Sroda admits, drive a wooden stake into the ground and strike it, creating a vibration that will make the worms exit their burrows, but he prefers more natural means to this kind of coercion.

If nightcrawlers are not surfacing in season, it is usually because it's too dry, he says. The best preparation for inducing their appearance is to sprinkle your lawn or gathering place generously all afternoon. Unless the temperature is under forty degrees or over eighty during the daytime, that evening should see a plenitude of worms coming up for air and to mate.

## Storing worms

The proper time to harvest your worms is springtime, about six weeks after the first worms start emerging. They are too soft to harvest before then, but preparation for holding and storage of worms will ideally take place during the winter months.

Sroda recommends constructing a master holding box that will accommodate from 500 to 1,000 nightcrawlers. A master box must have proper ventilation and ample worm bedding. For convenience, you might set the box on legs or some sort of platform to make it a good working height. The bedding must be organic and natural, highly absorbent, non-dusty, and resistant to being packed down. Sroda has experimented with paper, peat, bark, wood chips and various mosses to come up with his own "magical worm bedding." When this bedding becomes too worn out for the worms, it can become a valuable sideline for the worm farmer. Since worm castings are rich in plant nutrients, you can mix a great potting soil, bag it, and sell it to local florists and gardeners. One-third of your bag of potting soil should consist of your worm bedding; the other two-thirds should be regular soil.

Moisture is extremely important to worms, because they breathe through their skin. The top priority for the successful worm farmer is to keep the bedding moist at all times. Lake, river, or rain water should be used. Chloride- or fluoride-treated water can damage worms. Use one quart of water to each pound of bedding. If your worms start looking pale, you'll know you are using too much water—add more bedding immediately. The bedding should be moist enough so that the worms can wriggle about freely.

Like moisture, correct temperatures are crucial to our little friends. They need cool temperatures, and just stashing them in your basement won't do the trick. Most basements will get as warm as 75 degrees in the summertime. A thermometer tucked into the bedding should register no higher than 50 degrees for sensible worm care. Sroda keeps his worms in a special refrigerated unit, but if you haven't a spare refrigerator, you can keep the bedding nice and cool by surrounding it with ice cubes encased in plastic resealable freezer bags.

## Feeding worms

Sroda has developed a "magic worm food" that contains thirty-two important ingredients and is high in protein, carbohydrates, minerals, and vitamins. He also treats them to a little powdered milk and a bit of brown sugar every few weeks. His worms average twelve to sixteen inches. The natural diet of the worm is leaf, grass, and other organic material in the soil.

Because worms do not manufacture any acids naturally, they rely on outside sources to help them digest their food. Their food or bedding must contain some acids. If you find mold forming on the boxes, don't get too alarmed. A bit of mold seems to be beneficial to the worms.

## Breeding worms

As mentioned earlier, redworms are easily bred in captivity. They are hardier than earthworms and can survive at higher temperatures, though Sroda recommends directing a circulating fan on their bedding boxes at temperatures over 70 degrees.

One fertile worm or egg capsule can put you in business, but Sroda suggests you start with 200 to 300 worm capsules per cubic foot of bedding. Redworms lay capsules every seven to ten days, and these will hatch in about three or four weeks. It takes a year to get fully established and have adult worms ready for bait. As your bedding box tenants multiply, you should divide and provide more space. Except for that the care is generally the same as in the storing of nightcrawlers. Mites and flies can become a problem, since anything that will kill the insects will also kill the worms. But keeping the food covered with an inch or so of bedding usually controls the situation.

## Merchandising worms

An eight-year-old can establish a good clientele just by sticking a scrawled sign up on the lawn, but if you want to get into worms as a serious business venture, advertising is important, as is investigating all of the possible places to sell your worms. Laboratories, schools, and organic farmers are some of the other markets available to worm growers.

Presently, the United States imports over 239 million nightcrawlers from Canada, with others imported from Mexico, Great Britain, and China to be used as fish bait. So the market is there, if you decide to wriggle into it. Nightcrawlers are bringing from 90 cents to $1.50 a dozen in retail stores, which adds up to about $8 to $12 a pound. This means a good harvester can make up to $75 an hour.

For worm box blueprints, worm products and further details on worm farming, contact George Sroda at: Box 97, Amherst Junction, Wisconsin, 54407; (715) 824-3868.

—*Barbara Vroman*

# WRITING/EDITING SERVICE

**Start-up Costs:** $500. **Potential Earnings:** $10,000 or more part-time. **Advertising:** Direct marketing; word of mouth. **Special Qualifications:** Excellent writing skills. **Equipment Needed:** Electronic typewriter or word processor. **Best Advice for Success:** Be well organized to do jobs well but efficiently.

More and more people are leaving the corporate world and choosing freelancing as an alternative way of making a living. Many freelancers set their own work pace and gradually command an income that most companies could never match. Whether they are working for full support or pin money, freelancers share the same sense of satisfaction that comes from doing things their own way—and getting paid for it.

Karen Feinberg is a freelance writer and editor who works in her own home. She writes for businesses, organizations, and individuals who do not have the skill or the time to do their own writing. As an editor she corrects and makes sense of what others have written while getting paid for doing it.

The beginning writer has to be willing to write almost anything. Typical writing assignments include sales letters, handbills, ads, brochures, newsletters, catalogs, ghost-written articles, speeches, and how-to directions. Editing work includes correcting and re-writing articles, technical papers, and books.

When starting out, you can't pick and choose. Specialization comes later. Freelance writers often specialize in advertising copywriting, radio and television commercial scripts, and direct mail. Some write brochures, catalogs and other sales literature.

## Finding assignments

Getting started can be tough. You have to sell yourself and constantly "ask for the order." That means writing letters, making appointments, and making cold calls. Logical people to approach for writing assignments include executives in charge of advertising, public relations, marketing, and sales; store owners and operators; editors of company and institutional publications; and anyone involved with communications. Make yourself known and leave your card with anyone you think might need your writing help. Show samples of your work if you have them. Make up a portfolio or brochure describing your services which you can include with a letter and leave behind when you make a call.

Feinberg tried advertising in the business pages of the daily newspaper. The little one-inch-by-two-column ad brought her some attention, but not enough. That led her to try inexpensive ads in professional journals. Now Feinberg gets much of her work from professionals in the fields of criminal justice, health, and social services who want to publish articles about their work but need someone to edit their material.

## Knowing what to charge

You will probably charge most of your work by the job, but you'll also need an hourly rate to base your charges on. To know in advance how long a job will take, make your best guess and then double it. Don't be afraid to ask other freelancers what they charge. Ask advertising agency people and publication editors what they pay for services such as yours. An excellent guide for pricing is published in *Writer's Market*, available in libraries and bookstores.

A variety of rates have been compiled here; these should only be used as guidelines. Rates will vary depending on the local economy, the reputation of the writer, and competition.

| | |
|---|---|
| Ads | $75-$150 |
| Sales letters | $125-$200 |
| Ghost-written articles | $75-$100 per typed page |
| Speeches | $25 a minute |
| Brochures and catalogs | $50-$75 per printed page |
| Newsletters | $75-$100 per printed page |
| Editing | $10-$25 an hour |
| Hourly creative rate | $25-$45 an hour |

## Start-up costs

Some of the basic equipment required includes: a typewriter, a telephone, a dictionary, basic office supplies, business cards, and a space to work in. After the money starts coming in you can invest in files, a desk, a word processor with a letter-quality printer, and so forth. From the beginning you must keep books, carefully recording all your income and expenses, including auto mileage. You can deduct office expenses from your income tax, but follow the IRS's rules.

The standard advice to anyone with a steady job is keep it until you prove you can be successfully self-employed. Do your freelancing after regular work hours. Freelancers call it "moonlighting." Don't go into free-lance writing expecting to make a fortune, but you can make a good living with effort.

It won't be long before you will come to a crossroads as a freelance writer. A client will ask: "Can you illustrate this job? Get it in type? Get it printed? Can you write, produce, and place an ad for me?" As soon as you say "yes" you are no longer exclusively a freelance writer but a one-person creative studio or advertising agency. This is what many freelancers hope will happen. You are on your way to expanding your business if you de-cide to buy art, type, do printing, and place advertising in addition to your writing. You are also in a situation that requires much more working capi-tal and has greater risks.

## Rules for success

1. Do the best work you are capable of doing.
2. Be honest. If you can't deliver work when it is wanted, say so. Instead of losing the job, you'll probably get a longer deadline.
3. Explain in the beginning what the job will entail, including your fee.
4. Organize your time. Don't try to do too much.
5. Be firm. Don't let anyone intimate you into lowering a fee or do-ing what you don't want to do.
6. Never do work on speculation. Exception—writing you do for publication under your own name.
7. Don't leave messages with children.
8. Beware of unbalanced and unreliable types—they are probably slow pay or no pay.
9. Find time to relax.
10. Don't give up.

*— Van Caldwell*